"Sometimes, God will open your eyes in the middle of a life storm only to reveal your calling, a blessing more extraordinary and powerful than the disturbance, if you have faith." -Kala

# The Turning Point

Memoirs of Determination, Hope, Faith, Loss, Love, and Resilience

*Kala Jordan-Lindsey*

The Turning Point:
Memoirs of Determination, Hope, Faith, Loss, Love, and Resilience

Visit: www.kalajordanlindsey.com

For inquiries, please email: Write@kalajordanlindsey.com

*"If you don't have to start at the beginning of the race, keep going and don't fall. But if you do, stand up with wisdom and run with confidence. There is hope, help, and God's grace wherever you are—even in the middle of a powerful life event. Be bold and cope with the process of life as the Almighty leads you to where you need to be, and never give up."*

*-Kala*

# *Dedication*

To the love of my life, my husband, Anthony Lindsey, for his unconditional love and support since the afternoon we met at Lake Ida Church of Christ in Delray Beach, Florida. God sent me a humble, god-fearing man who continues to stick by my side and enhance my life. Honey, thank you for your prayers and daily text messages of encouragement and for embracing all the blood, sweat, and tears with me over the years as my amazing partner and best friend. I love you more than the number of times I have expressed it to you in person, on paper, and on the phone. You rock, handsome.

To my beautiful parents, Jefferson and Evella Grisby Jordan, for blessing me into this world, from August 14, 1986, to this moment. Before I was created, I was already a part of God's plans. Mama, thank you for carrying me until I overcame life into this world. Your lives inspired me to share mine to encourage others. I love you both more than words.

To my former teachers, professors, band directors, and students since grade school: You made a big difference in the world and an incredible impact on my life. Your inspiration and unique personalities will forever hold a special place in my heart. Thank you for the significant time and energy you poured into helping enrich my walk and touch my soul.

And to you, everyone everywhere who are believers or unbelievers. You motivated me to complete this book to offer you hope, inspiration, and insight into the love, power, and grace of God. Thank you for inspiring me with every reason to push through adversity, pain, and unexpected challenges in life. Be encouraged and blessed—and never give up.

# Contents

# Introduction

In November 2017, I was dismissed from my job. My second full-time music teaching position had been terminated unexpectedly less than a year after I started. I found this interesting because I was the only Black woman and educator working at this educational institution. For months, I was heartbroken and depressed but also hopeful about what unbelievable situation would arise next. I was confused about my next steps in life and how my family and I would survive this hardship until I had the courage to make one of the most difficult decisions ever—to have faith and trust in God's will and greater purpose for my life. Since then, my life has changed, but it didn't happen overnight. I am a work in progress—striving and growing each day with faith and embracing my new walk on purpose.

I was inspired to write this book because I want to give hope and wisdom to men and women experiencing a state of confusion about life, failure, or unexpected life events—unforeseen storms. Over the years, I've learned that wherever there is darkness, Light is in the tunnel if you're brave enough to seek, acknowledge, and honor the Creator of the world. God has purpose in your pain and triumphs, which He created to get you closer to where you need to be; to make you stronger mentally, physically, and spiritually; to position you on a healthier path so that you can grow and experience satisfaction; to bless you while you operate in your calling; and to enable you to connect with Him intentionally on a deeper level.

I wrote this book to glorify God, to express my gratitude for His grace, mercy, and favor over my life, and to leave behind a trace of expectancy for generations to come. I encourage you to embrace this collection of essays if you're experiencing unexpected circumstances or a lack of success or if you feel empty, worthless, overlooked, or discouraged. You are not alone. Expect better days, and never give up on your aspirations to rise above the hustle, grind, or experiences that are getting you closer to your breakthrough. God never makes mistakes. Trust His will, way, and word even when you're in a noisy and clueless fight. After I wrestled with my flesh to release these memories on paper, God sparked a fire in my heart and motivation in my bones to reveal my personal and inspirational stories of truth to comfort you where you are now.

Writing this book required time, energy, commitment, early mornings and late nights, sacrifice, an investment, and guts. It wasn't a quick commercial process, but I didn't procrastinate—and neither should you if you desire to accomplish your goals. For years, I had a vision to create this book no matter how long it took, how many fights I'd experience until it happened, and how many miles I'd have to walk to reach this goal. I was determined to write a book of memories without the stress and strain of hiring a ghostwriter to record my life experiences.

With a better understanding of my direction, I made a commitment to stay on the course no matter what trials or tribulations I experienced along the way. I had high hopes and knew my faith would grace me to reach the finish line. However, piecing together scattered words, the past, memories before birth to where I am now—the good and the bad, the fights, the happy and the sad days, sensitive details—required hard work, passion, deep prayer, concentration, and God's strength to provide the raw details. Furthermore, reliving my experiences was emotionally difficult, and I unexpectedly found it hard to let go. Some days, it was challenging to write in certain chapters. But I rose from fear and surrendered anyway. I moved forward and knew my stories were worth sharing, especially during times like now, when many are struggling to survive, eat, provide for their families, rebuild after COVID-19, and embrace the new norm. Therefore, I didn't give up on my vision to finish this book.

I motivated myself when I was down and experienced unexpected anxiety, and pushed through negative thoughts, excuses, weaknesses, and discouragement with prayer. I was determined to let go of valuable content to help you experience a better, healthier lifestyle and journey. If you think it's impossible to win a tough fight, watch the greatest boxers of all time. **Life isn't easy or a smooth boat ride, but with faith, God will give you the power and grace to overcome hard times if you trust in His word wholeheartedly.**

If you're curious about the turning point of my life, what happened, how I survived, or why I never gave up, here is the story you've been eager to read and add to your library.

During childhood, I sat on my parents' living room carpet with a notebook and pen and brainstormed what I wanted to be when I was an adult. As I grew, the list became longer—a professional basketball player, brain and heart surgeon, cardiologist, entrepreneur, FBI agent, chiropractor, and musician were all on my dream list. I made bracelets, necklaces, and rings and labeled them with price tags. Then, I carried my jewelry case around the community and sold what I'd made. Sometimes, I wore these pieces to school, which many loved. I gained confidence and knew there was nothing in life I couldn't overcome. If I put my mind to it, I could achieve great things and inspire the world—and it happened.

Years later, I developed an interest in music, which surprisingly became my life. I had no clue this universal language would grab my attention and take me on such a ride. Music was all I knew, and I pursued it since age eleven. I was in it for life. I said, "I'm never going to leave the music field." But that wasn't true. God's will, His purpose for my life, was more powerful than my hopes and plans. So, never say "never" because you never know what God has in store for you until He reveals it. Then, you will discover something worth pursuing and sharing with others.

Today, I'm in awe of the power of God's unfailing love, grace, and mercy. I didn't give up, nor did my Father. He picked me up from the lowest place in my life, rock bottom, and rescued me before I gave up when change impacted my plans. He blessed me in a safe and welcoming space, an environment where I'm comfortable, satisfied, and where I have the freedom to release my creative ideas and experiences on paper. My calling is that safe and comfortable space where I can let loose like a dancer in the studio or the most intimate spot in my home.

I am no longer mute like a caged bird fighting to be free. I am a thousand times more confident than when I first learned to walk. Be bold and stand up. Don't walk in silence before you're gone.

Shout with joy while God delivers you. Unmute your voice, shine your light.

I'm also thankful that God forgave me of all the foolish stuff that happened in my life and the roads on which I walked, ran, and jogged. However, I almost skipped this stop—an important one that many hesitate to stop at or fear because of what others might think. I almost gave up on sharing these words from my heart, but my "why" ignited my spirit to say "yes" and go for it.

I didn't know how to release "me," so I struggled with this veil over my life as if I were wrestling in the ring with my flesh for victory until God set me free. So, you're not alone. Let go of your untold stories to bless others, and God will continue to please your heart's desires—yes, the ones preventing you from experiencing love, joy, peace, happiness, and satisfaction in the Lord. Let God transform your mind before you rest.

I spent years sitting at my desk, unclogging hidden words, thoughts, and experiences stored in my heart. At times, it was difficult—I experienced mixed emotions—but I knew one day, before my final breath, I would heal enough to be free to help you find the strength to do the same thing.

Your journey isn't in vain. Let go of your desires and follow the Director of the world. There is hope in your dark state of mind. Never give up. Trust God's plans for your path and grow to appreciate your flaws. Be thankful for another day, chance, and opportunity to do better and be the difference. You're a star, so shine unapologetically.

I'm free, and it feels amazing to be able to let go of things that are out of my hands and thereby experience true life—life in Christ.

If you're in a tight situation, one that's stressful and draining the joy out of you, let go and let God control the situation; release unapologetically with confidence and conviction; give it to God and God alone. If it feels uncomfortable, embrace this moment, this temporary season—there's a reason for everything happening in your life.

I wasn't serious about life and my health. However, I'm healthier, stronger, and wiser than I was in my last stage, to God be the glory. I was off the map—different—and took my spiritual walk for granted. Today, though, I can see. I am no longer in the wilderness. I'm no longer tied up and confined to the old life that blinded me. I'm loose from those chapters and thankful because God blessed me in a mighty way, to arrive at a point in my life where many are afraid to turn and unclog and just be who God created them to be, to boldly deliver the most wanted stories on the planet like yours.

I let go and surrendered myself, my story, the one in which I almost lost my mind, but God renewed it so that He could use my storm, my chaotic story in a mighty way for His praise, glory, and honor—and to help you along the way. So, this is a safe space where judgment is not allowed. What you read is the truth and nothing but the truth; the pages of my life are unplugged, real, without "story edits," cropping, and clipping. I've been dying to share this book with you for years, and as much as I appreciate that you are reading my open book, I hope you have the courage to step outside the box and share yours one day, to help others experiencing low self-esteem and doubt, as I did for years. I struggled with the person in the mirror—though not with my hair and makeup or physical looks. It was deeper than that. At least, that's what I believe after having walked this planet for thirty-seven years. I struggled with releasing my identity. I struggled with the human being whom God created—with the newborn who developed into a teenager and then into an adult, a young woman. I wrestled in my sleep and shed tears the next morning. I slept on ideas and memories, and I carried flashbacks until I started writing.

A few years back, I submitted a three-hundred-page manuscript to a popular full-service publishing house with the intention of self-publishing. However, I chose not to publish *Opened Eyes*. I wasn't ready, and I pondered back and forth with a load on my shoulders, like a child confused about whether to get vanilla or chocolate at an ice cream parlor. I walked through the entire process for almost two years, and then I ended the contract with uncertainty. Something was missing in the memoir. The timing wasn't right. I also wasn't working, which created a financial burden when I submitted payments to the publisher. After my husband and I discussed the situation and prayed, I decided to wait until I was confident that I was ready to publish this book. Years later, The Spirit revealed the appropriate book title and subtitle for me. I was excited and felt good about the decision to wait on the Lord. I changed *Opened Eyes* to *The Turning Point* with faith more than ever, and God confirmed it.

I just didn't know where to start and how I'd ever have the strength to adjust to this new lifestyle, to this new thing, this new journey of life on a whole new level—one I never imagined in a thousand years.

For over a decade, my life has been a roller coaster, a ride of unexpectedness, ups and downs, and hardships. I'm sure you can relate, especially if you know me or have my other books. I've experienced everything from having a speech impediment to encountering failure to losing an unborn child and job to starting in a new direction halfway in my life. When I was thirty-two, I began taking baby steps again; with no intentions to start at first base or ground zero again, from the bottom, I did, and it was the greatest move I could have ever made. What an adjustment—one filled with grace and mercy and God's unfailing love; one that took more faith than believing in myself, and nothing less.

I've learned to embrace my past by keeping my trust in the Lord while looking forward one day at a time. And I am not the same woman. I have a new attitude and approach toward life; my outlook includes God in the picture. My heart is also healthier; I can finally breathe and hear my heartbeat. I can see without experiencing doubt because my faith is settled in Jesus Christ, who is controlling my life, mind, body, and soul. The Lord is my Conductor, and I'm thankful.

From battles to breakthroughs, struggles to success, God is continuously working in your favor and knows what's best for you. Have faith. **Your worst day could turn out to be the best experience ever.**

I wrote this book to encourage you in your troubles while you expect God's favor and solutions to enrich your walk. Let these essays bless you with your needs and grace you to experience a more fulfilling life for the rest of your journey. However, while you wait on the Lord, stay away from distractions, gossip, drama, or negativity. Don't let unhealthy company get in your way, destroy or take over your mind, and get the best of your love, joy, peace, and happiness. Don't let your circumstances ruin your best life. Look beyond your temporary storms and move forward with your life like a marching band.

Your soul is important. Nourish it with good stuff, positive people, hope, God's wisdom, love, and faith. This is the opposite of following your flesh, which can demolish every part of your body. Your life isn't in vain. Cherish your purpose. Let Christ be your firm foundation. Value wisdom. Take advice. You matter—the precious body God created. It's time to let God do great things in your life while you embrace the rest of your time on earth in His will.

Look beyond your unexpected circumstances and realize God will change your outlook on life and the way you handle and embrace situations out of your hands. You're one person with two hands. God is sovereign and has the power to do what you can't do. He can do the impossible and help you get your life together by the power of His grace. So, never give up on hope and your faith. Embrace where you are now while celebrating the person you are becoming.

Believe in Him and be ready to accept God's will for your life— the good and the unpleasant. Live on purpose while you explore and discover what God has for you and what He has blessed you with to give to others. If you do, you'll start to live a fulfilling life with gratitude for where you are now rather than despair at where you could have been, should have been, or would have been.

I've gained more than I lost from my journey despite difficult challenges and ups and downs. It's not over. I'm living and learning, striving and thriving, and I hope you love each moment of your precious breath and grace yourself when you make mistakes. They're part of life and the process of growing each day. I appreciate you and love you from the bottom of my heart.

By the end of this book, I hope that you will have taken away something from my incredible, God-inspired journey and embrace all the advice, encouragement, and wisdom to improve your life—mentally, physically, and spiritually.

May God bless you to prosper all the days of your existence, discover greatness while you're living, and thrive in your faith.

# Chapter 1

## Determined

*"I was created on purpose—without mistakes—with my heart fixed on overcoming life unconsciously, and I won because the grace of God built me on purpose."*

*-Kala*

On a lovely afternoon, I sat in the backseat of my mother's automobile and listened to her as she shared special memories of my sisters and me. We both smiled and carried on with the conversation. Then, my beautiful mother, Evetta, said, "You all were the love of my life, my joy and happiness—Jennifer, Allison, yourself, Heather, and Aimee. I struggled with my pregnancies, but each one was an enjoyable experience and unforgettable. During my pregnancy with Jennifer, I was sickly and lost fifty pounds, including my teeth. I became the most ill with her. My body experienced a lot of changes, and I stayed in labor the longest and screamed for nearly sixteen hours before I gave birth to her. Ten years later, I became pregnant with Allison, who was also small but born healthy and beautiful as you all were—doll babies. Heather had a twin brother, but, unfortunately, he passed due to unexpected complications. She was also sickly, including Aimee, who was born early and was my last child—your baby sister.

"However, my pregnancy with you was different. In July 1986, as I approached my ninth month of fertility, I suddenly felt contractions. So, your father and I rushed to the hospital for an examination. I was confident, without a doubt, that I was in labor and would finally give birth to a son that night. But after the obstetrician and nurses examined me, they said, 'No, you're not in labor.' *So, you all think I'm exaggerating?* Ms. Jordan, you can go home now. After they made these remarks, your dad and I left the hospital and drove home. But I knew I wouldn't be home for long. I had a strong feeling I'd deliver you soon. Well, the son I was prepared to bring into this world.

"It irked my nerves when we walked into the house, and it bothered your dad and me that the medical team didn't think I was in labor, as if it were a joke. I became frustrated and anxious at the same time because I knew my body and had experienced similar complications during my previous pregnancies. I knew I was going into labor, Kala. I expected to be admitted, without hesitation, but it was a fight. So, days later, my contractions became stronger, which led your father and me back to the hospital with the assurance that it was time to finally deliver our precious blessing. Finally, after the doctors saw me and thoroughly examined me again, they said, *Yes, you are in labor.* I knew that and was determined to give birth within hours. So, after hearing the wonderful news, I felt relief, even though it was emotionally frustrating, and they never believed me, prolonging your delivery.

We felt like no one listened except for God, who continued to keep us strengthened. We prayed and had faith that we were going to have a healthy baby boy. And we didn't give up. I stood strong and stayed calm through the process.

"After all, we were so excited about your expected delivery that nothing mattered to us except for bringing you into this world. But this happened until you experienced a series of obstacles. At first, your heart rate dropped. This scared me, but I knew everything was going to be okay. Then the nurses informed me that the umbilical cord became wrapped around your neck, which could have caused you brain damage or led to death. But, still, you didn't give up. Hours after, your body rotated in an unusual fetal position, but you were determined to succeed. Nothing stopped you from overcoming unexpected barriers because you were strong.

"However, I received more unexpected news. The doctors said that I was unable to have a natural birth. At that moment, you were already struggling for your life, so we agreed to have the doctors deliver you at their best recommendation. So, on August 14, 1986, weeks after your due date, they used forceps to bring you out safely. You were committed to push through unexpected trouble, stumbling blocks out of your control, being that you were unconsciously making your way to see this world. The moment you were delivered, the doctor pulled you out and we cut the umbilical cord. Then she said, *Oh, wow, you have a beautiful little girl. She's covered with hair over her face and ears.* Then, they placed you in my arms and I held you against my chest. I looked down at you and cried tears of joy along with your dad. Everyone fell in love with you and commented on how you looked like a beautiful doll baby.

It's funny because your dad and I purchased nothing except boy clothes. We told everyone that we had a little boy. Your daddy wanted a son, so when they informed us months ago that you were a boy, he was excited. However, I was content with a boy or a girl."

*Wow, really? The doctors didn't detect this early on, Mama?*

"Technology back then was different than it is now. During my doctor's visits and exams, they thought you were a boy, especially since your head was big. But we both accepted God's will and moved forward. Your grandmother, Maggy, helped us with your name, and we found Kala, which is a lovely flower in India. You represented strength, motivation, and determination. And we fought a heck of a fight, and so did you. Decades later, we're still amazed at your determination to overcome unexpectedness in life. We commend you for your character and accomplishments and drive to keep going despite adversity. You're a beautiful woman with a big heart."

After I sat down numerous times and listened to my mother's phenomenal story of perseverance and how she fought through her pregnancies, I knew without a doubt that God had placed in me a greater purpose, beyond my own reasons, for making it into this world. I was meant to see life and embrace all that God had planned for my journey. Making it safely into this world happened only by the grace and mercy of God, and it displayed my strength and ability to achieve anything God had already permitted.

I overcame a series of tugs-of-war in total darkness and isolation from the world except the presence of God, who designed and blessed me with determination. So, if you ever think you can't do anything because of the way you look or how many struggles you've experienced, you must change the way you think, and you'll succeed. Train your mind to be determined to accomplish anything with the grace and mercy of God.

What you feed your mind is how your body will perform. So, if you want to achieve a goal or attain an obstacle, adopt a positive mindset. If you crush doubt and leave fear alone, you'll get somewhere. Great things will happen. You'll be satisfied, and your soul will be pleased.

I also found my mother's pregnancy amazingly impressive because, in her womb, God planted greatness in my heart before I knew it. Before I saw my parents, I was blessed. Before I came into this world, God designed my life.

**Start with positive thinking. Block negativity from your brain or adopt a different way of creating healthy habits. If you do this, you'll boost your mental health. You'll feel better, look healthier, and speak with confidence when your heart releases words of good, encouragement, inspiration, or wisdom for the glory of God.**

We were born to lose, yet win—to experience trials and tribulations, hate, failure, discrimination, and depression. However, God also blessed us with wisdom and knowledge to overcome life, the uncomfortable events that disturb us, in His will.

Although receiving unexpected news or even coping with an unforeseen struggle is difficult, with faith and hope, you can and will get through the emotional, physical, and mental aspects of your battles. My parents said, "To this day, we're so grateful and blessed to have you as our precious, beautiful, and pie-faced daughter!"

What's also remarkably special and humbling, to this day, is that God hasn't given up on me. This keeps me going, and it should keep you going, too. Your walk and everything you experience in life is part of God's plans for your soul. There are no mistakes in your footsteps, your actions, or the outcome of a storm.

I can only imagine the mental and physical strain this obstacle had on my mother. However, because of her strong mentality, she never gave up. She persevered and kept going despite her sickness, her weaknesses, and the opinions she heard.

Have you ever run a two-day marathon that required you to start and finish, despite your outcome? How was it? Did you complete the challenge, or did you give up just before the finish line because you were sidetracked by the "noise" of life? Now, yes, the outcome of my mother's pregnancy could have been worse or unbearable, just like any challenging and unexpected circumstance in life, but she didn't give up. Because I was her hope and blessing, the struggle and the intense and challenging labor motivated and inspired her to keep going and persevere. If I had known that I was created in the "package of life" to win, to overcome every obstacle on this planet, would I have wrestled to be born? God saw fit with a far greater and more powerful purpose, one beyond human understanding. Do you honestly believe you were just born to live, or do you know without a doubt that you were created by the power of an amazing God who "Made all the delicate, inner parts of your body and knit you together in your mother's womb so wonderfully complex and formed you in utter seclusion, as you were woven together in the dark of the womb. He saw me before I was born. Every day of my life was recorded in His book. Every moment was laid out before a single day had passed."

It was not only a fight that had my name on it but also an obstacle created with a greater purpose beyond human imagination—just like the obstacle you're coping with now. I truly believe it was the perfect struggle that was destined to prove how human and imperfect I was, to train me for what lay ahead, and to give God the glory and honor. It was also guaranteed to develop and perfect my mental, physical, and spiritual strength in the Lord so that I could cope with the tough, painful, and lifelong process of persevering through every struggle I'd experience, like the unemployment storm I coped with a few years ago that turned into a Category 5 hurricane and then a mind-blowing tornado, causing me to almost give up.

You might become sad, depressed, doubtful, and fearful. You might have developed anxiety and thoughts of suicide. However, in the end, just before you were delivered, you stood strong and kept the faith, which gave you enough power to persevere and never give up. Psalms 139:16 reads:

> *You saw me before I was born. Every day of my life was recorded in your book. Every moment was laid out before a single day had passed.*

This is one of my favorite Scriptures in the Bible because it assures me that God knows more about my life, including my experiences, than I'll ever know. I encourage you to let this Scripture inspire you to live with more confidence than ever, with unstoppable hope and faith. Let God bring you comfort in knowing there's no mistake in your walk or your struggles with sickness, unemployment, singleness, financial status, and tragedies. Despite what you're coping with this very moment, now, today, just remember that you were born to persevere, to never give up winning. Now, you're probably wondering: How in the world could this be possible? How could my life have been planned centuries ago, way before my ancestors were born?

Though the answer is simple, it remains complicated, unbelievable, and confusing, to this day, for many around the world: that God, the Creator of man and this universe, could have planned out every single day and every struggle of one's life. The made me only one of at least a billion others on earth in 1986 who struggled to be delivered into this world and out of a multitude of unexpected circumstances and hardships such as poverty, health issues, financial debt, immigration, legal issues and confinement, unemployment, homelessness, depression, prostitution, drug and alcohol addiction, and spiritual warfare. However, there's more to the picture.

What blows my mind to this day is remembering the "process," the ongoing days and nights spent tossing and turning, persevering to overcome such obstacles to see this world for the first time, except for God, our Creator. However, what's eye-opening is that the same God who created man also blessed man with just enough strength and power to overcome the natural forces of life. My mother said, "Kala, up until you were finally delivered, I'd make weekly visits to the hospital only to be sent home every time I complained of being in labor. But I knew this wouldn't go on too long. The more you kicked, tossed and turned, and shifted your body, the more it agitated me, causing the umbilical cord to wrap around your neck."

It's eye-opening that though I struggled as an unborn and unconscious child to see this world, I overcame life by the grace and mercy of God. Now, you're probably wondering: Is that still the case today? Does this mean every human being in the universe struggles in life? Has anyone who is now deceased ever struggled or coped with adversities and challenges such as those that I'm experiencing today? The answer is yes—the dead also struggled. Therefore, everyone who's still alive will also struggle, no matter how obedient, disciplined, wealthy, rich, skinny, tall, short, and perfect one tries to be and no matter how many times one overcomes one single struggle after another. Mankind struggles with life daily. To be born on earth and never struggle and suffer is unusual and unavoidable, as every single human being who has lived since earth's creation—including Jesus Christ—has struggled.

The struggle is real, and you will encounter some form of trial and error, circumstance, tribulation, adversity, tragedy, or unexpectedness while on earth. However, knowing what to do and how to embrace times like this will help you cope with life and whatever it brings to your door. The process of God's will for me to see this world was a powerful struggle and everything that happened was expected to occur without mistakes. It was a difficult, yet exciting season for my parents, especially when they received the news that my birth would be delayed.

I encourage you not to panic or worry when life comes against you. Stand up and walk by faith, even when you face difficult moments. Or, perhaps, take a step back, inhale and exhale, pray, and continue mastering and "owning" these powerful and essential words you've been hearing for years: faith, hope, and perseverance, which strengthen your mental, physical, and spiritual health one day at a time. However, this won't happen magically. Overcoming life and experiencing God's best is an everyday, ongoing process—and, for most, it's a lifetime process. So, prepare to embrace the journey and stay positive. Think positively through it all.

I fought in this "ring of life" as if I were fighting with the person in the mirror, and you know what? I won the battle because I never gave up. Now, can you imagine a mental and physical fight like this with the very struggle you're dealing with now, today, at this moment? Is it challenging? Are you staying strong? What's motivating you and your loved ones to stand strong and never give up? What's motivating you and your spouse to be resilient despite hurt and hardships?

Today, many human beings find it easier to give up on love because it was never taught or it was lacking in their households. They weren't taught the importance of love and how to persevere despite life's unforeseen circumstances. So, when life goes against them, it becomes a lack and blemish in their hearts and mentality.

The beauty in this blessing, which is an outcome that all expecting parents pray for, is that the struggle or impediment "favorably" fueled and motivated my mother in submission to God's will. My mother experienced such unexpected pain and distress, complications, and frustration during her long-awaited and tense labor because her blessing was more powerful than the pain. Pain and struggle were needed to test her strength, abilities, and faith beyond her own, and by going through this test, she passed the minimum requirement, which is to never give up. My mother consciously obeyed the natural response of the beginning "process" of never giving up. Because she couldn't control her unexpected distress in labor, she exercised her faith to let go and let God bless her with a successful and favorable delivery and pregnancy.

Have you ever coped with an issue in life, and because you let go and exercised your faith, you were blessed? My mother consciously recognized this because she'd gone through this amazing and interesting process with my oldest sister, but since her birth as well. Without alerts of pain, shock, distress, barriers, worry, frustration, aggravation, weakness, sadness, depression, guilt, and fear, one would never react and persevere to victory. Without unforeseen complications or struggles, we'd never experience the beauty, blessing, and reality of what it really means to be firm about never giving up. The beauty is that I literally experienced a normal complication of "life," which started with the physical shift of my body. This triggered a sudden and physical change in my mother's body, causing me to fight against a natural challenge, which is life. The blessing is that I was already filled with enough strength and power to sustain the struggle against life. This allowed me to overcome my barrier and succeed by not giving up. Therefore, I was able to experience an extraordinary and God-inspired win.

Mothers, what kind of struggles did you cope with while you were pregnant? How was it? Were you in shock? Was it unexpectedly complicated, difficult, or tiresome? Did you stay strong despite the difficult process? If yes, then it's wonderful you didn't give up. You succeeded. You overcame a natural trigger and struggle of life. You're a brave and special survivor. However, just because you won this challenge doesn't mean it's over. It only means that you've gained a better understanding and awareness of the process of how to never give up, to never stop, quit, or sit down when things get tough or when you face adversities. Just remember, the secret sauce to never giving up is not rocket science or some difficult challenge if you just simply never give up. What's funny is that ever since I was a child, I've heard the words "never give up," as if this were the easiest task on the planet for a child. In fact, it was, because it was just that easy to be persistent.

However, I never knew that while it was easy then, it would get worse. But it certainly prepared me for the real challenges ahead. Often, I heard my teachers, my peers, my friends, the public, and, of course, my parents say "Never give up." It sounded as if they were saying "ABC" or feeding a young child a bowl of instant oatmeal. Little did I know its meaning wouldn't change, the phrase "never give up." When you are an adult, your mindset and way of thinking should not be those of a child. Life is not instant oatmeal. It takes a lifetime to overcome, to gain victory against life's natural triggers. This doesn't happen within a day, week, month, or year. It's a lifetime process that doesn't end until we finally close our eyes on earth. So, after unconsciously struggling as a newborn to infant in every way possible, I gained victory by overcoming every challenge that lay in front of me by simply never giving up. Yet, that wasn't it. It was just the beginning of a long and continuous journey of persevering, now as a child.

In 1991, I started kindergarten. This was a memorable stage in my life. I was an enthused, curious, and anxious little girl who loved learning. When I first learned how to ride the tricycle in kindergarten, I stumbled for days to stay on a bike that weighed more than I did. However, that didn't stop me. I persevered and refused to give up. I struggled with pedaling left to right without falling, which also took time. The more I resisted giving up and improved my pedaling skills, the more I became consciously aware and learned the secret to overcoming life.

My strength and determination were also shown when I was younger. My mother said, "You also had allergies to bees. When you were nine years old, you almost lost your life due to your first allergic reaction to a bee sting. But God covered you with His love, grace, and protection. When I arrived home one morning from work, I noticed your neck was swollen, which cut off your line of breathing. I guess your dad was asleep."

I struggled with other adversities in grade school that became noticeable and sometimes embarrassing for me. However, I stood strong and never gave up—not because I was forced to keep going or to never give up but because I made the decision to do so.

Think back. What obstacles or struggles did you face as a child that motivated you to persevere? What did you do? Did you give up or did you stay encouraged? Did you talk about it with anyone?

Why or why not? Did you have feelings for your parents? Why or why not? Was it because you were fearful? I faced adversities with regard to my reading skills. Was it strenuous? Yes. In fact, it was an ongoing adversity that led me to take remedial classes for extra assistance. It took a lot of patience, effort, and willingness to accept this hindrance, and it took a lot of perseverance to keep going and not give up. Also, the fact that I stuttered lowered my self-esteem and confidence to the point that I became very quiet. Sometimes, I wouldn't speak out of fear of what others would think of me. Still, I was hopeful and never gave up. I overcame this challenging obstacle that prevented me from speaking.

I'm an eyewitness to my own walk, my life experiences and reality, besides God Himself, for the simple fact that God created you and I for a greater purpose. Therefore, you have at least one out of a million reasons to push through unexpectedness. I have unapologetic faith, but I know without a doubt that you and I were created (perfectly and powerfully packaged) as human beings with just enough strength from our Heavenly Father to cope with and persevere through the waves and storms of life. So, though it's tough, difficult, stressful, painful, and confusing, and though it sometimes seems like life is unbearable because it feels like a huge laundry basket falling on your head, be grateful because you're a human being. Stay standing as I have because your strength, hope, faith, determination, willingness, effort, attitude, and heart of making it, of overcoming the natural and destined forces of life, has the ability to bless you and those around you.

Enduring adversity without quitting also has the power to produce the best version of who you were destined to be. If you're living in doubt, look in the mirror and be bold enough to say, "I love myself." This will inspire you with more confidence to omit negative thoughts and discouragement, and instead, replace them with positivity.

If I had not turned my life over to the Lord in 2004, I would not have been able to move forward with my life and cope with everything I have dealt with, including the unexpectedness that attacks man without any three-day notices. So, I understand the difficulty, hurt, pain, confusion, anger, frustration, sadness, and weakness when you're deciding whether to keep going or give up. The process of perseverance was designed for every human being to cope with, so, it's okay. You are not alone. If you're ready for God to take your life to the next level, bless you immeasurably, comfort you in ways that could have never imagined, or transform your mindset to a healthier state, one that's Christ-inspired, then, ladies and gentlemen, you must "take it like a man or woman" and never give up. This requires effort and a willing heart of obedience and discipline, which cost nothing, to make the most important decision in your life: giving your life over to the Lord.

Persevere, despite days when you want to give up, quit, or turn to your old ways of living. It produces a rewarding blessing that requires next-level hope, faith, and determination, beyond your own, to keep going like an unstoppable Duracell battery with unbelievable enthusiasm, determination, and unapologetic purpose. The power in your difficulties is specifically programmed to eliminate every blemish, sour and bitter taste, proudness, and human desire. You seek to embrace life by allowing your struggles, downfalls, or unexpected battles to inspire you. Accept the process of God making the best of you. Never quit, as you're living on purpose and in purpose. When creating you, God destined you to be all you can be and beyond, with an amazing story to share with others. Embrace a mindset of hope, faith, and love, and shine your light. Without faith, you will have trouble discovering and appreciating your purpose in life. So, dig deep and humbly, put self to the side, and learn about our amazing Creator, God. Meditate on His Word, day and night, until your last day on earth. Remember, we were designed with an amazing gift and purpose to cope with life and obstacles with the help of the Son.

"Why are you crying?" my mother asked. As I lifted my head toward the rear-view mirror, hesitant to share the worst news ever, tears ran down my black, slanted eyes and dripped on my dirty school clothes. I was a quiet and shy girl with so much to share.

I looked her in the eyes and said, "This boy in P.E. class keeps touching me and he won't stop. Every day, he sits near me and touches me in places where it's uncomfortable, and I don't like it. And he does it when no one is watching."

My mom turned down the radio and said, "Kala, how long has he been doing this to you?"

I was nervous and embarrassed to speak out about this issue because it was one of the strangest things that I had ever experienced as an adolescent. I felt like I was in a world all alone when I entered this environment—the gymnasium. The moment I sat on the ground, reality hit. I knew this kid was ready to do what he knew bothered the hell out of me. He'd walk over, sit next to me, move his hands between my legs, and touch me near my chest even when I asked him to stop. He thought it was a joke, so he looked me in the eyes each time and smiled. However, I didn't. I was speechless and began to hate this hour, this class period that seemed like *A Nightmare on Elm Street*. The other bad thing about it was that no one else—except for God—noticed this kid's actions. It was horrible, and it seemed like neither the teachers nor the coaches paid attention. By the time the class period was over, I was down and teary. Honestly, my only wish at that time was for this kid to be expelled or suspended and nowhere near me again. I was a little girl who loved school and just wanted to be happy and attend class without anyone sexually harassing me. This damn boy wasn't going to get away with his inappropriate actions. Growing up, I was very soft-spoken and disliked large crowds, but this time I was determined to speak up and tell somebody about the ongoing problem.

Like many who experience traumatic experiences or distress, I was so uncomfortable that I didn't know what the heck to do. I was frightened of the outcome, of how my mom would react. However, like many of you, I was also tired of holding in my feelings. I knew that, sooner or later, I had to tell her the truth even though I was terrified of opening my mouth. If I didn't, I would continue to worry until I exploded like a volcano. And she knew it because she knew me. No matter how long it took for me to gain the confidence to express my voice, sooner or later something would have happened or popped off.

She felt sorry for me as I gazed forward while we drove down C Street, one street over from where we lived. Thank God something in my brain calmed me down. I took a deep breath and said, "He's been doing this for a while. I didn't wanna say anything because I didn't know how to tell you. I knew you'd drive out to the school and have a one-on-one with the principal."

She didn't hesitate. Instead, she said, "We're both going back to the school to get this squared away today." So, minutes after I shared the news, my mother made a U-turn, and we drove back to the middle school. She spoke to the head principal without hesitation. I stood in the principal's office next to my mom, nervous but relieved that she expressed her concerns for me without waiting for something worse to happen. Before we left the school building, the situation had been handled successfully, and I was overjoyed.

I said, "Yay! I did it." My heart smiled as if it were my birthday. I felt good, and a weight lifted off my shoulders. It was one of the best days ever. But more than that, letting go of what troubled my precious little heart was one of the greatest releases ever—and I'm not just saying this for you to believe me over a decade later.

Like a college athlete who dreams of getting signed to the NBA or WNBA or competing in the Super Bowl, I was determined to disrupt this problem by speaking to someone, to get it off my chest—and I did. But I did it only by the grace of God, who gave me the necessary confidence. I was young, but the power of God worked in me and through my situation with His mighty and awesome abilities beyond your imagination.

The moment I was "ready" to get this burden off my shoulders as a thirteen-year-old girl, I felt better. It was a relief off my troubled heart. The burden that was on my shoulders, driving me nuts, no longer weighed me down. The awesome thing about making the right choice to speak out was that though I couldn't discern the voice of God, it was the Spirit of God and His grace and amazing power that gave me the confidence to let go. I wasn't pressured or forced. It was the power of God continuously working in me since the moment I began fighting in my mother's womb.

This beautiful woman was my mother. She was meek and soft-spoken, but she wasn't afraid to speak up for my sisters and me. She never held her tongue back from protecting Jennifer, Allison, me, Heather, and Aimee. My mother wasn't hesitant about speaking up on our behalf—especially for me, as I didn't like to talk. I preferred to stay on mute unless I had to speak, which in this case, I had to do. The situation was emotionally disturbing because I felt embarrassed and horrified. I felt as if I were walking into a haunted house in P.E. I dreaded walking onto the basketball court because I knew what would happen minutes later. This damn kid was a smartass. He knew where I sat, what I wore, and that no one would watch, but he was wrong. Enough was enough. I was fed up and ready to share this uncomfortable news with my mom, and I did, surprisingly. Not only was I the middle child of four sisters (Jennifer, Allison, Aimee, and Heather), but I was also the quietest. I wouldn't have said a word if I didn't have to. I stared at others and minded my own business.

When I spoke, I was hesitant and shy. I barely talked in school, though at home I was more comfortable around my sisters and parents. I wasn't popular, so at times, I felt like, "Who'd want to listen to a girl like me?" I didn't think anyone would care what I had to say, so I stayed quiet. However, deep down within, I had so much to share. Because I feared my own voice, I lacked the confidence to release these words from my heart. I didn't know what others would think, so I isolated myself from my peers. Yet, I was one determined little girl who wasn't going to let anything or anyone stop her from excelling and succeeding in life. I used unexpected situations like this as opportunities to grow and explore the young woman I was becoming. It's never too late to adopt this mindset. Use your most difficult situations, or all of them, as advantages to gain, grow, and overcome life. You have everything it takes to rise, to succeed from rock bottom or depression, or anywhere you feel buried in adversity. Determination is another key, so never lose it. Embrace it. Cherish it or you'll lose it. Be it—determined.

I share this relatable experience to offer encouragement that empowers you to trust in the Lord with all your heart when you face fear or the darkest moment ever; to motivate you to know you are not alone in whatever you are fighting and holding onto in your life; and to help you reach a comfortable level of confidence to let go of what is sickening and affecting your mental or physical health. You don't have to feel like a prisoner, which was what I felt like at this time and for years to come, during different seasons. It might feel challenging and overwhelming at first, but when you have the courage to rise and overcome fear with confidence, you'll experience peace like no other and strength to prepare yourself for the next unexpected battle. Now is the time—this moment—to make a U-turn for the sake of living on purpose and in your purpose, for the betterment of all areas of your life.

If you ever find yourself in a dark place, don't be afraid, back away, and run from what and where God will deliver you. Stand strong and unmovable when you face unexpected battles. Don't be a big baby. Open your mouth! Speak up and speak out! Go for what is right—unapologetically. Be courageous and bold. Let go of your flesh and let God handle the rest of your life before it's too late. Be determined from the start or else you'll feel worthless, below average, or unimportant. You'll feel stuck, as if you're at a dead end with no way out, no possibilities. Yes, you matter. Use your voice. Never be afraid to express your thoughts and feelings. Let it go or you'll be unhappy and unhealthy. Everything will be okay, especially when you feel that your back is against the wall or everyone is against you. As you continue to live, to experience failures and successes or ups and downs, remember to stay determined no matter what category of storm you face.

I'm certain you're experiencing uncomfortable situations or seasons, and you're scared. Problems are flooding your life like a pile of laundry baskets, and you're clueless. You are frustrated, nervous, and hesitant about doing anything because you are lost—spiritually. Or you lost your belief in God because life has not gone your way like the precious wind. Holding all this in is worse. You have so much to share that you do not know how to let go of what is valuable wisdom and encouragement to others. Or you are the one I keep reading about on the news who is trapped in a horrible, uncomfortable experience preventing you from releasing your heart. You feel confined in darkness; you are struggling in silence as quiet as your heartbeat. Well, it is not over, and you are not alone in this temporary season. And it hurts because I have been there and cried. I wanted to give up, not caring about anything anymore, including doing the right thing. I am certain you are reading this far because you are interested in enriching your life or determined to gain valuable knowledge and wisdom to help you on your journey.

I hope you stand up from rock bottom, rise from depression and doubt, and do something different with your life. Or be excited about taking your imperfections and crazy, chaotic experiences and embracing what is left, now, before it is too late. You will be happier and healthier spiritually, mentally, and physically in Christ Jesus. So, if you ever find yourself in an uncomfortable situation or circumstance, and you really have the desire to let go and give it to God, then release and let God guide you. He'll turn your pain into your passion and bless you with excitement to write a book. Let Him rescue you to safety, to a better place than being miserable, unmotivated, or frustrated because He will.

# Chapter 2

## My Neighborhoods

*"My environment never affected my outlook on life, except it inspired me to appreciate a roof over my head, clothes on my back, and food to eat; I embraced where I slept."*

**-Kala**

When I was growing up, my family and I never lived in perfect neighborhoods like those that the rich or famous live in or that the actors, actresses, and rap artists vacation in throughout the year. We never slept in a three-bedroom or four-bathroom home with marble floors, standup showers, a Jacuzzi, a big garage, a backyard pool, and a huge yard with perfect green grass. We were nowhere close to living in such a picture-perfect neighborhood. Our apartment did not look like the homes in a Hollywood movie.

However, we enjoyed our window-view experiences as we drove by two-story condominiums and mansions near the beach, on the east side of Delray Beach, Florida, near all the finest American and

Italian restaurants, fine wine, and expensive shops that tourists visited. This area had Caucasians and foreigners, with few or no Black people. Often, though, I saw Black men with White women together, holding hands and walking in this area.

We also traveled through the streets of Boca Raton, Florida, where we spotted beautiful luxury homes, condominiums, and mansions. They were huge and grabbed my attention the moment I looked through the window of my mom's blue Volvo.

At night, they lit up, and during the holidays, the grass was cut, snowmen were in the grass, or the entire property was lit up. When we drove past these residences, I was amazed at everything: the architecture and colors of these beach homes, the location, the types of cars that the owners drove.

My reality was real, and the good thing about it was that I appreciated life no matter where I laid my head at night. I was content with a hot meal, a warm bath, a blanket, a pillow, and my teddy bear. We lived in a community where many ate fast food, potato chips, hot sausages, and food from the corner store, sold drugs and drank alcohol during the day, had children out of wedlock, and hustled. As I reflect now, I realize my household and I were nowhere close to living in one of those rich neighborhoods or around families who *had it all together* or had a lot of money. However, while we were not wealthy or of the upperclass, we had clothes, food on the table, and a roof over our heads.

At thirty-seven years old, I have learned to embrace and lean on God's word more than I used to, especially in my new position and in such a world where a lot has changed, including both the economic and education system, the cost of living, housing, the healthcare system, people, and more. The word of God continues to guide me, restore me, equip me with knowledge and wisdom to navigate life, and reveals the goodness and love of the Mighty Creator. Philippians 4:13: *I can do all things through Christ, which strengthens me* is my living testimony, a word from God that has blessed me to get through many challenges and hard times in life to this day. And reminds me how serious and vital it is to stay rooted in Jesus Christ in order to stay spiritually and mentally sane and in good spirits at all times. God's word is the fire in my bones, the motivation that keeps me going and that gives me strength to overcome the battles of this world. God is sovereign and greater than doubt; never limit the possibilities of God based on your circumstances. He is greater than your environment and more powerful than your situation. If you lived where I did, you would be beyond grateful for simply having a roof over your head. So, get rid of doubt and fear. Replace them with a hopeful attitude and a heart of faith.

We lived in a semi-gated community, in a popular three-story apartment complex with African Americans, who were of the lower and middle class, in Delray Beach, Florida. Caucasians, Haitians, and Hispanics were not around except at a distance from us and in public. Most of the families who lived around us were on government assistance. They received food stamps, unemployment benefits, WIC, and cash support, and they lived on Section 8, which was not a surprise. We stayed around families who were poor or did not have much. Many lived in poverty and dysfunctional environments, and they struggled with life due to a lack of income, as well as to stress, violence, depression, substance abuse, and low self-esteem.

Life was hard for many around us, but they embraced their disadvantages and turned their disabilities into motivation to help them push through adversity. They kept going and persevered, and when they needed something, they were brave enough to ask others around the complex or do what they had to do to survive. Some sold drugs for quick money, stole clothes or food from stores, applied for government checks for loved ones, sold clothes or cooked dinners in the neighborhood, or borrowed money from neighbors.

With limited resources and financial support, we also experienced rainy days. However, after the storm, we saw the sun; joy came in the morning, and we had more than one reason to look forward to better days.

The hustle and grind were real, especially with those who were single mothers, unemployed, or on disability. If a neighbor cooked, I sometimes saw a handful of people in that apartment or heard loud music and talking through the walls of our two-bedroom, one-bathroom apartment. Making a dollar out of fifteen cents was easy if you had something, but if you didn't, you could trade food stamps for cash to buy essential items or pay bills like rent. It was easy to become hopeless and lack the motivation to do anything in situations like this because the struggle was real. Times were hard, and this affected many in our complex, including my mother, who gave to those in need, the homeless, or those lacking a sufficient income to buy their next meal. She opened her door to neighbors and gave from her heart because she had a big heart.

Many wore filthy clothes for days, knocked on doors for food, sold drugs, drank alcohol, played loud hip-hop and rap music, used foul language, and bought food with food stamps, which was common. Most families qualified for government assistance, so they took advantage of this blessing to support themselves. I always saw green, red, white, and blue square-looking paper in my mother's hands and wondered what it was, but I never had to ask because I heard her say *food stamps*. I didn't quite understand their purpose until I was older. My mom would buy food and share it with family and friends. She never liked to see anyone starve or go without food, and everyone knew it, including my little self, who unconsciously embraced the footsteps and actions of my parents—more so my mother, who was a hard worker and took on most of the load. She made sure the bills were paid and that my household had food on the table.

My dad was also present and did his best. I loved my beautiful parents no matter what conditions and circumstances we experienced. We were loved despite our upbringing and living conditions and kept unity in our family.

Besides my family and my mother's friends, my grandmother, Maggy Grisby, lived across from us until she passed. I remember watching my mother visit someone else seconds from our red door. My mom said, "Yes, I paid her electric bill and rent so she did not worry. But not only that, I found out others were taking her money, so I wanted to take a burden off her shoulders." I was young, so I do not remember much other than the days when I ran in the complex barefoot with a shirt and shorts and out in the grass and playground. My sisters and I loved to play so long as it wasn't near the spooky graveyard we lived next to. My mom said, "This is where people are buried when they die," which I could not comprehend until I saw a casket go into the ground one afternoon. It was scary watching a casket rest on the ground and then disappear minutes later.

Years later, we moved to an area not far from our first residence. It was a three-bedroom, two-bathroom house with a decent-sized backyard, a dorm-sized kitchen, a front porch, and a driveway. My neighborhoods were physically different from other parts of the cities, but I did not know this until years later. I only knew that while my neighborhoods were different from other miles away, our living conditions were the same. The outsides and, most times, insides of apartments and homes were either filthy, damaged, or abandoned. And it did not seem to get better.

The more we grew and traveled throughout Delray Beach and other cities, the more we noticed the ghetto. But that was not all. I also noticed unusual graffiti on complexes, highway borders, and street signs. It was strange but also shocking to see the words, "motherfucker, bitches, and shit" on these precious buildings. However, it didn't bother me as much as it probably did others. It became the norm to see the expression of human hearts, thoughts, and lifestyles. It did not influence my ability to live a normal life around these neighborhoods. I refused to let it impact my destination and desire to achieve goals. Instead, my surroundings gave me hopes of making a difference and inspiring others who were less fortunate than we were.

My mother, Evella, worked in hospitality and the banking industry. After years of serving as a faithful and dedicated postal worker, she retired. On the other hand, my dad, Jefferson, had been a professional title installer since he was a kid. When he was young, he wanted to become a doctor, but he said, "My daddy could not afford to send me to medical school, so he taught me the skill of installing tile in homes and business offices." Both my parents worked great jobs and earned good money until their personal lives and work situations began to change.

When I was a child, my mother worked two and sometimes three jobs to provide for my family and me. She also worked overtime to make sure the bills were paid on time and we were fed.

However, that eventually changed, except for our living arrangements. We lived in the good part of the hood, where it was quiet but loud on holidays and nearby streets. The folks around us had more than a wonderful time. They had a party, danced, drank alcohol, sang, and played loud music. Although a handful of the buildings around us were homes, the people inside were drug addicts and alcoholics, and they lived on government assistance. Down the street was a popular corner store. It was everyone's favorite, including mine because I loved pickled eggs, chips, and drinks. Sometimes, I got hot sausages. Walking to this neighborhood market was like a field trip. Sometimes, my sisters and I handed coins to the store worker, but other times we handed him food stamps. I was amazed at their value and how they looked. It was amazing seeing this worker take money from my small hands and tell me, "Thank you, have a nice day." I walked out of the store and smiled until we got back home.

On the other hand, the area of my elementary school was an upgrade from where I resided; it looked different from where I laid my head and played. And when I hopped on the bus, not only did some of the children have a different skin color than my brown skin, but they also talked differently. This didn't bother or affect me, but I noticed the difference. Their skin was pale, and they used different verbiage than what I was used to hearing. Listening to someone talk properly (other than my mother) was unexpected. When they spoke, I was immediately drawn in, just as I was when we approached this unique area, my first-ever elementary school, Calusa. It was located around thirty minutes from our home, in Boca Raton, Florida. I recognized the warm and welcoming roads, buildings, homes, yards, and people. Many of the people smiled, unlike in my neighborhood. Often, I'd walk by an adult or child whose facial expression was sad-looking, nonchalant, or unhappy. This other environment, which was in a different city, was like a dream world compared to the regular environment I was accustomed to living in. But that was okay. I continued to appreciate and embrace my environment, including our next move.

When we moved to Lake Worth, Florida, we attended Barton Elementary School, which was minutes from our house on South B Street. We loved it. Sometimes, we walked to school. My mom dropped us off and picked us up, especially if my sisters or I stayed after school for tutoring. In third grade, I struggled with math, so I stayed after school and received tutoring from my third-grade math teacher. He was one of my favorite teachers and supported me the entire school year. He was patient, kind, and compassionate, and he loved to help students learn and succeed. I struggled with multiplication and division, but I was determined to overcome these stumbling blocks. At first, I was afraid to ask for help, but eventually, I found the courage to do so and asked after class. That was one of the best days of my life because I did something that I struggled to do—have faith and speak up. He made time to assist me with my issues in his class. After school, I learned helpful strategies and memorized great tips that helped me solve challenging math problems and improve my reading skills. This success boosted my confidence and encouraged me to never give up. With great support and love, I was motivated to learn and figure out ways to win instead of quitting; I was determined to persevere no matter what I faced or how many miles I had to travel to succeed. I was happy and thankful my hard work paid off.

Life was good when I was around others who spoke properly and who didn't do the things I liked. It sounds strange, right? Well, it's the truth. I felt welcomed and had a sense of protection. But it didn't determine my abilities and work ethic. No matter what and who I was around, it didn't determine my success, nor did I ever try to compare myself to anyone. I was different. I was built to win, and unstoppable. I was focused and had confidence that I would overcome life no matter what I faced. It was a joy to ride on the bus and look outside the window at green grass, flowers, clean streets, and a beautiful school campus. Everything seemed perfect in my eyes when I walked on this campus. The classrooms were clean, the main office smelled good, everyone spoke to each other, and the field was well-kept.

Years later, after I completed my undergraduate studies at Florida Atlantic University, I had a desire to further my education. I browsed my options and asked around. I prayed and considered Florida International University in Miami. I completed the online application and auditioned in the music department for graduate school. Weeks later, God answered my prayers. I was accepted at FIU and received a graduate teaching stipend and financial assistance. However, I knew I'd eventually need a "real" job to assist with other bills.

In 2011, I took a leap of faith and moved to Miami. I had worked at Office Depot for several years, so I transferred to a nearby location. But I wasn't there for long, even though it was close to the college. I wanted to focus on my studies for the next two years, so I gave my two weeks' notice and resigned. My income decreased, but my faith grew stronger. I was okay with "change" because I knew God would open another door of opportunity at the right time. So, once again, I was determined to make the best of my time and embrace what was to come.

Thankfully, scholarships and my graduate assistant stipend assisted with my first on-campus efficiency apartment. However, after I noticed a lizard in the apartment, I lost interest. I also noticed a slight opening at the bottom of my apartment door. I was ready to move out and into a *real* apartment. Months later, I took another leap of faith and hired a local realtor to assist me in securing my own apartment in a nearby community. After performing a Google search, I located a local realtor's office a few miles from the university. They were expensive but well worth it. I visited the office and spoke to a realtor about my situation and housing desires. She explained the process and provided me with important details. I was confident that I would be moving into a new place after the realtor reviewed my information, discussed my options, and provided me with a list of potential residences. That afternoon, I walked out of the rental office with a smile on my face and the hope that I would receive a call back with good news. And I did. Days later, I received a phone call from the realtor with the message that she had found a condo nearby. It was one of the best days of my life and a relief off my shoulders. She had located a one-bedroom, one-bathroom condo in South Miami—the Kendall area—and reached out to the owner. The realtor was very helpful and professional, and she assisted me throughout the entire application process.

Hours after the realtor contacted the owner, she reached out to me, and we scheduled a date and time for me to view the condo. The realtor was available the following day. At the condo complex, she greeted me, and then we walked upstairs to the unit together. I noticed the parking lot was unusual—the entrance required a gate card, and the area was bushy. However, the community seemed okay. It sat across the street from a corner store and pizza restaurant. My unit was in the back area around other condos, which faced a train area and mall. The neighborhood seemed quiet and housed older people.

The owner unlocked the unit door, removed the lock, and opened it. We walked in and she showed me around, starting with the kitchen. Then, she showed me the living room area and walked me into the master bedroom, closet, and bathroom. The condo was nice and spacious, and it included a big patio. It also included carpet and a water heater in the master bedroom closet. However, I was content and needed a place to rest my head, so I informed her that I was interested in renting the condo. She provided me with further details. I also reached out to the realtor and informed her that I was interested in taking the condo. She was very happy for me and completed the paperwork on her end. I moved in days later.

The condo was in a safe and quiet neighborhood surrounded by busy streets and loud traffic. I lived alone, but I was certain it wouldn't be this way forever. I had faith that, one day, I would get married and have a beautiful family. I had to be patient and wait on the Lord.

I also noticed shopping centers, like a mall, grocery stores, a tire shop, a coffee joint, and gas stations, in my new area. However, there wasn't security at the complex. Still, I felt safe and knew that God would continue to watch over me and keep me safe.

The condominium complex had limited parking and tenant assistance as well as no pest control service, which eventually created issues. In fact, I found myself preparing to cut the lease after almost a year of being dissatisfied and unhappy with my living conditions. For personal reasons, I asked the landlord to replace the carpet with tile, but she refused to pay for this adjustment. I informed her that my dad was a professional tile installer and would be happy to remove the carpet and replace it with tile, but she stated that she would not be able to pay him for his services. I was shocked and motivated to move out. On top of these issues, I experienced problems with the air conditioning and saw a roach crawling on my dresser mirror one night as I walked into the room. I was frightened and reached out to the owner that evening. She explained that pest control was not included in the monthly rent. I also reached back out to the realtor and expressed my lack of interest in the condo. I wanted to move into an apartment that had tiled floors and where pest control was included in the rent. I had faith it would happen.

I also met with the owner at her house, and we discussed these issues, but she had no interest in making changes to the condo. So, after less than two years, I terminated the lease months early and moved out. I had to do what I had to do, and I did it with hope, faith, and prayer.

I reached back out to the realtor for her assistance. During an unexpected change, I lived with a relative as I began my appointment as an adjunct professor at Miami Dade College. I was set on overcoming my temporary hardship and certain that God would bless me with another place in due time. Because the drive was far (hours away from my job), I took a risk some nights and slept in my car, or I paid a high price for a hotel room. It was challenging, but I didn't give up. I used this as an opportunity to pray and ask God to help me get myself together.

One morning, I slept in the parking lot of McDonald's near my job and set my alarm to get me up the next morning. I was grateful nothing bad happened and no one knocked on my window to ask why I was sleeping in my car. However, I knew I couldn't do this for long. It was dangerous and could cause issues down the road. I could also have received a trespassing warning. I thank God I didn't. His grace and mercy protected me. I knew my change would come at the right time.

After I prayed and searched for an apartment complex with additional amenities, God blessed me to locate an apartment near my job. It was a small apartment and expensive, but it had a nice interior and included tile. It was located on the first floor and was in a gated community ten minutes from the college.

Driving from Palm Beach County to Kendall was a struggle mentally, physically, and financially. I experienced family issues, my body became physically tired on my way to work, and I paid a lot for gas, so I took another leap of faith and applied for the apartment. My income was low, and my credit score was poor, so I was denied. However, after I prayed, expressing my interest in the apartment and my commitment to paying twelve hundred dollars for a one-bedroom, one-bathroom, dorm-sized apartment, God graced me to get approved. The particularly good thing was that God blessed me to get approved for the apartment without needing a co-signer on the lease.

I moved to west Kendall, opposite where I previously lived. The complex had a pool, a tennis court, a clubhouse, a gym, and other amenities. I moved in and got situated after a few days. It was by far the most expensive apartment I had rented since moving to Miami in 2011. Everything worked out well, but water and electricity weren't included in the rent, which became an issue. The rent was expensive and required most of my income, which created issues with me paying my tithe and other essential bills.

By the summer, after a few months of staying at the complex, I could no longer afford it. I reached out to the management office and informed them of the situation. The next morning, I typed a letter of intent to move out of the apartment, which meant cutting the lease early. I had become overwhelmed and did not want things to get worse by struggling in an apartment I could not afford. If I didn't find affordable housing, I was in big trouble.

This was one of the most difficult seasons of my life. However, I knew it was a test of my faith and that God would deliver me once again. So, I didn't give up. I pressed forward despite the adversity I experienced in securing stable housing. I didn't let the situation overpower my spirit and purpose for persevering and rising above the real struggle, the fight to earn, survive, and be successful. I had faith that better days were on the way and that, one day, God would bless me with stable housing, a full-time job, a better credit score, marriage, and a family.

Once again, there I was, in the middle of an unexpected life storm. The Spirit led me to search for housing miles away from my job. He led me in a favorable location in the Miami area. I picked up an apartment guide at a local supermarket and searched for affordable and local apartments. This was around the beginning of 2014, and it was challenging because I had to stick to my budget. However, I was determined to find the one. By the grace of God, I did, after weeks of looking, contacting local apartment offices, and driving up and down the highway.

God blessed me where He saw fit—in a safe, quiet, and affordable neighborhood—and satisfied my heart's desires. At the time of my application, the complex was offering a rental special for a one-bedroom, one-and-a-half-bathroom unit, and it included tile, pest control, and water. Also, it was located near gas stations, the hospital, grocery stores, schools, the pharmacy, and more. However, I continued to drive a distance to church services until I was ready to move my membership to a closer Church of Christ. From time to time, I visited local Churches of Christ closer to the Miami area, such as Pembroke Park Church of Christ, Miami Gardens Church of Christ, and Hallandale Church of Christ.

Today I am humbled and grateful to share that by the grace of God, my family and I are blessed to have a stable roof over our heads, food to eat, and clothes on our backs. We're content. My unique communities and the people who lived around us motivated me to strive for better for my family. We have God's love, joy, peace, and happiness, and that's what matters.

But God's not done with us, nor does it end here. Over the years, I've learned to keep my faith and to trust in the will of God, not my own understanding or intuition. My situation could have been worse, but God's grace and mercy rescued me at the appointed time.

With God's wisdom, embrace what you have, or you could lose it. And appreciate life with or without. Be grateful for the pillow where you rest your head, for the bedrooms in your home or apartment, for the wooden fence and exterior color of your residence. Don't complain about what you wish you had. Instead, have faith and thank God for what you have, wherever you are on earth.

Decorate your space or add a twist to areas in your home; use your creative heart in ways you never imagined and have fun in the process! Create magic in your home with your abilities and passion. Add color to a dark room to strengthen your mental health or build your self-esteem and confidence. Build an office in your living room area or turn a space into your meditation area. Design something from nothing, and God will bless you to produce amazing things.

If you desire something better, pray about it. Let God carry you where you need to be, not where you think you should be. He'll never lead you astray or in an uncomfortable direction if it's purposeless. And remember that you're doing better than many others who might be struggling to find somewhere to sleep, take a shower, use the restroom, cook food, and call home. When you grow to focus on being more content with God's blessings and will, your faith will grow, and so will that of others. When you put your trust in God's hands to settle you where He sees fit, you'll learn to appreciate your housing situations and life in general.

# Chapter 3

## *My Music Journey*

*"From day one, the sound of music and everything about it captured my mind, heart, and soul like the moment I picked up the clarinet and blew my first musical notes. The sound of this instrument swept me off my feet and gave me goosebumps like the ones my handsome husband gave me when we first met, in 2014. What an experience. Playing music was my life until something unexpected interrupted my journey."*

*-Kala*

The next phase of my educational journey was middle school. In August 1996, I found myself back on the school bus, headed to an unfamiliar environment, a place I had never visited until my mother and I attended an open house days before the new school year. She enrolled me and my sisters in Lake Worth Middle School, in Lake Worth, Florida. The school was about twenty to thirty minutes from our small, two-bedroom, one-bathroom duplex on Sixth

Avenue South, which was next to a major highway. Sometimes, I stood on the porch and stared at the cars, trucks, and school buses passing by, including the ambulances and police cars. Boy, were they loud, especially in the evening when I looked outside the kitchen window above the sink at the train that passed every hour.

More interesting was a corner store that sat across the street from our residence. My sisters and I loved this store. Every time we walked inside it, the owner, who was Arab, looked across the register at us, smiled, and greeted us. Occasionally, we saw our friends and neighbors, who ran out of breath and sweating, as if they'd just run a marathon. We did not have money, so we'd ask our mom or dad for money to buy chips, a soft drink, or candy. Then, out the door we went. We looked left, and then right, and then we ran across the street.

In addition to the corner store, we lived near town homes and other apartment complexes. Across the railroad tracks were several food places, a pharmacy, and small businesses. Checkers, Walgreens, a gas station, and a hair and beauty supply store were all within walking distance. Blocks away was Lake Worth Beach along with banks, Chafin's Music Center, the Lake Worth Library, the Lake Worth Power and Light Company, etc. The beach wasn't within walking distance, but it didn't take us long to get there when our mother drove us on the weekends or, sometimes, during the week. Going to the beach was one of our favorite mommy-daughters spots. Our dad was elsewhere, so we spent most of our time with our mom. However, he stayed in contact with us when we weren't together. Sometimes, he'd carry us along with him to work or meet my mom to see us and give us money.

Before arriving at the beach, we had to cross a bridge, which I disliked. I was afraid of riding over it because it was huge, and the water was deep. Sometimes, I saw it tilt up toward the sky and wondered what would happen if we got trapped on it one day. However, ultimately, I loved it. We put our faces against the window and looked at the water, noticing that it was deep and we were up high. We also saw boats and ships traveling under the bridge. We were amazed at what we saw and who we spotted near the bridge. For everything we approached in this area, we sat up in our seats and looked out the window.

When we finally arrived at the beach, we saw people wearing their swim suits (bikinis, two-pieces, and full bathing suits), the pool area, ice cream and food shops, dogs, a bar with a deck, and one of our favorite spots to play—the park. When we got out of the car, we stretched our arms and smiled. Then, we held each other's hands and walked across the street with our mother to the entrance of the beach area. Before we walked on the sand, we removed our flip-flops. That way, we could walk on the sand barefoot, which we loved. There were also two showers, which allowed people to wash off before and after they entered the beach area. We ran on the sand, made sandcastles, and walked near the edge of the ocean with a bucket or small bag in which to collect seashells, rocks, and anything creative or strange that didn't frighten us. We were scared little girls, but some things we didn't fear. However, we never swam in the ocean because we didn't know how to kick our feet and balance our arms in deep water. We had hopes of one day learning how to swim, though only if we had the guts to overcome this fear. Our mother kept her eyes on us and instructed us to stay near her and not go into the water.

Spending quality time with my family led to some of the most memorable days of my life. We also spent Sunday afternoons at Piccadilly, a soul-food restaurant. It was located on the east side of

Delray Beach in the Delray Beach Plaza. We ate there after church services and sometimes during the week. My favorite was boiled chicken, yellow rice, green beans, salad, and macaroni. I loved food, so I never played over meals. The food was delicious. We also loved Red Lobster, Waffle House, IHOP, Denny's, KFC, and Bud's Chicken & Seafood.

On the other hand, one time, I almost lost my life after my sister's boyfriend attempted to teach me how to swim in the pool. This was one of the most shocking experiences ever. He picked me up and walked me close to the edge of the pool, then let me go. When I realized what had happened and that I was floating at the bottom of the pool, I panicked and tried to swim near the pool's stairway. I made it out safely by the grace of God. There was no lifeguard on duty that day. When my mom found out what had happened, she became upset, and we left the pool immediately. However, he did apologize for his actions, as he hadn't anticipated what would happen. After that traumatic experience, I was no longer interested in learning how to swim. Nor did my mother want my sisters and me near pools or anywhere near water, including the pools at hotels, motels, and resorts.

During the week, if we weren't at school for tutoring, a rehearsal, or a school activity or club, we were home or with our mother. On the weekends, if we didn't go to the beach, play with our friends, or go out to eat, we were content at home. We'd get up on Saturday mornings, eat breakfast, and watch television. In the afternoon, we enjoyed going outside in our small parking lot to jump rope, play, and run up the street to see our Hispanic friends. Some were also Blacks and Haitians. Race didn't matter. We treated everyone fairly because we demanded the same respect.

We also played around the apartment, studied, and did our homework. Often, we went to the local library to read books and participate in weekend activities. Because we didn't have a library or bookshelf in our home, visiting our local library gave me hope about building one. I enjoyed having the opportunity to browse interesting books. However, deep down, I didn't have an interest in reading books because they looked complicated to complete with so many pages. I often wondered how others could sit in a library or at a park and read a book containing almost three hundred pages without getting bored. To me, it was strange, but I'm certain everyone had their reasons why they loved to read books.

However, I loved to brainstorm ideas and write. Creating things with my hands, thoughts, and ideas interested me more than picking up a book and doing something I didn't want to do. I wasn't a book lover, but when I read, some things grabbed my attention. Meanwhile, some moved me to close the book without reading past the introduction or table of contents.

Spending time at the Lake Worth Library was an opportunity for my sisters and me to step outside the house and explore our area and the events that occurred nearby and in the city.

We had moved into this area after the passing of one of my uncles, Uncle Pliny. His death was difficult for my mom and my grandmother. He had lived with us in a small apartment complex near Lake Worth High School, and my mom had stood near his side during the darkest days of his life. We moved there because my mom wanted a bigger apartment. This was just before I started the next phase of my educational journey. The only risk of our move was the highway, which seemed okay at first. However, it wasn't the safest place.

At times, my mom argued with the landlord for several reasons, including when he raised the rent. Often, my dad visited us. He didn't live there, but sometimes he needed a place to stay, and he wanted to be with us, so my mom welcomed him. He helped my mom from time to time and watched my sisters and me when she worked at the post office. She worked at the Summit location in West Palm Beach, Florida, and she loved it. Some days were challenging, but we learned to love and support each other, including my mother, who we knew worked her buns off to take care of the bills, put food on the table, and provide love and support during our educational journey. She worked night shifts and arrived home in the mornings. As I mentioned, my dad was a self-employed tile installer. Sometimes, we'd hear them argue over money and rent and he'd leave or vice versa—she'd drive off for a mental breather. Sometimes, he left and didn't return for days. But it wasn't as bad as what others experienced. My oldest sister, Jennifer, lived next to us in the duplex. Sometimes, she'd walk over and check on us, wash clothes, or take us to get food.

Just before we caught the bus, my mother would bring us breakfast from McDonald's or cook us a warm, delicious meal. She did this for years and taught us along the way how to cook. She worked hard and did her best to provide a roof over our heads, food to eat, and clothes on our backs.

Days after my new chapter in middle school started, my mother took my sisters and me shopping for food, supplies, and school clothes. I was very excited and anxious about starting my new journey in sixth grade. I couldn't wait until the next day, so as soon as the alarm went off, I rose, used the bathroom, rinsed my face, brushed my teeth, put on my new school uniform, and prepared breakfast. My mom saw me awake, but my sisters were asleep. So, she walked into the room and said, "It's time to get up for school, girls." Allison, Heather, and Aimee awoke and performed the same routine. We were each a year or two apart in age. Aimee was the youngest and was still in elementary school. After we ate, we grabbed our colorful and stylish backpacks and made our way outside to the bus stop with the rest of our friends and the unfamiliar boys and girls.

The bus stop was at the corner street near our duplex. My mother met us at the bus stop and watched us until the bus driver arrived. Sometimes, when the driver didn't show up, my mom drove us to school. However, when the bus driver arrived, I pointed at the bus from a distance and smiled. We said, "Bye, Mama. We love you."

She replied, "Bye, babies. I love you all, too." She smiled, blew us a kiss, and waved.

Then, we stood in line. When the bus stopped at the stop sign, the door opened. We walked onto the bus and walked toward the back area. Everyone was quiet and looked around. Some held their heads down as if they were sleepy. Or maybe they were unmotivated or unhappy about going to school. Some of the boys played video games on their electronic devices or kicked pencils around the bus with their feet and smiled. The bus driver didn't notice or say anything. That morning, as I approached the back of the bus, I saw many of my old classmates from elementary school and familiar faces I had noticed in other classes. I sat at the back of the bus while my sisters sat with their friends.

After everyone found a seat, the bus driver closed the door. We passed stop lights, stop signs, apartments, government buildings, and familiar streets. Then, suddenly, after a bumpy, noisy, and quiet ride, I spotted a big, secluded, brown and white building when the bus driver turned right on Barnett Drive. The school was near one of the most popular fun spots in town, Fun Depot, and looked like a college campus. I saw medical buildings and a car lot on my left. I-95 was directly to the right side of the school campus. We entered through the gates of the school and arrived at the bus loop, which was next to the faculty parking area, the main parking lot. My heart sped, and I smiled for many reasons: I was excited and relieved that we had made it to school safely it was my first day of "big school," and I was anxious to meet old and new friends. I also looked forward to the many opportunities God had in store for me.

When I walked off the school bus with my new backpack and school uniform, things felt surreal. I walked through crowds of loud voices and laughs from a bunch of adolescents. They were tall, short, skinny, and overweight, and some looked to be my age, so I knew I was in the right place: middle school. However, a handful looked older. This intimidated me somewhat, but not for long. I had felt this feeling when I started kindergarten, but days later I was okay and comfortable. I was also a little nervous when I arrived at middle school, but not as much as my cranky peers and their parents. Several administrators shouted, "This way, boys, and girls. The office is straight ahead. Yes, walk this way and turn left."

As they shouted on their walkie-talkies, the police officers directed traffic, school buses, cars, and anxious kids who were dying to chat with their friends and rush to the cafeteria for a hot breakfast. At that point, I knew it was a reality, and I was ready for my new and exciting journey in a different place than Calusa and Barton Elementary School. I continued to explore the campus and search for my classes. "Yikes!" I said. The morning felt like an unexpected rush hour as I gazed at parents walking their nervous and crying sons and daughters to their classrooms as if they were college students who needed an escort to the main office. I didn't need my mother because we had attended an open house days before the start of the new school year. I was confident about having the courage to enjoy this day and embark on a new journey in my first hours as a sixth-grader. However, I didn't say anything. I kept quiet as I observed my surroundings and walked to my classes with a backpack filled with college-ruled paper, highlighters, pencils, and a Dr. Grip pen. I was set to go, ready to learn and get familiar with my new space, teachers, and peers. I knew it would take time to get to know everyone, but I was one happy girl and no one was going to change that. I was determined to stay focused, do well, and make the best of my new chapter as an adolescent.

Not everyone around me had the same mindset; their viewpoints about life and their desire for education were different from mine. Many didn't like school, and they expressed that fact, even on the first day of junior high. However, their outlook on education didn't affect my commitment to learn, strive, thrive, and succeed. I was blessed, and I knew it without a doubt.

I didn't know anything about having faith except what I heard at home and in school. I heard the word "faith" in church, but I couldn't comprehend its true meaning until years later. My teachers would say, "Believe in yourself. Have confidence," and I did, even when I failed or struggled as a youth. I knew there was something extraordinary about my spirit, attitude, and outlook on life—something special that I couldn't hold back and resist. I was that kid, the young girl who wasn't popular in school and around her neighborhood, but when you met her, you were inspired by her heart, her dedication to stay focused and learn, and her contagious personality. I gave when others didn't. I showed respect when some didn't. I encouraged someone when they were down, hurt, or hopeless. I inspired others when they quit or wanted to give up. I showed compassion to those who didn't know how to love and care for others. When I didn't do well in school, I wasn't lazy. I persevered and discovered ways to keep going.

I thought about my dreams, how I desired to get out of poverty and go to college. I strove to not waste my life and to do something with my gifts, talents, and creativity. Giving up wasn't an option for me because I was determined to rise above my generational curses, challenges, dysfunctional household, and oppositions of life. I was determined to win. With a growth mindset, I used my challenges and struggles as opportunities to strengthen my hope and faith, and they did. Every time I faced an obstacle or problem, I stood up and did whatever it took to gain, grow, learn, and succeed. Unexpected adversity like this helped build my resilience and shaped my viewpoint and character in life.

Humbly speaking, I had an innate extraordinary spirit to not make excuses when I experienced stumbling blocks. I had an attitude of confidence and a will to succeed and be steady on my journey. My parents never had to force me to go to school or to learn because I always had the motivation to gain knowledge about things, even if I had to self-teach and figure things out on my own. I loved challenges that tested my faith and abilities to figure out solutions to problems, no matter how long it took me to win. I was born determined, and nothing could change that.

Obstacles inspired me to look forward to better days and successful outcomes; the ability to work toward achieving my goals was the fun part. I took pleasure in every step of the process. After I won, I felt good. I felt more confident, stronger, and wiser than I'd been before I experienced the problems.

I was also committed to pushing through the waves, unexpectedness, and stumbling blocks of life. If I wasn'thadn't been, nothing would have changed. I would not have been able to climb and flourish as I did if I had chosen to sit in my storms and watch them overpower my abilities.

The first time I struggled to ride a tricycle I persevered until I got it. When I struggled to read and speak at a normal pace without stuttering, I was lost and experienced low self-esteem until I chose to look past my flaws and fight to win this battle. Eventually, I did.

I did everything I could to achieve my goals, even though it was hard. That was the part I held on to, embraced, and used for my own good—not because I saw others doing it but because I experienced a similar test and had faith that I would excel and accomplish my hurdles. In the end, it paid off. My desire to push through difficult times and use my storms as ways to improve and grow strengthened my focus and mindset ten times. **I learned to accept the girl in the mirror—the person God created and blessed—and to fly like a butterfly as I discovered ways to blossom like a beautiful flower.** I didn't need to fit into the crowd and wave my hands in the air like I didn't care for attention because I knew my worth and the value I possessed. I knew my lack of success would turn into success. I knew my impediments would open doors of opportunities to explore and enable me to discover some of the greatest secrets that would bless my life and help others avoid giving up. That was what mattered. It wasn't about me or the problem; instead, it was about learning to conquer life over fear or doubt.

When I fell or failed, God lifted me. When I stopped, I saw success before I experienced it. When I felt discouraged, I encouraged myself. I said, "I can do it. I will make it. I am an achiever. I have what it takes to overcome life. I am brave and strong." I refused to let life take me by the hand and bring me down. I was designed on purpose, with purpose, and for a greater purpose, and I truly believed that. There were no mistakes on my journey.

I was a quiet and courageous girl who walked with confidence, dignity, and an optimistic attitude toward growing and overcoming life.

In the next phase of my life, I was ready to explore more of the world—new things, new people, and my God-given abilities, i.e., my gifts and creativity. I had ambitions to continue rising beyond adversity, a dysfunctional household, and my neighborhoods so that I could succeed at whatever I faced along the way, even if it meant being brave.

When God presented me with an opportunity to do something I never dreamt of or imagined, I responded to the blessing and went for it—with a smile, unapologetically. After I said "yes" to making this extraordinary move, my life changed. However, this decision took me out of my comfort zone and required me to be disciplined and committed to my gift. I was young, with hopes of exploring great opportunities along the way. So, I was confident that I had made one of the best decisions ever. There was no turning back. I was all in and firm about making the most of one of the best opportunities of my life.

The reality of watching sixth-, seventh-, and eighth-graders was stunning and interesting, especially as I observed everything while smiling underneath my innocent heart and soundless breath. I enjoyed watching some boys and girls, like me, with matching uniforms, decorative backpacks, and creative hairstyles, approach the classrooms in silence. Meanwhile, others jumped with joy to see their old school buddies and best friends for life. I didn't anticipate seeing many of my friends, including my best friend for life, because I wasn't that popular, or perhaps because I was still an antisocial girl with the same quiet, shy, and soft-spoken spirit, content with being alone and away from the "crowd" if no one approached me.

I enjoyed my English class because I aced my spelling tests and became the top speller. It was fun and engaging, though I struggled on some of my reading tests and quizzes. I still smiled and laughed, though. The teacher was hilarious, and he knew it, which made learning more engaging, motivational, fun, memorable, and special. I also liked my science class. Creating volcanoes and experiments with food was the best.

When I heard the words "sex" and "reproduction system," I felt uncomfortable and embarrassed if the teacher called on me. Yet, I was curious, and I was moved and enlightened by an entire class learning about the body and how babies were created. Despite being quiet, I had a mouth full of words at the tip of my tongue to share. Instead of raising my hands, I wrote down my questions and asked the teacher to answer them in private. She did, without hesitation. I was thankful and learned a lot by simply having the courage to do something I feared. I'd try to look the other way or hold my head down, but that didn't work. In fact, my science teachers always called on me to answer questions or read in the textbook. Class participation was a grade, so most times, I participated. However, when I felt uncomfortable about answering, I stayed silent and spoke with the teacher after class. They understood and encouraged me, telling me that everything would be okay. Their understanding strengthened my confidence and, eventually, helped me feel less fearful about participating in class.

Then, the moment I didn't expect happened: My palms began to sweat, my legs stiffened, my heart raced, and anxiety kicked itself into my immature and naive brain when I looked down at my first class schedule. It looked like an unusual restaurant menu with subjects organized by days, times, locations, and instructors. However, one stood out, like me, as the only Black woman and educator at an educational institution filled with mostly Latinos. Somehow, I exhaled and accepted my reality by embracing the opportunity to explore and experience something new in my life.

I was the brown-skinned, quiet-spirited, and antisocial girl on the block who was ready to explore and embrace life—to be all that I was destined to be, despite the odds. So, in 1996, I smiled as I walked into a big, bright, and unusual band room. It looked like a movie theater and was filled with black plastic chairs, musical instruments, instrument storage, and an area with pictures, plaques, and other awards. There were speakers at the front corner of the room, a white board, and the absence of sound, until I discovered that the lifeless instruments were hidden inside their coffin-looking cases for protection and beauty sleep (rest). But that wasn't all.

My life didn't become interesting and meaningful for me until I trusted my gut and followed a schedule that was totally beyond my control, interest, and wildest dreams. This convinced me that I was making the right choice to embark on a fresh, new, and amazing journey. With a smile and silent enthusiasm, I sat in one of those black plastic chairs, unlike what I sat in during class and at the dinner table. The seat was stable and comfortable and felt as if someone previously sitting in the chair had warmed it up for me without even knowing my name. Besides the welcoming atmosphere, the seat kept me focused on listening as my new band director gave an overview of the class. The speech was very detailed and welcoming to the array of boys and girls who felt the same way I did—puzzled and amazed. Sitting in this special chair also helped ease my mind, preventing me from standing up and walking out of the room before the bell rang and everyone raced to the door. I stayed and listened like an eleven-year-old was expected to behave.

What I enjoyed the most was standing up and walking around the band room to view and choose an instrument. Percussion instruments were my least favorite because I figured they were too simple. It looked like a boy's job—to hold wooden sticks, bells, mallets, and maracas in their hands, stand in the back, and lead the band.

Instantly, I fell in love with a tall, heavy, black-and-silver, twenty-four-keyed clarinet. The moment I discovered it, I was hooked, and my heart felt good. It looked easy to play, unlike the other musical instruments I saw, and it weighed as much as I looked for a while. When I first picked it up, it felt right, like God had chosen it for me before I'd even put my hands on it. I was clueless as to what to expect. I was now the young person behind the clarinet who was no longer shy about carrying around an instrument that weighed about as much as I did. I was bold; I didn't care who stared, whispered, or laughed. I was excited and determined to continue pursuing music. My confidence was stronger than ever.

It finally happened: I began my musical journey. Nothing interfered with my decision to welcome my newfound love, the clarinet, into my life. I was determined to embrace everything expected of me to learn this instrument. I was excited and felt like I'd made one of the best decisions ever. My entire life was now centered around my music education and band. This four-letter word was stuck in my mind morning, noon, and night—and, sometimes, in my dreams.

The clarinet grew to be very important in my life—so much so that I loved doing things that others disliked, like cleaning it and buying supplies I needed to play the instrument. Also, I carried it with me almost everywhere I went. I loved holding it and felt a deep connection with it. The clarinet became my new best friend, which I rarely had. I felt I could embrace the clarinet whenever I sat behind it but also while I was in class.

Studying music and learning to play a musical instrument helped me with my academics. When I struggled, I visualized the clarinet and applied strategies I used for the clarinet to my problems. During class, I thought like a clarinetist. To every test, quiz, project, and reading and writing assignment I was given, I applied my learning and wisdom from music. My clarinet gave me comfort and hope when I needed it the most. I felt good, like I could achieve anything I put my mind to if I persevered. I became attached to it and was very engaged in the process of learning how to move my fingers while reading black-and-white notes. It was amazing and did my mind and body good. Studying the clarinet kept me focused and inspired my desire to stay in shape mentally and physically.

Though I was no longer the girl who walked around without accompaniment or something to talk to as if it were human, there was still only a limited number of boys and girls in my circle whom I'd converse with. I was still the quiet and shy girl from grade school who preferred to be alone and avoided talking unless she had to. I was different, but not only did I accept this difference, I embraced it. So, I continued to isolate myself from big audiences and wherever there were lights, cameras, and action. I didn't care about being seen.

I was okay being the girl who stood behind the curtains. Not only did I sit, eat, and complete most of my schoolwork solo, but I also sat in the last seat in the auditorium during performances or educational events. I wasn't focused on accumulating a large number of friends. Instead, I wanted real relationships with others. I wanted to know my friends, to chat, talk, and laugh. I wanted to get to know others and build friendships, all while being a real band geek. I stayed focused, had goals, and wanted something in life.

Walking down a hallway filled with students, peers, administrators, and security, without a fan crew or group of middle schoolers screaming in my ears and throwing bubble gum at my face was my continued norm. I was okay without the extras. I kept it one hundred, in today's creative language, and lived.

I enjoyed my studies, including band, though sometimes I experienced obstacles that affected my confidence and motivation. However, instead of giving up or quitting, I let my circumstances inspire me to keep going with hope and faith. The more I noticed a consistency in my perspective in life while sitting behind this new experience, this new instrument, the clarinet, the more I fell in love with and embraced even my challenging days of blowing meaningless sounds. I was never done with learning, as I knew there was room for gain, growth, and improvement, no matter how many A's and B's I received.

I continued to persevere and embraced even my failures with a positive attitude and outlook. I took pleasure in my failures and adversity because they motivated me to press forward and stay focused. I was determined to get things done, even if it meant practicing more and doing extra work.

At times, I became down and regretted staying in the band. I began to dislike this four-letter word as part of my daily life. I wasn't a pro. However, I also started to like hearing cluttered sounds because I knew that, with faith, one day, those sounds would transform into pleasant or normal sounds that attracted the ears of both amateurs and professionals.

I was short, and my clarinet reached a little below my belly button. I enjoyed holding this instrument, looking down at my fingers in class and in the mirror to make sure the key holes were covered, and embracing every moment I was blessed with the opportunity to hold this baby girl with care, concern, and commitment.

However, weeks later, my adrenaline began to arise when I found out that I needed to rent or rent-to-purchase a clarinet. I thought my eyes would pop out of my head when I arrived home and shared the news with my parents. My dad was cool with it, but my mother was hesitant at first. Soon, though, she realized how passionate I was about playing the clarinet, so she made the sacrifice—on a fixed income and budget—to rent me a clarinet at a popular music store in our neighborhood.

The owner of the music store was a musician. He not only gave me clarinet lessons on Saturdays but also played just about every instrument he sold in the store. He was special, loving, caring, supportive, giving, and compassionate. I also noticed his sense of humor as he conveyed his personality during my lessons. For example, he'd play loud and encourage me to do the same. After each lesson, l continued to improve. Most of our lessons took place in a quiet, secluded room, but his passion for playing the clarinet was never unnoticed; it was recognizable to all the customers and, of course, the staff and the entire music world. If the only technique we worked on was breathing and learning to project one musical note through the bell of the clarinet, then he made sure we accomplished this. It's funny, but I was both nervous and excited about each lesson. It seemed like I was walking to the back of a long and quiet maze as I strolled through the store's music library storage to arrive at a small, nearly empty practice room.

The sound that exited my clarinet could be heard from the rear of the store, where silence seemed defeated by loud sounds from a young Black girl, a human being with a big heart carrying a speechless voice, a girl who was determined to succeed, improve, gain, grow, develop, and embrace this instrument that was now her companion. I carried a clarinet that wasn't quite mine while still being mine; it would remain a rental until my mom could afford to pay it off. This motivated me to be more thankful and appreciative for the love and support my mother gave and showed to my sisters and me while we were growing up.

I fell so much in love that I was attached to my clarinet. I loved it and, eventually, became so attached to this tangible object that my surroundings felt weird and unusual without it. My clarinet was now a part of my life, and nothing on earth could separate us.

So, after I spent an amazing year in sixth grade, and having navigated through doors of unexpectedness, I started getting the hang of things. I was prepared to take on this journey called life. I wasn't as fearful as I had been when I began; I became more confident and comfortable about my new educational journey. However, something stood out to me. I realized that I no longer had my own schedule—one that was simple. I had a set schedule that I wasn't accustomed to, but I adjusted and went with the flow of things.

During this season of my life, I began puberty, which was a shocker. However, my mom gave me a heads-up: "Baby, soon, you'll be having your period, and you'll start to bleed. When this happens, let me know and I'll give you pads."

I was nervous but not surprised the day I ran to my mother and said, "Mama, I'm bleeding." I walked to her room, showed her the blood on my panties, and froze. My eyes almost popped out of my head, but I was able to control myself.

She looked at me and smiled. After she handed me a couple of pads, I went into the bathroom and put a few in my panties. Then, I pulled up my panties and walked out of the bathroom. She called me over and we had a mommy-daughter chat. She said, "Each month you're going to have a period around the same date, so try to remember this day." I kept a mental note and remembered what she said moving forward. What an experience, an unforgettable moment that happened near the end of sixth grade.

I was successful and passed all my classes. That meant I was one happy camper and looked forward to the following year. I said to my parents, "Yay! I passed all my classes and I'll be going to the seventh grade next school year." They congratulated me and we celebrated as a family.

In mid-August 1997, I began seventh grade. I looked forward to my new classes and playing in the band. I was also ready for whatever obstacles were bound to come my way. I was ready to overcome life with the same mindset and attitude that had blessed me to win in my previous struggles.

My first day of seventh grade was okay, and I enjoyed all my classes except Computers. I didn't have an interest in it except when I began realizing how fast I could type my school papers. Because I played the clarinet, I developed good muscle memory and finger strength, which was a plus when I typed papers and other assignments for class. Weeks after I started the class, I could type without looking at the keyboard. This, in turn, helped me play the clarinet even better. I was faster than I ever was, and I started to embrace this ability.

I thought it was boring and useless because I had to learn how to read the keys from memory and all this other stuff, I knew I wouldn't use this information later in life, but I didn't fuss. I kept a positive spirit and did my best. When I struggled, I asked for help, and my teacher not only helped me but also encouraged me. She was very nice, polite, and quiet.

As a band student, I walked around the school with a black case—one that looked like a briefcase or tool case. It was odd but interesting because most of my friends and classmates weren't in the band. They chose choir or other electives. But I was okay. I was excited about playing music this year, which continued to boost my confidence and allowed me to shine my light. I was a dedicated band member and attended almost every rehearsal during the week and sometimes after school and on weekends if there was a performance. I also auditioned for music competitions like the All-County Honor Band and Solo & Ensemble, and I was successful in both. I was the only student chosen at my school to play in the honor band, which was a huge accomplishment for me and the Lake Worth Middle School Music Department. Weeks later, I performed a prepared clarinet solo, for which I received Excellent and Superior ratings.

I was excited and motivated more than ever to practice and improve my overall musical skills on the clarinet. That year was one of my favorites and one of the most rewarding years of my life. I was determined to succeed and work hard, and it paid off.

Just before the school year was over, I remembered my last rides on the bus, which were fun. I loved watching the go-carts fly across the gated roadway. They were loud, and each go-cart was colored. I had hopes of visiting this fun spot—Fun Depot. Every time we turned the corner toward the school, I'd see Fun Depot's big, eye-catching sign from a distance. I'd stare at it and smile. I knew that one day I'd have a chance to visit and have some fun. Finally, that happened. My sisters and I visited Fun Depot and, oh, what a time we had! We had a blast and thanked our mother for the amazing experience.

The next exciting phase of my life was the summer before high school. I was clueless as to what to expect. I was now the young person behind the clarinet who was no longer shy about carrying around an instrument that weighed just as much as she did. I was bold, and I didn't care who stared, whispered, or laughed. I was excited and determined to continue pursuing music. My confidence was stronger than ever.

The sounds of music caught my ears and soothed my heart. I loved it no matter what I heard and what I played. It was pleasant to my spirit; it quenched my soul and made a big impact on my life over time, which I knew was a blessing from God. After a while, music was all that I knew. It synced with my heartbeat, like being in sync with the Creator. It became one of my greatest joys and passions, and no one could have led me away from it. It allowed me to escape the world and express my feelings.

My life was centered around music, church, and family. Music was my first love, and I wouldn't miss a practice or performance for anything in the world unless it was necessary…but it was deeper than that. The more serious I became in my studies, the fewer friends I had. However, I wasn't shocked. I was okay with not being around the crowd. I wasn't popular socially, but I continued to succeed. I loved music so much that I invested in professional clarinets. I had respect for music education and educators, and I gained more confidence than ever. I was certain I wanted to pursue music for the rest of my life.

When you have a strong mindset and the determination to achieve your goals, great things will happen, and you'll experience favorable results every time. Explore and discover all the blessings God has for you, even if you fail or experience adversity on your journey. At least, you'll gain wisdom and take away powerful lessons to help in your new chapter, your new direction. So, pat yourself on the back. I am proud of you and commend you for your efforts; for being bold and courageous; for taking risks; for doing what others aren't motivated to do; and for being brave and an overcomer.

You are on track to experience more success than you think. Keep up the great work and continue to embrace your unexpected doors of opportunities—everything you can't see or feel until you have faith. Never give up, no matter how difficult it seems; no matter how long it takes you to accomplish your goals; no matter what battles you face along the way to your destination. God has the power to turn fifty cents into a dollar or your messy finances and depression into books that will inspire others to embrace their journey and be relentless, strong, and hopeful.

# Chapter 4

## High School Years

*"Obstacles encouraged me to never give up and became my motivation to reach for success no matter what I experienced in life."*

**-Kala**

Another stage of my life was in the books, and now I looked forward to what I called "the reality before the real world." I knew that after middle school, I was in for a major period of my life and that every grade, second, and year counted. There was no room for slack, failure, and distractions, as otherwise I was bound to experience a setback. However, I was ready for the challenge and everything else I would experience in the days ahead. I didn't know who, what, when, or where, but no one does, not until it happens. I set my mind to do the best I could and to stay away from negativity and trouble. I knew that high school would be completely different from my previous years, including the teachers.

I was more excited than ever and certain that I wanted to pursue a music career. However, I was shocked when I saw my ninth-grade schedule. It included math, English, earth science, social studies, French, choir, and band. I wasn't interested in singing, especially because playing music was my main interest, but I could give it a try. Nor was I interested in learning a foreign language, but it was required. So, I had no choice, as I needed a certain number of credits in a foreign language to graduate. Spanish was the second and final foreign language I needed before graduation.

At the start of the school year, I also explored sports, like basketball. It was my favorite, as was track and field. However, ultimately, I was more interested in basketball—I loved the technique and shooting the ball. So, I tried out for the team, but I didn't make it. I was down for a few days, but I rose and stayed confident with hopes that if it was God's will for me to play, it would happen. After I spoke to the coaches, they recommended that I participate in the annual basketball camp in the summer. I was excited to share the news with my parents that afternoon, but more so, I was excited to share the experience of my first day in the high school band.

In ninth grade, I played in the marching band, concert band, and pep band (the group that played during basketball games). In addition, I continued to participate in annual music competitions like Solo & Ensemble, All-County Honor Band, and other small competitions that would enhance my musical growth. I played music with friends, practiced at school and home, and performed each month, and I loved it. I was a fan of education, so being involved in education-related activities and tutoring was never a problem. Whatever I could do to excel in my academics and music studies, I did it; I pursued it—every day—with joy and a willingness to thrive, no matter how many hurdles I faced.

My passion was music, and I was convinced of that, without second guessing. My intuition confirmed it, so no one could discourage me from pursuing my dreams. I liked it, and it felt good to do things that interested me. At times, it was challenging, but my objections and visions motivated me to push through what I knew were temporary obstacles and aim for success.

Music was all I knew and what my heart desired, so I stayed focused and devoted myself to my passion. If anything related to music was going on in town or scheduled at my school, I was there or involved. Traveling was my favorite. During marching band season, we traveled to Tampa and local high schools to compete against other bands. My bandmates and I had a blast. After each competition, we laughed, joked, and met up for dinner that evening.

As mentioned, besides music, I sang in the choir. However, I loved playing music and moving my fingers across the bridges of the clarinet more than I did using my vocal cords for singing. So, the following year, I decided that I wouldn't join the choir. I realized that my passion for music was stronger than ever, and I was more serious than many others.

I did well in my first year in the band and improved over time with faith, determination, and resilience. My goal was to graduate from high school and play professionally, so I regarded my education seriously and took the necessary steps to stand strong and overcome my obstacles. I crushed doubt and let my faith overpower my fear to rise and win. I motivated myself and looked beyond the struggles.

My upbringing and environment influenced my character, outlook on life, and mindset when it came to reaching my goals and never giving up. They played major roles in my success while in school and motivated me with the hope that I could achieve anything if I put my mind to it and let God guide me. So, nothing and no one distracted me because my heart and mind were set on staying focused and experiencing my destination and other blessings along the way. I knew that if I wanted to do well in school and get to where I desired, I had to study, seek a tutor if necessary, manage my practice time on the clarinet, and stay away from negativity and drama—bad influencers, crowds, boys and girls, and those who didn't desire the same things I wanted in life. Surprisingly, many of my classmates and friends didn't express that they had goals. A handful did, though. They aspired to do well and be successful, so they strove and worked hard. They wanted to go to college after high school, to become nurses, doctors, or professional athletes, so they maintained good grade point averages and exercised self-discipline. They were determined to break generational curses, do better than their parents, and succeed at being the first to graduate or go to college.

My motivation to succeed and go to college was inspired by my environment but more so by watching the behaviors of my parents. My mother hustled and struggled in life and sacrificed her time, love, energy, earnings, and strength to do the best she could to take care of my sisters and me. When we didn't have, she put herself last and put us first. She made sure we had what we needed and rewarded us with things we wanted. My mother strove to do her very best as a wife, mother, sister, friend, and co-worker, and she did. She succeeded, and I will always admire and honor her, including my dad. My mother strove to do better and to make life easier for my sisters and me, and she never gave up. She persevered, and God blessed her. Over the years, I witnessed the blood, sweat, and tears, which inspired my outlook on life, love, determination, and hope. I knew it wasn't over and God was doing something greater and more powerful in our lives. Both of my parents gave me hope about experiencing a healthier life, a future filled with love, grace, mercy, and favor from the Lord. I looked forward to a bright and healthy future.

The next stage in my life was another unpredictable one but an exciting one as well. During my junior and senior years of high school, I continued to play in the band and auditioned for other ensembles, like the jazz band, which I made it into. I played the alto saxophone, which I loved. It was a big jump. The clarinet and saxophone were different but also similar. The fingerings were almost identical, but with the saxophone, the keyholes were bigger and a different color. Also, I had to use more air support, which at times I struggled with. However, the more I practiced, the more I improved. When I was confident enough to take my music skills to the next level, I participated in Solo & Ensemble and All-County Band. I was that other girl, an ordinary teenager who loved to learn, succeed, and try new things, and no one stopped me.

My mind was set on rising above my different but common surroundings. I aimed for better, not more, because I knew money couldn't buy love, owning a lot was bound to create junk and unhappiness, and pretending to be someone I wasn't would take more energy than just being genuine and honest. Besides, I was never a materialistic person, not because I didn't have a lot but because it wasn't as important as living a simple and satisfying life. I was okay with not being rich and not having the best clothes and things that my friends and classmates valued.

My education, love, my family, learning more about God, having a career, and having a family were what mattered to me. If I failed or bumped my head, I rose and kept it moving. My struggles pushed me more and gave me motivation to strive for a win.

My long-term aspirations were to perform in the Chicago Symphony Orchestra and teach on the side. Therefore, I isolated myself from the world and things—anyone and anything who was a distraction, possessed a careless attitude about life, or was potential trouble, or whom I didn't need. If they weren't my friends or in my circle, or if they opposed education, I didn't care to socialize with them. However, if they initiated a conversation, I listened and gave my two cents, and if they talked about topics I opposed, I didn't comment. I excused myself from the discussion or, sometimes, I encouraged them if they were down or needed advice. I protected my surroundings and feelings on purpose. I knew that if I got involved with the wrong crowd, I would become sidetracked and confused. My outlook on life and attitude might have changed. I wasn't going to let others take advantage of my kindness, smiles, and caring heart to discourage me.

I desired to be more than somebody. I wanted to be someone, a young woman who worked hard to get where she desired. Because I was unique in my own way and stood out from the popular crowds, I was a natural role model—a young lady who just wanted to do good and do well in life. I hated drama, violence, debates, and arguments; I strove to make peace and to have peace of mind. I succeeded in this because I made the choice to surround myself with a positive environment. I was eager to stay away from any hurt, harm, and danger. If that meant distancing myself from others who were negative-minded, violent, or cursed, or who loved drama, I did it. I minded my own business and kept moving.

I understood that practicing good habits and pursuing God's instruction would bless me to achieve my goals. My hopes were to one day get married and have a family. I always laughed about that and knew it would happen in due time. So, I was wise even with the guys I talked to or who I gave information to. I didn't want to date anybody or anyone. I had enough respect for myself and my body to show it love. I desired commitment and true love unlike what I sometimes saw on television. I knew it was love but not real love. I wanted a husband, children, a home, and to be successful. So, I was motivated to do everything it took to experience my goals and dreams even at this stage in my life, especially before I stepped into the real world. I worked hard with the intention to make it and succeed on purpose.

Music was my life and joy, and nothing would stop me from excelling and furthering my knowledge and experience in this field. I kept a firm attitude because I was heading somewhere, and that somewhere was where I desired to settle. I had faith. I breathed, ate, and slept to music, and I didn't bother investing my time and energy into those who weren't in my circle or who didn't appreciate the same values I did. I was thankful for what I had and for what lay ahead of me before the big move. I had a bright future.

However, my life changed the afternoon I met a guy who was almost ten years older than me. He was a handsome young man, who had a child, and had been in previous relationships. That was all I knew at the time. We met through someone else who worked at a nursing facility in my area. We spoke and, the following day, this average-size, attractive, blue-eyed man showed up outside my mom's house. He arrived in my dream car, the one I always loved. It was white, had shiny rims, and looked new. I remember hearing loud music from my mother's living room the day he stopped over.

He knocked on the door and told me his name and who had sent him to our home. I was shocked, but I'd also expected him to stop over. We talked and asked questions of each other. I laughed. He gave me butterflies, but I had no intention of doing anything more or even having a relationship with him. During this time, my mother was in jail, preparing to be transported to a prison out of state. It was difficult for my sisters and me, but we couldn't give up. We stayed strong despite not having our mother around. It was painful to watch her experience this unexpected life storm, especially because she was innocent and older with health problems. My sisters and I had little supervision and looked after each other. Our father was a few blocks away from us in a nursing facility, recovering from a traumatic brain stroke, so because our parents weren't home, I made the choice to talk to this man. I did what I wanted to do because it felt good, and I thought it was okay.

My friends and classmates had boyfriends, so I thought this was the perfect time to start dating. But I didn't consider my actions— I followed what my flesh craved, which was to follow the crowd and take a chance with life. So, that afternoon, I got dressed and rode with this stranger in his fancy, four-door car. I was amazed at how it looked inside and how it smelled. During the ride, we talked and got to know each other. I briefly explained to him where my mother was located. I also told him about my family background, my age, and the high school I attended.

When we arrived at his two story home, I was surprised at what I saw. It was spacious and beautiful, and it included stairs. He showed me around and took me upstairs. Then, we sat on his brown leather couch. It was comfortable and smelled brand new, but it wasn't. I noticed he was a neat freak and loved nice things. Next, he showed me around his bedroom. His bed was neatly organized and looked comfortable, so I sat on it and jumped up and down. He walked over and sat next to me, looked me in the eyes, and kissed me. I didn't resist. I let him have his way. Then, he removed my clothes. He started from the bottom and removed my pants, underwear, and top. Seconds after that, he unfastened my bra and set it on the bed. He laid me down on my back, and we shifted to the center of his king-size bed. Then, we made love, which was my first romantic experience. I had never imagined that my first time having sex would be with a man years older than me. At that point, I was in love, hot, and ready to do anything to experience love. That evening, I had my first orgasm, and I was in heaven, blown away at how good this man made me feel in bed and in his presence. Inside, I felt like I was in love, but I wasn't sure if he was in love with me.

When we got together, we had sex before the day or night was over. Our friendship turned into a serious romantic relationship, and nobody knew. He wanted me and I wanted him, so we expressed it through text messages, in person, and on the phone. The sad part is that he had no interest in meeting my parents, visiting my church, or committing to a serious relationship. Before we met, he had experienced a difficult breakup and he didn't want to jump into a committed relationship with anyone. He only wanted to be friends and to take control of my mind and body— which, sadly, he did. I didn't know what to say or do. I was lost and confused, so I acted carelessly.

I wasn't concerned about living right because false love made me feel good. His presence made me feel secure and good about myself. I was shy and didn't feel comfortable sharing my personal business about my new relationship with anyone except my best friend. Still, I didn't share it even with her—I didn't want to be judged by anyone, so I kept quiet and kept my personal business to myself.

At sixteen years old, I was naïve and wanted to explore life and new things. I wanted to have a relationship. I'd known several guys and I'd had puppy love relationships but none like this one. I didn't know if this could lead to a real relationship and marriage. I was happy and nervous at the same time. I finally had a boyfriend and was no longer a virgin. No one except God and my partner knew how I felt and the heartache, stress, and pain I had experienced for years. I was too shy and felt uncomfortable about sharing my personal business with my family and friends, and I certainly wasn't going to tell anyone that I had slept with a man almost ten years older than me. That would not have been a great sight. I didn't know what to do, so I kept quiet. Years passed before I was ready to share anything personal about my relationship with anyone.

With this major change in my life, I did my best to stay focused in school, on my academics, my goals, and getting to know God. I worked my first part-time job at an ice cream parlor and did my best to balance this adjustment and school. It went well and I loved it. I worked across the street from my high school, which made the job convenient. However, at night, I walked, rode my bicycle, or I called a taxicab. Months later, the owners—who were from Switzerland—left, and the ice cream parlor's name changed to Java Joe's. The owner was weird but caring. Sometimes, he left me to close the shop with another worker. I also got paid under the table, and sometimes I didn't receive my full paycheck. I told my mom, and she thought it was strange. I expressed my misgivings to the owner, and he apologized. He got his act together and started paying me my full earnings. Besides, it was temporary; I knew I'd be graduating soon and heading off to college. At my job, I prepared burgers, fries, nachos and cheese, chili and cheese, banana splits, sundaes, and a range of fast food and desserts.

My favorite ice cream flavors were rum raisin and vanilla, and I loved the cheeseburgers. Everyone who stopped at Java Joe's was appreciated and became a loyal customer. They shared our location with family, friends, and co-workers. I had a ball and looked forward to working more hours in the summer, which was around the corner.

The summer before my final year in high school, I worked more hours, practiced on the clarinet, and spent time with family, friends, and my boyfriend, who worked all year.

I had more time on my hands, so sometimes I worked seven-hour shifts or longer during the week and on Saturdays. On Sundays, I went to church. During this time, I also practiced more hours and took private lessons on Saturdays with the clarinet instructor at Chafin's Music Center. Music lessons were given in the back of the music center in a small bathroom-sized room, which included a piano. It felt claustrophobic, but it worked, and I gradually adjusted. A typical lesson included breathing exercises, scales, technique, and long tones, which were the most important. I struggled with my scales and articulation, so my instructor recommended that I spend more time practicing long tones. Weeks later, not only did he notice a significant improvement, but so did I, and I patted myself on the back. I motivated myself when others didn't (not that I expected anyone to), and I had confidence and enjoyed celebrating my accomplishments.

As always, he was very talented and supportive of my musical journey and wanted the best for me. After he learned of my mother's financial circumstances, he did something probably no one else would have done—he offered me free private clarinet lessons.

In the summer, I also spent more time with my parents, sisters, and friends. We traveled, went out to dinner, and had fun at the park, Boomers, Fun Depot, and the Palace Roller Skating Rink in Lantana, Florida.

In addition, I spent time with my boyfriend, who never took me out in public unless we checked into a hotel or met up for fun. We watched movies, laughed, talked about life, and had sex— protected and unprotected. The next morning, he would jump up and shower. Sometimes, we would have sex again. Then he would leave for work. At times, I was okay when he left, but most of the time, I didn't want him to leave. Sometimes, I cried after he kissed me and walked out of the hotel room. We had only temporary fun because we didn't seem to accomplish anything. Every time we met, he played with my emotions just to get between my legs. It almost seemed like having sex was his addiction. I brought this to his attention often, and he denied it, but it was the truth. Each time we met or texted, he wanted to make love, even if he had to travel from one city to another or meet me at my home. He found a way to meet up with me to get me into bed and have his way, and I fell for it every time. I was young and spiritually blind, so I thought that having premarital sex was okay; I was in a wilderness, and I wanted to do what others were trying or experiencing. However, this way of life wasn't me, and if you asked around, you'd get the same answer. I didn't wake up one day and want to start having sex with a stranger who was somewhat my boyfriend. I wanted to have a real relationship, to be hugged, kissed, touched, and treated like someone special, a young woman with respect. I observed it on television, where the couples looked happy and in love. They kissed, cooked breakfast and dinner, had cars and homes, and had bedroom fun, each night. I saw what I wished to experience, so I gave in to temptation and did what made me feel good.

Later, I developed a strange interest in watching pornography. I Googled a list of videos and explored new ways to have fun in bed and experience more satisfaction. I also watched videos on YouTube and sometimes shared the experience with my partner. He smiled and laughed at me the first time I informed him that I watched pornography. He thought I was hilarious. However, I became uncomfortable and nervous watching others have sex. I figured I would discover all the many ways to embrace the bedroom, so I went for it without understanding my actions. I didn't know it was a bad thing to watch others have sex at my age. I was almost an adult, so I enjoyed exploring topics, information, or subjects in which I lacked understanding. I was addicted to it, to the point that I became distracted; I always thought about sex and imagined having it with my boyfriend until it happened. From the setting of the video to the moment the couples had their last orgasm, it all entertained me and aroused my hormones. However, over time, I prayed to God and asked for forgiveness and deliverance from my unrighteous behavior. I was ready to put this foolishness away and do better with my life. So, months later, I stopped watching pornography and thanked God for rescuing me from destruction and ungodly conduct. I never looked back.

However, *false love* felt good, especially when my partner whispered sweet words in my ear. He gave me goosebumps when he touched me, spoke to me on the phone, texted me, and looked me in the eyes as we made love. I fell in love with his beautiful blue eyes, his facial hair, his soft skin, and every part of his body that he used when we joined together and became intimate. I loved him, and he told me that he loved me, but he really didn't; he loved my body more than he embraced my heart.

We had sex everywhere—outside his workplace in the backseat of his truck, in the front seat of his vehicle at a park, and in an empty parking lot minutes from where I attended church service. When he texted me, I didn't waste time meeting up with him. I loved him and wanted the best for our relationship. I also expressed my desire for marriage and a family if it was God's will, but only time would tell. It was too early to figure out if he was the one or a potential spouse. My focus was on doing well in school and making it into a college or university.

*Finally!* It was August, and I was weeks away from starting my senior year in high school. I couldn't wait—not only to start my final year but also to apply for another job. After careful consideration, I decided to resign from Java Joe's and pursue a higher-paying job in my area. Weeks later, I completed a job application at Wendy's and was hired. However, it didn't last. I left the job after the first day because the work atmosphere was busy, and I had to learn a lot in a short amount of time. Days later, I prayed and called a local Office Depot, asking if they were hiring. The manager said, "Yes, we're hiring. Come into the store and complete the job application." I told my mother the great news. She drove me to the store, and I applied for a part-time cashier position. I knew this job was for me, and I received a call back for an in-store interview.

Days later, I received a phone call from the store manager. They had reviewed my application and wanted to bring me on board. Before that, I would have to complete a drug and alcohol test and background check, which I did the following day. I was happy and didn't know what to do except thank God for His grace, mercy, and favor. Then, days later, I started my senior year in high school while working part-time at Office Depot.

At the same time, I was under stress to pass the Florida Comprehensive Assessment Test (FCAT) in reading. I had passed the math portion the previous year, but I struggled with reading. So, I took remedial reading courses and stayed after school for tutoring. This helped, and I enjoyed it. I also gained a lot and loved the challenge. I wanted to be as prepared as possible for college, so I had my mind set on overcoming this obstacle, and I did, to God be the glory.

It didn't matter where I attended college. I hoped to get somewhere near home. I was never fascinated with attending an Ivy League or prestigious college or university; they were all the same to me. Just walking through the door would be a blessing and honor.

I wanted to pursue a career in music performance and teach part-time. My mom advised me to speak to the administration at the high school and contact two local colleges/universities in our area, which I did. The following day, I walked into the career center and set up an appointment to meet with the career advisor. Days later, we met and reviewed a list of local colleges and universities. Also, she provided me with information about financial resources like scholarships, grants, and student loans. Work study was also an option, but I wasn't sure if I wanted to work on campus during my first semester in college. I didn't want any distractions to prevent me from succeeding, so work study was my last resort.

By the end of my senior year, I had received several scholarships and grants—the George Snow Scholarship Fund, a scholarship through the Community Foundation for Palm Beach and Martin Counties, the Coca-Cola Scholarship, and several more. I also received more blessings. Days before I graduated, I attended the end-of-the-year scholarship program at my high school and received an additional college scholarship.

When they called my name, I smiled and said, "Thank You, Lord." I was overwhelmed with joy and excitement about sharing the great news with my family. They were amazed at how far I had come and my accomplishments.

I was gearing up to receive my high school diploma, which happened in May 2004. This was one of the most memorable and special days of my life. That morning, I got up extra early, prayed, put on my clothes, let my braids down, and headed over to FIU's arena in Boca Raton. When my parents and I arrived, the arena was packed with students and their families and friends.

I also played my last performance that morning in the band as tears fell down my cheeks. It was a moment of joy and happiness for all that I had accomplished—from my failures to my successes. I worked hard and deserved to experience this day. When my name was called, *Kala Jordan*, I stood. As I walked to the front of the stage, I looked around for my mom and waved. I spotted her and saw the huge smile on her face. I was so happy and thankful that God had blessed her to be present on such an important day in my life. She had supported me and made every effort to be there to celebrate another amazing accomplishment and milestone. I accepted my high school diploma with gladness, gratitude, and appreciation for God's grace and mercy and for His bringing me through some of the most difficult times of my life. His favor allowed me to be honored and blessed, and that was what mattered. I was satisfied and felt good.

After everyone clapped their hands and cheered on their loved ones, I stood up and hugged my bandmates, band director, and friends. Then, I looked for my mom. I couldn't find her, so I called her. After I squeezed through a herd of families and graduates, I saw her standing on the outside of the arena. As I went toward her, many had balloons and gift bags and took a million photos. "Hey, baby. Congratulations! Here, these are for you," said my mom.

I smiled and said, "Thank you, Mama! Glory to God. I'm officially a graduate. I am done."

She laughed and handed me balloons, a gift bag, and a graduation card. They were beautiful. Then, she hugged me and kissed me on the cheek. Handing me the most beautiful flowers ever, she said, "I love you." That was one of the best days of my life and the beginning of a new journey.

That afternoon, my family and I celebrated at one of my all-time favorite restaurants, Red Lobster. We enjoyed the rest of the day sharing memories, laughs, hugs, and smiles. I had a fresh plate of salmon, shrimp scampi, garlic bread, mashed potatoes, broccoli, and a house salad. It was delicious, including the strawberry daiquiri!

Nothing and no one would stop me from embracing the rest of my day and the days ahead.

# Chapter 5

## *College Life*

*"I was determined to rise above where I lived and succeed beyond statistics on young, Black women who lived around poverty, drugs and alcohol, molesters, and single-parent households. My mind was set on doing something with my life, and it happened by the grace and mercy of God."*

*-Kala*

In the summer of 2004, I met the orchestra director, who greeted me with a smile and open arms and auditioned for the symphony orchestra at Florida Atlantic University in Boca Raton, Florida. I played excerpts from a selection of works, including musical scales, and then she provided me with additional information about the orchestra program, including rehearsals and performances. I was satisfied and hopeful about my audition results. Days later, I received an email of congratulations on doing well and making it into the orchestra. Also, I was honored to receive a music scholarship. I was excited and grateful, and I shared the great news with my family and friends. My hard work, practice, and confidence had paid off. I was overwhelmed with joy and looked forward to playing the clarinet in my first orchestra as well as participating in other music ensembles. However, I was also nervous because this was my first time being away at college; I didn't know what to expect and how things would turn out on the first day and throughout the term. Still, that was the exciting part—adjusting and embracing change. I anticipated amazing things and the opportunity to play with like-minded and talented musicians.

In August 2004, I began my undergraduate studies at one of the top universities in the United Sates. I thanked God for being the first in my family to go to college to further my education and study music. It was also a blessing because it gave hope to those in my community, graduating class, and others around me who were hopeless or poor or who desired to do something with their lives. In addition, my acceptance at a university after I'd encountered difficult conditions growing up showed my sisters and other youth that with hope, faith, and determination, you can accomplish your dreams, touch lives, and walk through doors your ancestors couldn't. I felt good setting a positive example for others who aspired to walk in my path. They knew it hadn't happened overnight. They observed my actions and the goodness and grace of God over my life. Some knew about my family history and the hardships I experienced. So, when God blessed me to go to college, they weren't shocked but celebrated with me and embraced the awesomeness of God. Their faith grew stronger, and they gave life another chance. Achieving something in their lives and breaking generational curses was their hope, as it was mine. In this new environment, I strove each day to find ways to improve my life and health while seeking to get closer to God. This wasn't easy, but I didn't give up. I saw the Light in the middle of too many fights and knew my God was real.

Unfortunately, not everyone in my circle or my 2004 class ended up graduating. Some failed, dropped out, started businesses, or went in another direction—far from where I was headed. Some preferred to go out of state for college and others chose to study abroad. However, their decisions didn't impact mine because my mind was set on furthering my music education and getting to where I wanted to be regardless of the cost or struggles along the way. I had a thirst to pursue music and stay focused on where God was carrying me.

Now that I was officially a freshman, I was ready to experience the "real world" and be independent. The university was huge, so it took me a while to adjust to my environment. I saw tall buildings, dormitories, a thousand parking lots, security, lakes, and everything you could imagine finding on a college campus. It was like I'd walked into another world, a new atmosphere. It was on and popping! I was young, fine, and ready for the ride of my life.

After I walked into my suite, I settled in my dorm room and roamed around the campus. It was noisy, and I observed nothing but smiles and laughs. No one cried except for some of the parents, who embraced their loved ones as if they weren't going to see their children again. I smiled and kept quiet until I became a bit more comfortable with my surroundings.

Later that evening, I met my suitemates. I didn't expect to meet everyone at once, like a class of first graders. It was college, so no one had a curfew. I certainly didn't, and I was happy, once and for all. On the other hand, I looked forward to meeting others in my field of study and sitting in my first semester of music classes. I was confident about this next phase of my life, and I was ready to take on the world. I was an excited young woman.

My baby (clarinet) and I were inseparable. I couldn't picture myself not holding this musical instrument and performing on it. Playing the clarinet was all that I knew and strongly desired, but deep down, I also longed to express more than my ability to play on the clarinet. I knew this because, after every concert, I said I could have performed better. There was more, and I was determined to reach this climax no matter how many hours I had to practice and how long it took. One day, I was going to discover this missing piece in my life.

I was fixed on doing whatever it took to reach my goals, whether small or big. I knew it was a process and that progress was acceptable. It was better than giving up and wasting my precious life. This was my pet peeve for years. Sometimes, I sat and watched others do what I desired to do and accomplish with no understanding of God's will for my life. I wondered and walked with curiosity hidden in my heart as to whether I would ever experience that "oh yes" moment—the second when everything lights up in your head, clicks together, and makes sense, when something satisfying and great happens. I became frustrated, but I didn't beat myself over the head. I knew it wasn't the end of the world and that there was hope every time I practiced, displayed grit, and worked toward reaching this experience. I gave myself grace, but God comforted me with more. There was no turning back if I wanted to move forward with my life and discover what God had in store for me, including my true passion.

The start of the school year was sweet, a blessing, especially because God blessed me to receive scholarships and grants to cover my college education. However, I realized it wasn't enough. If I wanted to stay on-campus beyond a term and survive with less worry, I needed more money. Unfortunately, I didn't have college savings or funding set aside for my education, as my friends did, nor were my parents rich. That meant securing loans was my only choice. I saw this easy and convenient way to obtain money as another avenue to get guaranteed funds in my pockets without having a perfect credit score, stable employment, and a co-signer. I was okay with that, but it bothered me that my boyfriend didn't give me anything toward my college education, not even a gift card. That hurt, but I didn't beat it over his head, nor did I allow it to take the best of this season of my life.

With zero dollars in my pockets to help pay for my college education, except for food and gas, I applied for student loans to assist with my meal plans and future on-campus housing. I went to Google on my laptop and applied for student loans in a heartbeat with faith that I would be approved, and I was. When I saw the amount, I had the biggest smile and thanked God for helping me find a way out of my predicament. I received thousands of dollars within days, and I was one of the happiest women alive. I didn't realize I could receive money as fast as applying for a loan at the bank. I shared the news with my beautiful mother and helped her out. I knew she could use the extra money to help with bills, gas, food, and savings, so my heart was led to be generous to her.

If I hadn't applied for student loans, I would not have been able to stay on campus and use the funds for other necessities. So, like many other broke, poor, or underprivileged individuals and students, I did what I had to do and sought money and other resources to the best of my ability and knowledge. I didn't want loans, but the lack of a stable job or full-time income would have caused challenges. The big plus is that before I started my studies at FAU, I was blessed with a used, four-door Saturn—an on-time blessing. I knew it was only by the grace of God that I received a car as a graduation gift from my supportive parents. However, others were unfortunate and couldn't afford things for college, like a car or reliable transportation. I was blessed by the Best and grateful for what I had, my new environment, and my parents, family, and church family. However, I was on my own when it came to car insurance and credit card bills, as well as other things I wanted and needed.

This next chapter in my life was interesting and certainly an adjustment beyond elementary, junior high, and high school. I was a young Black woman with her head together and her heart fixed on overcoming generational curses, hardships, the hustle, and the grind that I was exposed to for most of my life. Watching my mother sacrifice her time, freedom, and love for my sisters and me motivated me more than ever. I desired better and to provide for my family, and I knew this was where it started—not in the streets, lying on the couch, walking around town with my head down, or locked in a bedroom. There was more to life than what I observed, what others wanted to do, and where many chose to settle or end their lives.

This decade was my time to shine and be the example beyond what the world and statistics portrayed a Black woman's life to be and end as. I was determined to beat the odds of life, the drama, struggle, and grind I lived around. I refused to be another African American victim who became a single mother and walked down the streets without an education, common sense, and a job. I had faith that I would make something out of my life; I was certain that I would succeed beyond just obtaining a degree. I was committed to rising above where I had come from, making a difference for those less fortunate, and creating history.

I also had hopes of giving back to my parents. My mom had always wanted a house with a garden, a car free of payments, and money in her pockets. My dad just wanted money. Ha-ha! Each day, hearing from my mother reminded me to keep going and never quit; to stay focused and succeed; to make something of my life; to be a leader, not a follower of the world; to show love and compassion; and to always have faith and never give up. Also, my dad and I always laughed together. He encouraged me to keep up the great work and to succeed so that I could make a good living. I thanked God for both of my parents and always told them, and my sisters, that I loved them.

"Yay!" I said in my inside voice. It was mid-August, the time of year when many children, adolescents, and adults were either preparing for school or, in my case, college. There was no turning back. The beginning of the semester finally came, and in less than ten hours, I would experience the first day of this new journey.

*Beep, beep, beep.* I woke up, looked over at my alarm clock, and set it for five more minutes. Then, in the blink of an eye, it was time to get up for real. I rose, prayed, got dressed, ate breakfast, gathered my purse and class materials, and walked downstairs to the computer lab. It was cold, and no one else was inside at 8 a.m. I saw soda bottles and snack wrappers on the side of some of the computers. I thought to myself, 'There must have been a party in here last night or somewhere in Indian River Towers.' I sat down anyway and logged into my student portal, where I viewed my schedule. I didn't see many classes, but I realized that my first semester would be slightly different than the following terms only because I was required to register for remedial reading and math.

Once I passed these classes, I'd be permitted to register in ENC 1101, or English 1, and non-remedial math classes. So, I dual-enrolled in these classes at Palm Beach State College, Boca Raton Campus. Also, I was registered in the symphony orchestra, an intro college course, and a few other music classes. It wasn't much, but it was a start. I knew my course load would build one semester at a time, and I was okay with that. Every phase of my education was important and would help me reach my goals.

My first semester at FAU was quite an adjustment, but overall, it was a great experience. My classes, the orchestra, and my grades were pretty good. However, I knew this was just the beginning of a long, unpredictable journey. I had faith in He who covered me with grace, mercy, and favor—my Heavenly Father—and who made all things possible.

I was grateful and thrilled about all there was to learn about music and the clarinet, but I also understood that my life wasn't about just college, my major, and doing work or even obtaining money. It was about living, learning, and growing as an individual and a young Christian woman despite what and who was in my circle or environment. I socialized with others, but for many, it didn't go further because our values were different. I was a young woman who loved God, prayed, and read her Bible when she had a chance, but some of my friends and the people in my environment didn't have the same interests. Naturally, we didn't connect beyond conversation in a classroom, in the dormitory, or in music rehearsal, or beyond just a "hi" and "bye" in public. Still, it was cool. I knew my worth, and God blessed me with great value to encourage and inspire others. I was on fire, ready to explore and experience this new setting. So, I walked around the campus and the music building—upstairs, downstairs—and browsed the music halls and practice rooms. I was excited at what I saw and instantly fell in love with my new environment. Even better was that I lived seconds away from not only the music building but also the cafeteria, the on-campus bookstore, the health and wellness center, the gym, and other interesting buildings. However, I walked behind the university in the evenings to take remedial reading and math classes at Palm Beach Community College (now Palm Beach State College). It was tiresome, but it also motivated me to reach the finish line.

The good news was that despite my having to take remedial courses and walk to Palm Beach Community College, my first semester was a success, including my participation in the symphony orchestra. The director was amazing and one of a kind. I admired her cheerful attitude and big heart. Her spirit touched my life and enriched my musical journey. I quickly adjusted to my new environment and became more comfortable as I branched out and met others. Sometimes, I isolated myself from others to read, study, pray, and relax, but I met a lot of students around campus, in class, in orchestra rehearsals, and in the cafeteria, which I loved. The cafeteria was one of my favorite spots to hang out and chat with other students because the food was fresh and delicious. I didn't have to walk or drive off campus to eat a hot meal.

Sometimes, though, in the evenings or on weekends, I ordered food off-campus. I'd walk across the street to a nearby plaza and purchase food, or I'd drive to the Boca Raton mall and eat a plate of hot Chinese food or a meal at The Cheesecake Factory. It was fun and I enjoyed my getaways. I had the chance to explore other places away from FAU and around Boca Raton. However, typically, I traveled alone because most of my friends, bandmates, and acquaintances had different schedules, worked, or lived off-campus, far from Glades Road.

Reality hit the moment I realized I was out of work. So, I cut down on my spending and made a greater effort to use my resources wisely. I didn't want anything or anyone to interfere with my college experience. Therefore, I contacted the Office Depot branch where I'd started in Palm Beach County and requested a transfer. I needed the money and didn't want to depend on student loans and grants to keep funds in my pockets. So, days after I reached out to the store manager with my request for a transfer to the Boca Raton location, it was completed. Before the week was out, management at the Boca Raton site had contacted me for an in-store interview, which I scheduled. The interview went well, glory to God. I was so happy that the transfer had gone through and that there were no issues. As a result, I had hope for a better financial future, and my motivation to succeed was reignited. This opportunity humbled my heart and strengthened my faith. Most of all, I was certain my unemployment storm was temporary and a test of my faith, so I didn't worry. I celebrated before I started the following week. I worked in the evenings and closed on weekends except for Sundays. I attended church on this day. All went well and I met great people. The job was less than ten minutes from the university, which was a blessing. I received medical, dental, and vision insurance, including employee tuition reimbursements, discounts, and a 401(k).

At Office Depot, I worked as a customer service associate (cashier) in the ink department and Copy & Print Center. However, special holidays and back-to-school seasons were hectic and demanding. As mentioned, I was part of the closing shift unless I was unable to work some evenings. However, this didn't interfere with my studies. I had an advantage because I was a student—

management created a flexible schedule for me and others who were in college. My co-workers were amazing. I became good friends with several of them, and we had lunch and meetups. I enjoyed working there and gained valuable experience and knowledge on the cash register, with clients, and with everyday situations. There were no full-time openings, only seasonal and part-time availability, which was fine. I was a full-time student and did not want to work full-time quite yet. I didn't want anything to interfere with my studies.

My faith was greater than a mustard seed, so God had opened another door of work for me without hassle. I thanked Him for being the solution to my problem, and I became motivated to read my Bible more than I did after I was baptized in 2004.

Studying God's words of wisdom, direction, and discipline took my thoughts off worldly things, including my difficult and toxic relationship. I needed Him more than I realized, and no one, including this man, would cause me to stray from following my Lord despite my weaknesses and lack of understanding as a young woman. At times, it was challenging, but I strove to balance both my personal life and my education with the strength God graced me with. I wasn't perfect; I fell and failed along the way, but my Heavenly Father picked me up and gave me comfort and hope to get through each day without giving up.

During my college experience, I received routine check-ups at the FAU Clinic, met with my major advisors, and practiced daily, usually in the evenings. It was amazing, worth the experience, and memorable, but it required hard work. I also had the chance to watch performances, participate in on-campus and local music events, and engage in all there was to know about music.

I put in the extra work to excel in my academics, and it paid off. However, my lack of money was the real struggle. Working to earn money wasn't the issue. Learning to manage the financial resources God had blessed me with was the challenge. At this age, I viewed money as just another piece of green; I loved to hold it, and I loved it when it was deposited into my bank account. But I didn't value it and save like I should have.

After I began taking out student loans, my "financial mindset" traveled in darkness, and I experienced the consequences of it along the way. I had my first credit card in high school. Then, when I started college, I applied for another one. The question I've sometimes asked is: Did I need it? Well, yes and no; it was money, and that was all that mattered.

At eighteen years old, I cared only about the fact that money was "available." I received grants and scholarships, but I became addicted to taking out student loans each semester like an alcoholic drinking Corona every Friday. Nothing seemed to stop my anxious heart because I was spiritually weak and lacked financial discipline. I wanted money, and that was it. I wasn't concerned about how I would manage it, keep it, and grow it, nor did I seek to invest it.

Unconsciously, I created debt on top of debt because I focused on now rather than the long run; I didn't realize what I was doing would affect my financial future. I didn't see the disadvantage because it "felt" good to receive money without earning it. To receive thousands of dollars, I didn't have to work 9-5; I only had to read, click, and sign. I was blind, but I didn't know what the hell to do with my brain. I know this because I didn't choose to make a difference. I didn't choose to learn how to handle money. I didn't want to attend financial workshops because I thought they would be boring. I was further from "wanting" help than from "wanting" to spend whatever was in my name and in my pockets. My "bad habits" continued even after I got my first job.

I was clueless about saving money, so when I earned it, I spent it in a heartbeat. I had no monthly budget or detailed list of bills I had to pay. Then I would receive a notice in the mail, an email, or a phone call from creditors. It was hard, and I was lost. However, in the middle of darkness, I saw the Light; I had hope and faith in the Son, Jesus Christ.

I experienced financial hardships throughout my studies, which created more issues. It affected my health and caused me to stress out, worry, and experience anxiety. It sucked, especially at the beginning of the month or when most of my bills were due. Eventually, my late payments impacted my credit score, which was between poor and good. Every time I applied for a credit card or loan, I was denied for one or more reasons: My income and credit score were low, I didn't have enough credit history, or there were delinquent accounts in my credit file. However, I wasn't discouraged. Rejection pushed me to do whatever it took to overcome life and encouraged me with hope. I embraced denials and used "no" as an opportunity to reach for success. With faith, I knew I was going to get there no matter how long it took.

Because I had faith and hope that God would deliver me and change my circumstances, I didn't give up. I continued to work, apply for scholarships and grants, and perform gigs to earn money. I was determined to rise above stumbling blocks and failure and experience a financial breakthrough.

The next phase of my educational journey arrived, and I looked forward to my second year in college, as a sophomore. After I passed my remedial courses, I was approved to register for major courses like Music History, Sight-Singing, and Music Theory. Signing up for these classes was a smooth process.

That term, I played clarinet in the wind band and symphony orchestra, participated in weekly private clarinet lessons, enrolled in College Math, Beginning Music Theory, and Sight-Singing, and practiced my butt off nearly every day in practice rooms the size of my bathroom. It was a lot of work, but studying music, performing in concerts, socializing with others, and being in a different setting was worth my time, energy, and effort. I enjoyed the experience and looked forward to discovering more about college life. However, months into the semester, I began to struggle in Math, Sight-Singing, and Music Theory. I wasn't shocked, but I was speechless. I prayed about the situation and decided to work fewer hours so that I could refocus on my studies. I didn't fight for long. After I made slight adjustments to my schedule, obtained assistance, and improved my time management, my grades improved. This wasn't the first time I struggled in school, and I knew it wouldn't be the last, so I used my challenges as opportunities to gain, grow, and embrace the journey of overcoming life, which inspired others. The more I struggled, the more God blessed me with strength and His word to strive and excel. I became more resilient and noticed growth, and I used every hurdle as a blessing to receive God's grace and mercy through my faith. At the end of the semester, I reaped the benefits of hard work, dedication, faith, and perseverance. I didn't give up, and neither should you.

In 2006, I experienced a very difficult, emotional season after the loss of my first, unborn baby, my precious angel. It was another time in my life when I became depressed and isolated myself from the world, including family. I was lost, confused, and clueless as to what I had experienced—an unwanted and unexpected abortion. I almost lost my mind, but God's grace, love, strength, and comfort prevented me from giving up and losing my precious soul. I was afraid to tell anyone—even my parents—because I didn't feel comfortable sharing every detail of this difficult experience and the days leading up to that point.

I was young, naïve, and in the dark. I was hurt and in pain because I was embarrassed and didn't know what to do. I didn't know how to gather the courage to share the news with loved ones. I also felt empty and worthless. I didn't want to be judged and looked down on, so I didn't know whom to talk to. I didn't want anyone to dislike me and picture me as a horrible young woman; I was young and lacked understanding. I just didn't know what to do, so I stayed quiet in prayer with the hopes that, one day, I would have enough confidence to open up to someone who was also walking in silence because of this experience. I knew I wasn't the only young person who had experienced this, but I felt alone—in a world of my own. I was down beyond the depths of the ocean. However, God prevented me from destroying my life before my time was up.

Every time I tried to share my experience with someone, I was uncertain and remained silent. However, I had hope that one day it would happen, like it is now. Sharing this personal experience took more than you'd ever imagine.

I walked in worry because I feared others, who looked like me, who were imperfect like me, and who had experienced trauma like I did. I also feared God, but at the same time, my Heavenly Father gave me strength to overcome this agitation and confirmation that He knew the details before I had anything to say. I prayed and asked God for forgiveness, and His Spirit gave me confirmation along with His word. This helped me realize everything would be okay.

However, I knew this experience would be a lifetime journey of healing; I was certain each day God would guide my steps, comfort my spirit, renew my mind, and inspire me to surrender my life to Him. If you can relate, you are not alone—ever.

I have sympathy for you; I understand how you feel and what you are experiencing or have experienced. Healing is different for everyone. It's a season for some, months for others, and a lifetime for most. However, the One who gives the healing is the same God who rescued me in a time of need, and He will do the same with you. Never give up. Take a deep breath and pray. It's not over. Trauma is a scar, but you can use your uncomfortable experiences to uplift, help, and encourage others who are facing similar difficulties. You have much to offer others, especially wisdom, positive advice, and spiritual guidance. Don't be afraid to express yourself and uplift others who are down. Share your life storms to comfort others, and you will be encouraged. God will transform your heart every step of the way if you let go of your life and give Him access to yours, to heal you one day at a time. God is help, so turn to Him. Our Creator is strength, so seek Him. He will restore your confidence when you are weak and grace you with favor to get you through unbelievable life events like this.

Stand up and unmute your voice to the world. Every day, a young teenager and woman struggles to cope with and heal from this trauma, including sexual harrassment, sexual abuse, rape, and domestic violence. Share your voice with them. Speak to others to help save a precious life. Educate young ladies and women about your traumatic experiences. Write a book to help you on your healing journey. I'm grateful that God graced me with enough strength, courage, and comfort to share the story of this traumatic event that I experienced over a decade ago. Everything will be okay.

Have faith, even when it's dark or you are walking in the valley. God knows your story, hears your cries, and understands your pain. Meditate on His word in all seasons of your life, including this one, and always pray. You are not alone, dear. You are loved, and I love you.

After this experience, I was no longer the young woman I'd been the day before. Life felt more real. I felt an inch taller, and my muscles—including my heart—grew stronger. However, I was still spiritually blind; I had no vision. My flesh led me into the wilderness. On the other hand, I felt the Spirit of God working in me and guiding my steps, especially when I experienced my difficult loss. I studied the Word and found strength to get me through the moment as I continued to serve God, attend Bible study, and participate in the worship service experience. I sang, gave my offering, prayed, listened to the word, and fellowshipped with others, all while coping with a thorn from hell, pain from a scar. I pushed forward and embraced each moment with a purpose: to be resilient, unbeatable, and fly like an eagle despite my situation.

Life went on, and it was hard to white out the voices that ran through my head days before I lost my baby. However, deep down, I saw a pinch of hope—Light to guide me on this healing journey. I looked up and thanked God for another chance and day to gain a closer, more intimate relationship with Him so that I could live rather than continue walking in sin. At that point, I was comforted. I wiped the tears that ran down my face, and I took a step forward. Weeks later, I purchased a beautiful sterling silver bracelet of hearts from Banter by Pagoda Piercing to represent my life-long love for my precious angel in Heaven, who's with me always, everywhere in spirit. I was proud of myself and humbled before God that I had been brave and continued my studies at FAU without taking off a term, quitting, or giving up on life. This decision was an achievement in itself, and I gave God all the praise, glory, and honor. As I approached my third year in college, I celebrated. My grade point average was 3.5, and I was on track for graduation. My angel motivated me and encouraged me more than ever.

As a junior, I extended my practice hours in preparation for my clarinet recital at the end of the term. I also studied extra hours, especially because I was near graduation. I didn't want anything or anyone to hold me back from earning my Bachelor of Music degree.

The next few months became a challenge to earn income as a performer, so I began teaching private clarinet lessons at a local elementary school. I also played side gigs. That was interesting and fun, but it wasn't easy. I had to commute and pay for gas while working part-time as a full-time student. Still, I pushed through it because I loved music. I also loved helping others understand this universal language and how to play the clarinet. Then, reality hit again. I began to struggle, which was strange, but not a surprise. My relationship with Christ was weak and not in sync with His Spirit. This included my faith. I had faith, but it wavered like a boat on the ocean. I wasn't satisfied. I was unhappy at times. However, I kept going and embraced life.

I had no idea about the miles I would have to walk for God to turn on the light bulb in my life, His will, and my calling, which I longed to discover and experience. I had hopes that one day it would happen.

I was certain I knew everything as a young adult, and I wanted to enjoy life my way, not the right way or the Christian way. I wanted to make my own decisions and go wherever I desired without the need to exercise self-discipline. Living on campus gave me the freedom to be an independent adult.

I enjoyed living on campus because I could meet up with my boyfriend, who swept me off my feet. Our romantic relationship was consistent but also uncomfortable at times. Some evenings, he sat in my dormitory, and we talked, but then we left for a hotel to have sex. That was one of the strangest things I experienced. However, most of the time, we met off campus and hung out together. Sometimes, we had lunch. However, because we met a lot on the weekends and evenings, we had a bite to eat before we had our alone time. It became tiresome because we rarely did normal things that ordinary couples did. We texted each other daily, smiled when we met, and made love. He loved it, and so did I, but I hoped one day we'd have a normal relationship, not a "friends-with-benefits" one. In the back of my head, I knew things would change in a matter of time. Because I rarely attended on-campus parties or nightlife activities, I relaxed with my man. We were like two birds sitting in a tree, k-i-s-s-i-n-g. We met up at local hotels, at his job site, at the park, or during his break. Some days or evenings, I drove as far as beyond where I lived—for his love.

I maintained a positive attitude despite my strange and unhealthy relationship. I made the best of my time and moved forward. I was happy that I didn't have to report to anyone, at least until I got married. However, my faith was tested on many occasions. While I wanted to do right or refrain from sin, my body craved the opposite; I was spiritually lost and blind, so it felt good to do anything and live carelessly. Everyone else lived loose, so it was okay, in my eyes. However, that wasn't what my heart desired. I was a lost young Christian woman who wanted God to rescue her from darkness and the difficult world of ongoing struggles that she was experiencing. So, I continued to pray and motivate myself. I was convinced that I was built on purpose, but I didn't truly understand my reason for living. This was hard, but I was determined to overcome life and keep a positive attitude.

I prayed, participated in worship service, helped with the baptism ministry, attended other church functions, and digested as much of God's wisdom as possible. However, at the end of the day, I continued to let my flesh take over my life; I was a Christian woman and desired to be freed from sin, but my actions weren't Christ-like.

I hit rock bottom—in the dark—and cried many nights, which inspired me to start a journey about my experiences, especially my unhealthy relationship. I was fed up with his actions and lies. I had never experienced anything like this before, so I walked to the school's psychologist and scheduled an appointment. Days later, I went to my appointment and met with a nice young woman. She sat next to me in a small and quiet room and asked me a load of questions about my life and this relationship. I became uncomfortable when she asked me certain questions, and I shed tears. By the end of our session, my hope was stronger, but I was hesitant about ending the relationship.

I didn't know which way to turn because his love made me feel loved. His touch made me feel good. His smell gave me butterflies. His eyes made me fall in love, and the way we made love hooked me to hang on to this handsome man. That evening, I reflected on my visit with the psychologist and decided not to return. I knew I was stronger than my battle and wiser than what this man might have thought. I had confidence that my days ahead would be better than yesterday. Besides, this visit didn't solve my main issue. I knew God was my Solution, but it was difficult for me to accept my reality. Instead of wholeheartedly, purposely seeking God for direction and deliverance, I continued to satisfy my flesh, which hurt me more than it helped. Deep down, I was desperate for a breakthrough and change like never before with my weak faith. So, I continued to pray and persevere. All I desired was to discover true love, joy, peace, and happiness, but I knew change would have to start with me; I would have to leave this man who I thought loved me more than my body. But he didn't desire my heart. His actions proved it, and that hurt—facing the truth.

Have you attempted to do something on your own, but it didn't work out? Were you upset or angry that the situation didn't go your way, or were you content and thankful? I experienced many instances in which things didn't go my way and it wasn't easy; as a matter of fact, it was hard to accept because I really desired it to go as "I" planned. However, what I learned over the years and through trial and error is that sometimes God says no for greater reasons. Now, you're probably wondering: Does that mean He doesn't care? No. It simply means that it wasn't His will and that you should never give up.

If you're experiencing doubt or uncertainty, don't worry; I understand. You're not alone. Be patient and give yourself grace and the OKAY to be human. Even better, let God transform your mind. When He does, your perspective about life will be clearer and you'll start to embrace all the many ways grace continues to bless you. Your situation will get better, and you'll overcome your unexpected obstacles in life one day at a time. Embrace the bright side of things and learn to appreciate the process; if you live across the bridge but don't embrace the obstacles, unexpectedness, delays, or all the things that could affect your experience, you'll complain and be ungrateful about every uncomfortable experience in life. Deal with the process God designed for you, and you'll gain peace of mind on earth. Nothing will take away what God has for you. Love in the process because there is comfort and hope in what God has planned for you to face in this world. Crush your intuition and be the best example you can naturally be. In doing this, you will attract others to your spirit, enrich the lives of your neighbors, and inspire others to have more confidence, especially on your journey. I wasn't perfect then, and I'm not perfect now. However, I strove to find peace, to be a peacemaker, to help others embrace life and love their passion, like music was to my heart. It was medicine to my soul that uplifted me when I was anxious about life and needed to release tension. It relaxed me when I was overwhelmed with the things and situations of this world. I expressed myself unapologetically, which motivated me when I had doubts. Music was my voice, my way of communication, and I embraced it. It was part of my life like every heartbeat and the oxygen I released. Music opened doors I never experienced and surrounded me with loving and caring human beings who wanted to see me excel, grow, and succeed. My teachers and professors respected me as a person, a woman, and a Christian, and they cheered me on both when I failed and when I triumphed against adversity. They gave me positive advice and spoke highly of me. When I needed help, they made time and supported me until I accomplished my goals.

However, every time I triumphed, I faced another fight. I never thought my romantic relationship would interfere with my studies. I wanted the best of both worlds: to be a good woman and to serve my flesh. However, it didn't work out. I noticed my partner's actions and attitude toward life didn't change, so I had to, especially after I experienced ongoing trials and tribulations and mental and physical hell, including depression. I was a caged bird, a woman who was trapped inside a relationship wilderness and who desired to be free. I knew our relationship wouldn't last—I felt it in my bones. However, letting go and leaving behind something that I might miss was difficult to imagine; letting go of someone so dear to my unconscious heart was my greatest fear. So, I continued to pursue this relationship despite the chaos and the mental and physical pain I put myself through. I was determined to make it work if it was God's will. Only time would tell.

My second year at FAU was another year of ups and downs, but it was memorable, and I enjoyed each moment. In my sophomore year, I struggled with Music Theory and Sight-Singing, but with help and guidance from friends and professors, I succeeded. Music theory was fun, but each term it advanced. Sight-Singing was my least favorite course in college because I had to use my voice, sing musical scales, and memorize so much that I lost interest in the course. I enjoyed playing in the wind ensemble, the orchestra, and my private lessons. I had the best professor of clarinet in the world, and he knew it as much as I expressed it. He was very patient with me and gifted, and he always wanted the best for me.

Most evenings, I spent at least an hour in the practice room polishing my craft, technique, and skills and practicing repertoire. Sometimes, I helped others if they needed assistance and vice versa. Each summer, I stayed on campus and commuted to my mom's place, visited other relatives and friends, and registered in either Summer A, B, or C. I loved studying and furthering my music education, so attending school year-round was never an issue for me. However, I took breaks, had fun, and relaxed on weekends and throughout the week.

As I reflect on these years of my life, I don't know how I got through what I experienced, but I do know it was only by the grace and mercy of God that I survived and didn't give up. I could have quit a long time ago and wasted my life away until it was destroyed, but I didn't; I held on to God's word, hope, and faith and to my determination to make it through unpredictable storms on purpose and with purpose.

As I lived, gained, fell, and failed on the mountain of life, I grabbed on to something I could embrace from every circumstance and matter, and I used it as motivation. I pushed forward and learned many lessons during the first three years of my college experience. Difficult experiences made me stronger, wiser, and more resilient. The more I struggled, the stronger my faith became. Never stop praying when it's dark, and no matter what you experience in life, never give up. At the end of the day, my college experiences helped shape my perspective on life by making me a better, stronger, and wiser woman, wife, mother, and Christian. So, don't ever think your life is such a mess that God can't help you bring it together or get you together. He has the sovereignty to do anything. Believe in yourself, but have faith in the Almighty.

# Chapter 6

## *Adversity*

*"I walked, ran, shed tears, and failed, but I didn't give up when I faced difficulty. Before the fight was over, I won."*

**-Kala**

I was in my final year of undergraduate studies at Florida Atlantic University when, days before the term began, I looked over my final grades and noticed something strange. I saw that I was in good standing with all my required music courses except for Music History. I was shocked because I had never expected to receive a D in any of my music classes; I thought it was a mistake, but when I looked closer at the computer screen, I saw that it was, indeed, correct. So, I walked from my dorm room, across the street to the music building, and into the Music, Theater, and Dance Department. I told the secretary that I had an urgent matter and I needed to talk with the chairperson as soon as possible. The secretary phoned her and then told me to walk back to her office.

We greeted each other. I sat down and explained my reason for the visit. She saw the look on my face; I was upset and needed answers. She asked for my student ID number, reviewed my grades and the undergraduate course requirements, and then informed me that I could not graduate without passing the class with a C or better. I was only a few points away from a B.

There was nothing she could do to allow the professor to adjust the grade in this class. However, she suggested I speak with my instructor about ways to improve my grade in the class and on future tests in the following semester.

I was speechless and frustrated because my plans were to graduate in four years, on time, without any complications, and to begin graduate school the following August. That didn't happen. When I spoke with the professor, she informed me about the reasons for my grade and what I needed to do to improve it on the test and in class.

I thought receiving a D was something horrible as a music major. However, after I took a step back and reminded myself that I wasn't perfect, I felt better and more confident about overcoming this obstacle. I gave myself grace and thanked God for bringing me this far on my journey. The setback also strengthened my hope, faith, love, and patience in the Lord and my outlook on life. This failure taught me to wait on God despite the circumstances and appreciate His will even though it didn't make sense at first.

Summer 2010 was around the corner, and I was interested in participating in a summer music camp. I browsed the internet and noticed an opening for a clarinet teacher position with the New York Music Festival in Oneonta, New York. I submitted my application along with a recording of myself playing the clarinet. I wanted to take a break from school and do something different, and it happened. Weeks later, I received a "congratulations" email from the camp director. I was accepted to attend the New York Summer Music Festival over the summer. It was the opportunity and experience of a lifetime to meet world-renowned band and orchestra directors. After days of prayer and full of excitement, I decided to accept the paid offer. However, airfare and hotel were not included. I shared the great news with my family, friends, and professors. Everyone cheered me on and congratulated me for such an achievement.

That summer, I experienced my first airplane ride, which was not pleasant at first. However, after I relaxed and attempted to rest and shift my thoughts to this opportunity, I was okay. Yay! We finally arrived in Oneonta, New York and landed safely. "Wow. I'm not sure if I'll ever get back on an airplane," I said. But I wasn't a hundred percent—I expected to return home by plane.

For the next two months, I had the opportunity to experience the reality of a dream. I met a ton of wonderful and gifted individuals and musicians at the festival. I also had the chance to teach others on the clarinet and receive lessons from incredible clarinet professors. Every day, I explored new things, activities, and places and met new people. Every moment was worth the experience, time, and energy. I even met new friends and spent time with them throughout the festival. The first evening was the best. We carpooled, gathered at a local Chinese restaurant, ate a delicious meal, and socialized. When we returned to the college campus where the festival was held, we practiced, roamed around, and met in a lounge, where we shared special memories and laughs. I had a blast and enjoyed assisting the band directors and meeting one-on-one with top clarinet professors.

Every night was a rehearsal, and most performances, masterclasses, and other special events took place during the week and, sometimes, on the weekends. However, there wasn't a nearby Church of Christ, so I pulled out my Bible each day and read Scriptures. On Sundays, I took communion and paid my offering. I was determined to carry the Lord everywhere I traveled, no matter what I had to do to get to His Word. God made a way for me to get chosen to participate in this summer event and inspire others through my spirit, passion for music, and dedication to serving others. I took away great memories from this festival—from the morning I left my apartment to the day I arrived back home and shared my experiences with everyone. I praised God for His grace and mercy and for this once-in-a-lifetime opportunity.

When I returned at the beginning of August, I experienced blood pressure issues for the first time in my life. My general physician referred me to a cardiologist in Palm Beach County, and I was prescribed a low dosage of high blood pressure medicine. I took one pill each morning and adjusted my diet: I implemented exercise, got more rest, and read the Bible more than usual—all for the sake of improving my health. I embraced change and welcomed my next term that August.

My fall 2010 schedule was lighter than ever. I had Music History, wind ensemble, orchestra, conducting, private lessons, and a general education course. Most of my time was spent preparing for my final clarinet recital and gathering paperwork and materials for graduate school, as well as meeting the requirements for my Bachelor of Music degree. I hoped to start at Florida International University in spring 2011, which had been on my radar for over a year. I was excited and certain I would be graduating soon, so I spoke to my supervisor at Office Depot and requested that my hours be cut. Walking across the stage in December was more important to me than working more hours or doing anything that could delay this goal.

It was November, one of my favorite months of the year, and things started to become real—a lot more than in previous months. Thanksgiving was around the corner, and I was less than two months away from graduating with my Bachelor of Music degree while preparing to audition in the FIU Music Department. I celebrated in advance, not only because I was about to complete yet another milestone on my educational journey but also because I had passed my Music History course. I jumped with joy. Yay! I thanked God and shared the great news with my mom. However, I still had a way to go before this happened.

In early December, I performed my final clarinet recital and passed. Everyone loved it, including my parents, friends, and professors. I received a standing ovation and was blessed with flowers and cards after the performance. I was pooped but enjoyed every second of pouring my heart out through this instrument. My hard work, dedication, commitment, and long hours in the practice room paid off, and God opened the door for me to further my education at another prestigious university, Florida International University in Miami, Florida.

Weeks after I graduated with my Bachelor of Music degree, I completed the graduate studies application and reached out to the Music, Theater, and Dance Department to arrange an audition. The following week, I received an acceptance letter from the university and drove down to Florida International University's Modesto Campus to audition for a seat in the graduate music program. Within a couple of days, I received the exciting news that I had performed well and been accepted into the Music, Theater, and Dance Department. I thanked God for another blessing and shared the great news with my professor of clarinet. He was very excited and congratulated me on a job well done. I also thanked him for the recommendation letter and expressed my excitement for this achievement.

Days later, I received an official acceptance email and a letter through the mail regarding my audition and stipend for a graduate teaching assistantship. I was super excited because the stipend was set to cover my music classes and provide me with financial assistance for the next two years or until I obtained my Master of Music degree. So, days before I transitioned to graduate school, I began shopping for supplies, new clothing, and items for on-campus housing. I decided I would rather stay on campus than in a regular apartment. There were vacancies for the efficiency apartments, so I applied and received notification of my move-in date and time, which was a few weeks away.

Yay! "It's move-in day," I said. My amazing uncle packed items in the back of his truck and helped me move in that morning. We drove from Palm Beach County to South Miami on the turnpike. It was a quiet and smooth ride. I was very excited about embarking on another milestone in my life, and nothing was going to prevent me from making this happen. I was determined to climb the ladder of success to get to where I desired, no matter how far I had to travel. I had a vision, and I was going to experience it. To make it this far was a blessing and an opportunity that few experienced, so I was thankful beyond what I could express in words, deeds, and actions.

My schedule included fewer classes than my undergraduate studies: Graduate Music Theory, Music History, private clarinet lessons, wind ensemble, orchestra, and a few others. During this time, I met other graduate music students, performed in ensembles, practiced, and performed off campus. In mid-January, I traveled to Pittsburgh, Pennsylvania on Amtrak to participate in an audition with a professional orchestra. I traveled solo and loved it. My travels and experiences were memorable. I didn't make the cut, which sucked, but it was worth the effort. I was grateful for the opportunity to do something and travel outside of Florida. I experienced snow for the first time, stayed in a luxury resort, Westin Pittsburgh, and met wonderful and talented individuals. When I returned to Miami, I shared my experience with friends, family, and professors and was determined to thrive and succeed.

After my return from Pittsburgh, reality hit, and I realized my assistantship wasn't enough to cover my monthly expenses. The little that I did receive was a temporary cushion until I sought employment. I noticed a Chili's on campus, so I walked in, spoke to the manager, and applied for the on-call waitress position. Days later, I received a phone call for an interview, and before I walked out, I was offered the on-call position. I was excited, but I didn't know what to expect. It looked fun, but that was only my window-view perspective.

The following week, I started my first afternoon at Chili's. I worked mostly in the afternoons and sometimes on Saturdays if needed. I received less than ten dollars per hour plus tips, which wasn't enough to pay my bills. After careful consideration and prayer, I provided management with my two weeks' notice. Days later, I initiated a transfer to another Office Depot, which sat across the street from the university—that was a blessing. A week later, I received a call that my transfer had been successful. An interview was scheduled, and it went well. The following week, I started as a part-time cashier. My position was the same, including the pay, and I worked twenty-five hours or less per week unless I covered someone else's shift. I always sought ways to earn extra money, especially because I didn't receive holiday pay and, some weeks, my hours were cut.

For weeks, everything was smooth, including the commute from my efficiency apartment to work. There were no issues—for the time being. However, business became slower. The meant, sometimes, I was sent home early, which affected my income. I began to lose interest in the position and sought employment opportunities elsewhere—primarily in the music field. During the week, on my off days, I searched online for clarinet teaching positions and performing opportunities. I was consistent no matter what time I performed my work search. I was committed to pursuing my dreams in the music industry despite the rejections I had faced. I knew, sooner or later, I would get the call; I had faith and kept a positive attitude.

After I browsed through over fifty employers, I saw a clarinet teaching position opening with the Miami Music Project, a non-profit organization that exposes children to music, musical instruments, music education, and performances as an avenue to help develop social transformation. It was perfect timing! I thanked God for guiding me during my search and for presenting another door of opportunities and blessings to enhance my life and the lives of others. This position seemed like a winner, an opportunity that would touch lives and help me grow as a musician and an individual. I was moved by its mission and purpose to use music as an instrument to help develop children's social and general life skills. Plus, the time frame worked with my schedule.

I notified management at my current job that I was no longer interested in the position for several reasons. I left in less than two weeks. Then, that evening, I applied for the music position. Within days, I received the great news that I had been accepted for the clarinet teaching position. I was excited and thankful, and I anticipated every opportunity ahead. Weeks later, I joined the staff of the Miami Music Project, which was about twenty minutes from the university depending on the traffic. I met great staff members and individuals, caring families, and bright students. I taught in the evenings and had opportunities to share my expertise in music, instruct students on the clarinet, encourage and motivate their precious hearts, and perform side-by-side with the participants. I developed great relationships with each family and provided them with updates on their child's progress. It was such an honor to become a part of these children's lives and leave great memories with them, their families, and staff members. I worked there for over a year but less than two years. In the meantime, I discovered other opportunities in the music field and began preparing for my final year at FIU.

I wanted to focus my attention and time on my thesis and graduate performance, so I resigned from the Miami Music Project with hopes of returning if it was God's will.

Shortly after, I began to struggle in Graduate Music Theory and Music History, so I received assistance from my professors after school to help me get back on track. My academics were more important at this point, and I looked forward to graduating on time.

During my final semester at FIU, I continued to play in the music ensembles, perform my graduate assistant duties, take private clarinet lessons, study Music Theory, and prep for graduation.

However, things became challenging. Not only did I struggle with my thesis, but I needed additional rehearsals for my graduate recital. I also experienced another financial hardship. I accumulated debt, and when I applied for personal loans, I was usually denied. I was also denied many credit cards because I had insufficient income, and my credit score was unbelievably low. It was eye-opening and difficult to believe, but it was my reality. However, I was determined to overcome my obstacles no matter how long I fought on the battlefield. I prayed, stayed hopeful, and embraced my faith in God. I knew my Father had me and change would come one day, in His timing. Some days seemed like a roller coaster, and others felt like a dream. I struggled to keep money in my pockets through almost every season of my life, especially during the summer when I had little to no work. I always looked forward to the summer, but I also knew it would be a temporary season of financial struggle. It was the most difficult time because I had little to no work. Often, I scraped up change or borrowed money from loved ones or friends. I was embarrassed and felt ashamed about borrowing money, but I had courage and spoke up. I set aside pride and everything that discouraged me, including thoughts of guilt, and I did what I had to do. Many had sympathy and helped me out without judging or criticizing me. That encouraged me to not give up and to keep striving and persevering.

I thanked God for my circle of real friends and family support, and I never took His grace and mercy for granted. Unexpectedness seemed to haunt me; after I overcame one life storm, I faced another. I continued to fight like a song that played over and over on the radio to the point that, on some days, it didn't make sense; I was lost and down in the wilderness. I became frustrated and anxious for change, but I knew it wouldn't happen overnight. I looked forward and never stopped praying. Some days were worse than others—mentally, physically, and financially. However, God turned my hurt and pain into motivation to lean on His word and trust that He would provide for my every need no matter what situation I experienced. Most importantly, I knew there was something greater, more significant that God was trying to tell me in the middle of my life storms; there was more to my struggles with life, but I didn't understand His messages. Times like this strengthened my faith and drew me closer to the Lord. I kept the faith and expected God to reveal my real purpose in life and my breakthrough in due time.

It was the last semester at FIU before I would walk across the stage with my Master in Music degree. I had fewer classes and focused on completing my thesis and clarinet recital. It wasn't easy for many reasons: I no longer received my graduate assistantship, I didn't have much savings, and I didn't know my next steps after graduation. So, I applied for unemployment benefits and food stamps, which I received by the grace and mercy of God. I continued to persevere and push forward, which required more mental strength than physical power. I set my mind to endure hard times even though it seemed impossible to survive with little. I knew that with God, all things were possible, which encouraged my spirit to embrace what God was already working out in my life. I knew He had me and wouldn't let me fall without picking me up. Besides, I had no time to think about giving up; I was certain that nothing was too big for God to handle and to grace me to overcome. He'd done it before, so I had faith that He would grace me again. So, I did what I could do and left my worries in God's hands, especially when I experienced rejection, isolation, and loneliness. My trials and denials made me stronger and wiser, and they opened my eyes just a bit more than they'd been the previous day.

My credit score was good, but not perfect, so every time I applied for loans, credit cards, and, sometimes, cash advances, I was denied. It sucked and was difficult to accept. Sometimes, I felt embarrassed and down, but I lifted my head and prayed to God for deliverance. I didn't give up because I was certain my situation would improve. When I got settled and worked a stable job, God would send me a breakthrough and my life would be better than it had been the day before. So, I continued to work side jobs to pay for rent and food, and I saved funds if anything was left over (which there was but not much). Sometimes, I'd have a hundred to two hundred dollars remaining, but I tithe, so at the end of the week, I was nearly broke. Sometimes, I shed tears because I didn't make enough to put back what I desired.

I hoped to make enough money to build a savings account, but it was difficult. My responsibilities were to put aside ten percent for the Lord and funds for rent, my car note, life insurance, credit card bills, and other expenses. However, in my circumstances, saving was a big challenge, one that was almost impossible. I did my best. What I find mind-blowing to this day is that I had enough faith that God heard my prayers for change. My obstacles made me stronger and gave me hope for better days and financial stability.

On the other hand, I was excited and looked forward to graduation and having a real job. After sleepless nights, hard work, tutoring, and, most importantly, the grace of God, I passed my graduate courses and completed my thesis and graduate recital successfully. It was a long journey that I looked forward to completing each day, and it happened. I was excited and grateful for my accomplishments and motivation to make it across the finish line despite the obstacles I faced.

Weeks before I received my master's degree, the Spirit led me to reach out to the Director of Music, Theater, and Dance at Miami Dade College Kendall Campus, and I did so without hesitation. I

Googled the phone number and spoke with the Chairman of the Music, Theater, and Dance Department. I informed him that I was months away from graduating with my master's at FIU and that I was interested in teaching music classes, clarinet, and whatever else was available. He was delighted to receive my call and enjoyed the conversation.

After this call, he invited me to the college to meet with him to discuss upcoming adjunct teaching opportunities. A few days later, I drove to the campus and parked near one of the faculty parking lots, which was next to my destination: a big gray building with glass windows and stairs. When I stepped outside my car, I saw students sitting on the curb playing on their trumpets and flutes. Then, I saw other students with musical instruments exit a room that looked like a band room, so I walked inside and asked about the Music, Theater, and Dance Department. The gentleman whom I spoke with was very nice and helpful. He welcomed me with open arms and informed me that his office was upstairs. So, I exited the band room and walked up stairs.

I walked through the door and saw a herd of students walk out of classrooms. Some exited the door through which I had entered. It must have been the hour when students switched classes. I smiled, turned left, and saw door-sized rooms where students played musical instruments, studied, or chatted with professors. I walked down farther and looked up at the room number. I'd made it! I was excited and thankful I had arrived at what I expected to be my first workplace after obtaining my Master of Music degree.

The room's sign read "Music, Theater, and Dance Department" in bold. I walked in, and immediately to my right was the chairman's office. He was sitting and typing on his computer.

He looked over at me, smiled, and said, "Hello, how can I help you?"

I said, "Hi, I'm Kala and I have an interview with the department's chairperson."

He said, "Well, that's me. Welcome. I'll be with you in a few minutes."

After a few minutes, he called me into his office and thanked me for reaching out to him weeks ago. He said, "You contacted me at the perfect time, around the corner from the upcoming semester." He provided me with a general overview of the college, the Music, Theater, and Dance Department, and music courses offered at the campus. He also shared his music and teaching journey and encouraged me with stories of his childhood and professional teaching and performing days. I was touched and motivated by his unique and caring spirit, and I loved his attitude.

Then, he printed out a list of music appreciation courses he needed to fill and showed me the required book for the course. There were a lot of slots open, which was great. This allowed me to choose a course section that fit my schedule and that had the possibility of filling up with students. He also provided me with pay rate information, including several forms to complete for payroll. At this point, I knew I had won the position. It felt right, and I seemed to be a great fit for the role.

He said, "The fall term is around the corner, so you'd have plenty of time to review the course book and prepare a course syllabus and lessons for your students."

I looked at him, smiled, and said, "Okay, awesome. Thank you. I look forward to my new music teaching journey at Miami Dade College."

He asked me if I had any questions, and I did. He answered them. Then he said, "Well, congratulations. You've been offered the position."

I was thrilled and thanked God. I said, "Wow, thank you so much. You made my day."

He said, "You're welcome. I knew you were the one. This position was yours before we met. Complete the rest of the hiring paperwork and submit everything to me by next week." We stood up. He shook my hand and said, "Welcome, Ms. Jordan. We look forward to having you on board in the Music, Theater, and Dance Department in a few months."

I said, "Thank you. I look forward to starting in August. What a blessing."

It was one of the best mornings of my life and an honor to have met such a warm and good-hearted individual—someone understanding, a human being who showed compassion because he understood my situation and career goals. We instantly connected, and before I left the the chairperson's office, he offered to let me teach some music appreciation courses starting in the fall of 2011. I was overjoyed and shared the exciting news with family, friends, and my boyfriend.

During my first semester at MDC, I had a blast and met hundreds of students with different personalities, attitudes, and backgrounds. I loved it and earned a decent income. I worked part-time, at least twenty-five hours a week, and performed small gigs on the weekends. However, at times, I was still short of funds. To make extra money, I helped colleagues who needed a substitute on days when they were absent or unavailable. I gladly taught additional music courses in the Music, Theater, and Dance Department when needed.

In addition, I was offered the opportunity to play the clarinet in the Miami Wind Symphony, a local and professional wind band that the chairperson directed. I prayed and took the offer, then attended evening rehearsals during the week and morning rehearsals on Saturdays. I received a small stipend a week after I performed each time, which I used to help pay for rent, food, gas, and other important bills.

On occasion, I performed in local symphony orchestras if a substitute was needed. That was fun, and I met a lot of great and talented musicians and individuals. It wasn't stable, but I enjoyed the experience and blessing to network and perform with others. I was certain my financial situation would improve; I had faith that someday I'd teach full-time and perform in more concerts. I prayed for consistent income with the hope that God would deliver me and make it happen.

However, my personal life was still weak. A few years before my sixth and final year at Miami Dade College Kendall Campus, I was still in a difficult relationship. It was time for change, and I deserved it. I wanted peace and to live a normal life. I knew my worth and the value I possessed; I had endured twelve long years of mental, physical, and emotional abuse, heartache, stress, drama, frustration, and unhappiness. My body was used like a toy; it was taken for granted and used for fun and pleasure. Many days, I cried at the edge of hotel beds after my mind and body had been used by a man who didn't love me for who God created me to be. I longed for a normal relationship and to do regular things like ordinary people, but it didn't happen. I stayed trapped in a dark world of my own, longing to be free, to breathe and live Christ-like; I desired to be a better woman than the truth, my walk, my reality, not an undercover Christian. I looked forward to experiencing the rest of my days with a God-fearing man who would love me for me and accept me for my flaws, strengths, and weaknesses.

I was worn out and tired beyond fed up with another man's lies. I desired to better myself. So, after praying to God for change in my life, a breakthrough, a healthier relationship, to experience true love, joy, peace, and happiness, I was finally brave and confident enough to walk away from this unhealthy twelve-year relationship. I had peace of mind, hope, faith, fulfillment, happiness, and empowerment in the Lord.

This was the first time in years I could breathe, spiritually see, and concentrate. I felt refreshed and stronger than I had felt yesterday. My body was no longer in mental and physical chains, a dark and hopeless wilderness. God had rescued me safely and without hurt, harm, or danger. God certainly did something extraordinary in the days leading up to my departure from this ungodly environment where I had lived for years, and my heart was happy. My spirit was renewed. He transformed my mind. My soul was restored by the love, grace, and mercy of God.

The years I spent at Miami Dade College Kendall Campus were a special and memorable blessing. Though my journey wasn't perfect, I embraced every obstacle and life storm I experienced. I worked hard, was dedicated, and made an impact in my role and the community. I also blessed my colleagues and vice versa. Yet, I knew this wasn't the end. God was preparing me for an advance, a greater door, and an opportunity to grow in His will for my life. It wasn't about earning a higher salary and having any job to meet my needs. Rather, it was about finding the fit that God destined and desired me to experience. So, I kept the faith and kept it moving until years later, when God did a new thing in my life.

No matter how your journey seems or what it looks like, keep going and never give up. There is hope even in the eye of a life storm, a job loss, doubt, pain, a low credit score, denial, or fear. You must desire a closer, more intimate relationship with Christ and glorify Him the rest of your life; you must praise Him and thank Him for where you are now; you must have confidence that God will deliver you to a better place, where you need to glorify His name and experience peace and satisfaction.

It's hard to embrace life and your problems when God is out of your desires, schedule, plans, environment, or lifestyle. Let Him open your eyes, turn your perspective about life around, and bless you to be satisfied, content, and appreciative of His will.

Prepare for unexpectedness with faith, knowing that, in due time, God will get you through whatever you are dealing with. Be encouraged to know there is hope in your confusing situations, like the ones you don't understand and fret over. God will open your eyes if you let Him and will bless you to experience unimaginable things on your journey. He will bless you with amazing grace and make a way out of no way when times are hard and you feel like quitting or giving up. Embrace your days of being down, feeling empty, being broke, or feeling like it's all over. If you're one to worry, read Scripture or stop and pray wherever you are—no matter what day or time it is. Turn to Jesus, and He'll strengthen you more than any doctor, psychiatrist, psychologist, or mental health physician could. That's a fact. I've been there and experienced the other side of walking in Christ and embracing His grace, mercy, and favor.

God will bless you in mighty ways when you turn every difficult or challenging circumstance over to His hands and leave it there with faith. If you are in a rush, don't have time, or want it now without waiting on the Lord, you'll crash or continue to experience life in darkness. However, even if you experience life in darkness in Christ, He'll carry you through in a way that will blow your mind and keep you standing no matter what disturbances or distractions you encounter along the way.

Take it one day at a time; don't be anxious about tomorrow, about what you don't have, or about what could happen if you don't make it to work on time. God is never late; He's always on time and keeps His word. Live for today and let the future arrive in God's timing. And never give up. God will bless you with all your needs as you continue to trust in His will, way, and word. Leave the world to Him.

Whatever happens will happen no matter how many gates you jump, fences you climb, or struggles you overcome. God is in control and has the mighty power to create unimaginable surprises and miracles in your life. Trust in the Lord more than your intuition and the drama on the news.

God knows what's best. Remember, life is a mindset journey, so turn your life over to God and start training your thoughts to focus on His word, exercise His word in your life, and embrace His will, and you'll be safe and secure. You won't lose your mind or go crazy like many around you. Life in Christ will keep you safe despite the battles or chaos in your backyard. His inspirational and life-changing words will sustain you even in the middle of a Category 5 hurricane. So, get in Him; surrender your life in His hands before it's too late. If you don't, you'll be miserable, stressed out, or always frustrated with the way things turn out. You won't have peace or be pleased with your purposeful life condition.

When you experience fights with the world or at your job, in your community, or at the unemployment office, stand still and let God handle your situation. Let Him bring you out on the other side stronger than when you were at rock bottom. Also, encourage someone along the way.

Stay hungry to study God's word and exercise His wisdom in your life daily. If darkness overpowers your faith, embrace the Light with hope. Glorify God in your weakness, mentally, physically, and spiritually, and never give up.

Anger depresses the heart, but when you nourish your mind with positive thoughts, hope, or the Word, you'll learn to cope with situations with power out of this world—power from above with every breath you take.

Let God carry you to where you need to be without trying to hold on or stay where you are, as it just might take you out—in day light, while you're shopping, sleeping, walking, or reading a disturbing message. I'm certain He'll shift you where you need to be with purpose. He never makes mistakes.

Every time I faced obstacles, I saw *the Light,* Hope, and my deliverance before God blessed me with victory. I encourage you to wholeheartedly seek Him. Worship and honor the Lord and have faith. You will be delivered. However, you must believe it more than you hear it and read it. When God rescued me on my journey, His unconditional love and mighty power blessed my life, and it continues to do so. When God delivers you from hardship, a health issue, or depression, talk about Him with the world—praise His name and share the Good News. Also, encourage someone along the way. This offers hope to those who are down or hopeless. Exercise your faith without wavering and never give up.

When it feels unbearable, rest assured that God will take care of you and bless you with your needs and desires. He will satisfy your anxious, hurting, lost, or lonely heart. Persevere when you experience burdens or feel like problems are on your back. Let God change your way of thinking for a clear spiritual vision. Desire to be resilient and stand strong no matter what you face. And keep it moving.

I thank God that I chose not to give up, as otherwise, this book would have stayed in my heart. The world would have edited my story or talked about my experiences from their viewpoints. Instead, God blessed me with every reason to write this book, to share my story of truth to bless your life beyond your wildest dreams, and to offer you hope and encouragement in your darkest moments.

# Chapter 7

# Our Love Story

*"He ran to me with the sweetest poems and handed them to me. We looked each other in the eyes and smiled. At that point, I knew he was the one—the man I desired to spend the rest of my life with and start a beautiful family."*

*-Kala*

When I least expected to meet a handsome young man with the most attractive smile and dimples, I met Anthony. After he and I spotted each other at a worship service one Sunday morning, he ran outside the church building and handed me what I thought was a love note. I took it from him and smiled, then walked to my car and drove down to FIU to participate in a performance. I arrived on time and felt more cheerful and excited about performing; I think it was due to the surprise note this man had handed me. He certainly made my evening.

It finally happened—the moment I had been waiting for after a two-hour concert. I unfolded the paper and realized it was one of the sweetest collections of poetry and prose I had ever read. The best part about it was that he was the author! Never in a thousand years had I imagined a young man would run up to me and hand me pages of love notes full of heartfelt thoughts, feelings, and prayers. This stuff happened only in movies, especially romances or those with happy love story endings. But I was blessed and thankful; I'm living proof that not only can your dreams come true, but God has the power, strength, and understanding to answer your prayers in the right season and time of your life if it is His will.

Days later, in 2014, Anthony and I officially met and talked at my uncle's and auntie's home after worship service. My family and I always stopped over to chat and eat a hot cooked meal. We laughed, told stories, and met other relatives. So, when Anthony and I met, he joined us and visited the sick-and-shut-in with one of my uncles. We ate lunch, walked at the park and on the beach, and learned more about each other. During one conversation, he shared that he had never met his father, who had passed away when Anthony was two years old. I pitied him and felt his pain. I told him he'd always be in my prayers. Then, I hugged him, and we continued our interesting conversation. When he stood, I noticed he was tall and skinny and had the most adorable dimples. It was funny because, when I was a child, I'd always pocked myself in my cheeks to create dimples. So, when Anthony smiled, he gave me butterflies and goosebumps all over.

He was the right size, a perfect height, and very attractive. I also noticed he was quiet, with brown eyes and wavy hair. He was respectful, humble, and God-fearing, and he had a beautiful spirit, which captured my heart. Plus, he didn't wear his pants past his underwear. I loved the fact that he didn't have gold on his teeth and wear heavy gold chains. He was the perfect match, and I was thankful I hadn't met him online or on social media, unlike another young man I'd met. That latter friendship didn't work out, and I was glad, as he lived out of state and lied about visiting. My relationship with Anthony was meant to be, and I was so thankful I hadn't pursued the other man.

Anthony lived in Delray Beach, about forty-five minutes to an hour from my home in Miami. On weekends, he traveled down to my place and relaxed. He lived with his auntie and worked during the week. However, he hoped to move out, so I invited him to stay with me at any time, which he did. He visited me on the weekends and, sometimes, at the end of the week. He enjoyed being in Miami with me. It gave him a break from home and time to spend with me. I loved it when he was around. He was company whom I truly missed and who made me feel safe. His presence also seemed "right," like "He was the one, God-sent."

We spent several holidays together, went out for dinner, and embraced our relationship. He also surprised me with my first cruise. We enjoyed riding on the Jungle Queen Riverboat, in Fort Lauderdale, Florida and looked forward to returning, Lord willing. Well, I wasn't sure, as I wasn't a fan of being on top of water. He laughed and said everything would be alright. It was memorable and we had a blast, but I wasn't definite about returning.

Months later, I missed my cycle and purchased a pregnancy test. When I got home, I took the test and was amazed, but not surprised, at what it read: YOU ARE PREGNANT. I ran into the living room and shared the great news with Anthony. We looked at each other and smiled. I thanked God, and Anthony congratulated me. However, we wanted this to be official, so I visited my primary doctor. It was true; the pregnancy test was accurate. We were on our way to having our first beautiful child together. From day one, we had talked about marriage and having a family, so we were thankful.

During this time, I continued to work part-time at MDC Kendall and to perform. However, I experienced morning sickness for months, and my blood pressure became elevated. I visited my gynecologist several times during the week and did my best to maintain work and everyday tasks. However, things became hectic, and I spoke to Anthony about resigning from the college. We wanted a healthy pregnancy, so we prayed. Then, I put in my two weeks' notice and prepared to take a break from work. I was sick and needed to adjust my schedule and lifestyle.

After I resigned, I applied for unemployment benefits, WIC, and cash assistance. My family and I were approved for unemployment benefits and WIC but not for cash assistance. However, we were blessed and thankful for the assistance we received. Weeks later, my 401(k) retirement benefits were electronically deposited, which was an on-time blessing. Despite my work status, Anthony and I praised God and continued to celebrate and embrace life. After all, our little bundle of joy and blessings was on the way, and we were excited about meeting her.

Weeks later, Anthony proposed to me at Lake Ida Church of Christ before the worship service ended in front of the congregation. I was shocked but not really because I was expecting this day to happen. After the minister called me to the front, I walked up to the pulpit, and Anthony got down on his knees and smiled. He ended with the question, "Would you marry me?"

I said, "Yes, of course!"

This afternoon was one of the most memorable, sweetest, and best days of my life. I was patient, prayed, and had faith that God would bless me to meet the right man—not just anybody but someone special and chosen. God made it happen.

On October 24, 2015, we experienced our big day. We walked down the aisle at Lake Ida Church of Christ before family, friends, and our senior minister. I also invited a close friend of mine, who performed the flute at our wedding. She played beautifully and was such a special addition to our special day. We had studied music together at Florida Atlantic University and continued to hang out and make music. Our immediate families, including brothers and sisters in Christ and friends, were present. The wedding was small but unforgettable. My best friend and my sister, Allison Henson, were my maids of honor, and my other sisters, Heather and Aimee, and my niece, Gabriella, were included. Of course, my parents, Jefferson and Evella Grisby Jordan, were present. We had a great turnout and support. Anthony and I were excited and grateful for our precious bundle of joy—Kamaria—lying in my belly.

Now that we were married, Anthony joined me in the apartment, which he loved. From day one, he had said that he looked forward to having his own place or joining me. When it happened, he was the happiest young man and husband on the planet. Weeks later, we enjoyed our honeymoon in Orlando, Florida. It was our first long-distance road trip together. Through prayer, planning, and saving, God made a way, and we thanked Him for His grace and provisions.

Our family and friends joined us in celebration of our first baby shower, and it was a blast. Our church family also supported us and prepared a second baby shower. We were so overwhelmed with gifts that we couldn't fit everything in our car. So, we made two trips up and down within a few weeks. We then spent the next several months embracing each other, praying, and planning for the coming steps of our lives, including the birth of Kamaria.

We were blessed and beyond two lovebirds. Anthony and I were a God-fearing couple. However, our lives weren't perfect, nor did we expect them to be. I struggled to make ends meet during this transition in my life, especially after I resigned from the college. We had more bills than income, but God continued to bless our household. We worked together as a team, prayed together, and had each other's backs. God provided and blessed us with our needs, even when we had little to nothing. Our faith strengthened every day.

During times like this, we were certain God was near our sides like peanut butter and jelly; we had faith that God was carrying us where we needed to be, which gave us hope and enhanced our marriage. We never had the desire to copy someone else's marriage or have the same relationship as our neighbors because we knew that what we had was special and blessed. No matter what we experienced in our relationship, we found ways to thrive and seek God's will and wisdom to strengthen our marriage and household. Our faith was greater than our problems and unexpected life storms.

At this time, I'd worked part-time at a private school in Broward County, which was about thirty to forty minutes from home. I taught general music education to children who were underprivileged and experienced behavioral issues, and I loved it. Some days were difficult, but I embraced every moment I had with these children. It wasn't the best job, but it was something—a job that helped pay our bills.

However, after months of working, the distance became a challenge, and my pregnancy affected my health to the point that I had to call out from work or go to the hospital. Driving from Miami to Broward County began to take a toll on my health, and I knew I'd have to resign from the position sooner or later. Finally, I did.

On Sunday, October 20, 2016, immediately following church service, I experienced strong back pain. I informed Anthony and, hours later, he checked on me again. I was fine the rest of the night. However, on the morning of October 21, I felt pressure in my lower belly—contractions. This time, they seemed serious. It happened as soon as I stood and walked to the bathroom. I screamed out to Anthony, and we grabbed our bags and sped to the hospital. When we arrived, we entered the emergency room, and they rushed me to the back. My heart sped and my blood pressure rose. Minutes later, I was relaxed, but Kamaria wasn't. The nurses informed me that I'd need an emergency C-section once my gynecologist arrived at the hospital. They also informed Anthony, who was in the waiting room. With this being my first delivery experience, I was anxious. Minutes before they took me to the back, Anthony and I prayed. Then, seconds later, I was given anesthesia. Ultimately, I awoke in the NICU area, and Anthony and I had the amazing blessing to hold our beautiful bundle of joy, our precious baby girl, Kamaria. Holding her near our chests, against our flesh, was one of the greatest feelings, moments, and blessings ever—an experience we'll never forget.

I reached out to my immediate supervisor at the school and informed him about my emergency. Days later, I prayed and decided to resign. Then, I applied for unemployment benefits. I was without work and needed money to survive, so not only did I apply for unemployment, but I also applied for food stamps while I searched for a new job. This was new to me and uncomfortable, but I had no other choice. So, I took a deep breath and dropped my pride. I wasn't used to sitting on the couch, so I did my part by searching for work while I applied for other financial resources; I was jobless and had no other income coming in.

Because of her early birth, Kamaria had to stay in the NICU for a week. Because I'd had a C-section, I had to stay in the hospital as well. Anthony stayed with us the entire week. Our parents visited us a few days later. Everyone adored Kamaria and talked about how beautiful she was. We were very grateful for a successful delivery and a beautiful daughter, as well as for the great hospitality at our local hospital. Everyone overwhelmed Anthony, Kamaria, and me with love, care, support, and phenomenal service.

During my final week at the hospital, my gynecologist met with us and removed my C-section stitches, which was painful but a big relief. I was happy that I could now stand up and walk. I visited Kamaria and breastfed her for a few days. However, she no longer tolerated it, so I stopped breastfeeding her and prepared bottles.

Days later, we took photos of Kamaria and placed her in a car seat to finally head home. We were excited to embrace new beginnings and a new journey with our precious little girl, Kamaria Grace Lindsey, whom we knew was blessed with life by the grace and mercy of God.

During this time, I was still out of work, but Anthony and I discussed my future return. After a month and a half of staying home to recover and care for Kamaria, I used my time wisely and applied for work. I noticed a full-time music position opening at a private school near home and applied for it. I was particularly interested because the school was next door to a daycare center.

After a week, I received an email from the principal, who asked me to stop in for an interview. The school was about thirty minutes from our residence. So, I stopped in, looked around, and met the head principal, who provided me with full details of the position, including requirements, pay, benefits, and general information about the school's background and mission. The interview was a success, and I looked forward to sharing the great news with Anthony. Afterward, I stopped in and met the teachers at the daycare center. I loved the atmosphere, organization, and cleanliness of the daycare. The teachers were Hispanic, and some of them spoke English. I took information from the center and drove home.

When Anthony arrived, I told him the great news and about how excited I was to return to work and earn an income. The salary was great, the distance was okay, and, best of all, the daycare center was next door to the school and accepted babies as young as six weeks. We prayed, and I decided to accept the music teaching position and register Kamaria at the daycare.

Weeks later, I started. My first day was different but great. I taught kindergarten through eighth-grade general music in a single room. Meanwhile, I sat next door with Kamaria daily and helped feed her. She was the highlight of my days, as was my handsome husband, who had supported me since day one. Everything seemed to work out well except for my pay schedule. I received monthly pay, which was unusual for me. However, I was content and grateful for the income.

My students met with me at different times during the day and experienced a quality music experience. However, at times I struggled with their behavior issues. Many were underprivileged, lived in single-parent homes, and experienced mental issues. Still, they were determined to overcome their obstacles and gain knowledge to succeed. What made this setting more special was my understanding of their upbringing and difficult journey. They rose and, over time, with patience and adjustments on my end, improved and started to appreciate the blessing of education. Their attitudes and hearts inspired me to pour out more of what God blessed in me, and they thanked me for it. I stayed humbled and gave glory to God.

My group of kids was on fire to learn, strive, thrive, and succeed, and they did. I also created a band, and students played the recorder and percussion instruments. They enjoyed making music and discovering their gifts and talents. Many sang, while some loved drawing, painting, and fashion. Some wanted to become instrumentalists. The kids also participated in local field trips and special events at the school. In December 2016, they performed at the school's Annual Holiday Extravaganza; they played recorders and sang. We had a blast. It was a memorable day of fun, food, and performances.

I really enjoyed my new environment, the students, and certainly the pay. I had a pleasant experience. However, I wanted health benefits, a 401(k), higher pay, and a normal pay schedule, so I spoke with Anthony, and we prayed. He supported me a hundred percent as I moved forward with hopes of God turning around my situation and blessing me with my heart's desires.

Days later, I walked to the school's main office and spoke with the principal to give her my two weeks' notice. She was speechless and thanked me for my hard work and dedication as an educator. It was a relief, and it felt good to have the courage to do what I did that afternoon. I had enjoyed my experience at the school, but it was time for a change that would help my family, financial situation, and professional aspirations.

I was hopeful about my future, with better employment, a healthier lifestyle, and my spiritual walk. I was convinced I was closer to experiencing my dream job than I imagined.

# Chapter 8

## The Unexpected Day

*"Well, that moment when all seemed fine and the birds chirped, hell broke loose like an unexpected earthquake. It was a shaky moment like no other— not even a day like yesterday or a thousand years from now where on a sunny, hot day in South Florida the usual happened; when dogs barked through the walls of my neighborhood and outside my window until an ordinary day turned into an unforgettable, unimaginable scene like watching the most shocking movie ever."*

*-Kala*

During the last week of 2016, my family and I enjoyed ice cream and dinner at one of our favorite spots in town and looked forward to celebrating New Year's Eve with other family members and our church family. It was the most wonderful time of the year—a month of excitement and expectancy of the future with Christmas, New

Year's Eve, new beginnings, and tax season around the corner. I envisioned working at a higher-paying job, having the perfect full-time teaching position, and all the many blessings God had in store for me and my family. I knew it was my time, my season to gain, grow, and fly higher—to discover and embrace what I really prayed for with hopes of sharing my passion and creating special memories with others. However, I was uncertain about when and where this full-time opportunity would arise; I had no clue where I was going to work next, but I was certain I would find a full-time job with benefits and all the other good stuff that comes along with working thirty-five to forty hours a week—paid vacation, health, dental, and vision benefits, personal time off, a 401(k), and bonuses.

In my spare time, I searched for full-time music openings in my area. I was confident that I would find a great-paying job that satisfied my needs. Anthony agreed, prayed with me, and continued to encourage me. He had faith that God would answer my prayers, and so did I. We patiently waited and enjoyed our New Year's Eve at church. It was a blessing. Everyone smiled and hugged each other the moment 11:59 pm approached. There was a countdown, and when midnight arrived, everyone shouted, "Happy New Year!" Anthony and I did the same. We looked at each other, hugged, and kissed. We thanked God for carrying us through another year of grace, mercy, love, and favor.

However, the first week already seemed like the middle of the year with a rocky and stressful start. I was in the middle of dealing with unexpected legal matters after I had experienced an in-store problem the previous year. The case was close to being settled, which was great, but it was still a load on my shoulders. Thankfully, God blessed us to get through this unexpected life storm successfully and with peace of mind.

I never thought in my lifetime that I would struggle with so much. Sometimes, it was unbelievable. However, I was unstoppable and pushed forward with hope and faith that things would improve. At this point, I knew God was up to something. I also knew this time was a test of my faith, so I didn't quit. I kept going and prayed. Anthony and I kept the faith and stuck together because we were determined to get somewhere, to embrace all that God had in store for us without distractions, drama, and negativity. This required gorilla faith and God's mighty power every step of the way.

Beyond my blurry vision and uncertain thoughts about the future was hope—a lot of it the moment I came across a full-time music teacher position at a local educational institution. The best part was that it was full-time, with a higher salary than my current job, and included great medical, dental, vision, and retirement benefits with an annual bonus. Immediately, I said, "Thank You, Jesus," and texted Anthony about the great news. He was also excited and praised God.

When he arrived home from work, we prayed. Then, I sat down at the computer and applied for the teacher position. Days later, over the weekend, I received an email from the school principal requesting an interview for the following week. I prayed again and replied, "Yes, I'd be glad to meet you for an interview."

The next day, the principal followed up with me, as did the assistant principal. During the middle of the week, I received another reminder about my upcoming interview at the school. I was excited and gathered my driver's license and copies of my resume for the big day. I looked forward to this great opportunity and to meeting the staff at my next potential workplace.

On the day of my interview, I clocked out of work at my current job, turned on my GPS, and entered information about the interview site. I was surprised because I arrived at the school in less than thirty minutes, which was a blessing; it was nearby, and traffic was smooth. I arrived in good timing and prayed before I walked in. I loved the location, although it was a distance from our home. Still, at that point, it didn't matter. I was excited about a new opportunity that would bless our household tremendously.

Days later, I received a "Welcome and Congratulations" email, which advised me to report to a specific location for a background check and fingerprints. I completed this within days, and the following week, I was notified of my start date. I put in my resignation at my current job and prepared for my next journey without any reason to look back.

At the beginning of 2017, I began my new full-time music position—a new chapter. It was a dream come true and perfect timing; everything seemed to fall into place. The position was a blessing for many reasons: I received health care benefits for me and my family, as well as a great retirement package, other financial bonuses, and an outstanding teacher's salary—one that was higher than any job I had ever worked since high school. Because of His awesomeness, we didn't take His grace for granted. Plus, I had the blessing of teaching kindergarteners through fifth-graders. I taught general music and helped students learn to play the recorder, as I'd done in my previous position. I loved it, including the students, who were predominantly Hispanic. There were only about five Black children at this school, which was no surprise, yet interesting because I was the only African American woman and teacher at the time.

My family and I continued to struggle financially until I got back on my feet and earned my first paycheck, which happened in late

September. I was excited and super thankful for God's triple blessings. That first paycheck covered our rent, lights, car and life insurance, tithes, and more than I could imagine for savings. It almost seemed surreal, but it was real. It felt good to be able to spend again. However, after a few months into my contract at the school, I noticed my health and marriage began to suffer. My diet was weak, and I barely exercised; I ate more fast food, sweets, and processed food than home-cooked meals, and I drank less water than I should have. Some days, I felt dehydrated and sick, but making a living was more important. My health, personal life, and walk with Christ were secondary; my career and making money were my priorities. Looking back, I realize I didn't know that because I lived to please my flesh, my relationship with the Lord was not the best; it was weak, dry, and dead—even with the money.

My marriage was also impacted. I awoke at around five-thirty in the morning and didn't see my husband until after I got off work, which was sometimes after five in the evening. Kamaria attended daycare minutes from my workplace, so after I clocked out, I picked her up. Anthony also picked her up from school, which was a blessing.

Before the school year was over, all the teachers and staff were treated to a local hotel to celebrate a successful year. I had started in the middle of school and continued until the summer, when I worked for a few weeks. It was a blessing because I also received checks in the summer, which I expected as a full-time employee. Therefore, we didn't struggle like we had in previous years. I had income for the first time ever during the summer, and I thanked God for His provision.

It was now August and the new school year had begun. The open house was a success, and I was excited about meeting and teaching my new students. On the other hand, I was informed that I would not receive my first paycheck for the new school year until late September. It wasn't easy, but God continued to bless my family and me; we were stable and thankful.

After I received my first full paycheck for the new school year, I was overwhelmed with joy and gratitude. It almost felt like I had won the lottery. We were grateful, without a doubt, but I understood that I didn't earn what I earned for nothing. I worked hard, sweated, and sacrificed my time and energy to reap the benefits. In humility, I was one of the most dedicated and committed teachers at the school, and everyone knew that. But not everyone cared.

Stepping into a new role at an institution, an environment where I had never worked, was an exciting yet different experience. Not only did I work in a city where most of the population was Hispanic, but also the educators and students were predominantly Hispanic. Surprisingly, I was the only Black woman and music instructor. It was weird and interesting because I had never worked in this type of atmosphere. I went with the flow of things and did the best I could. However, never in a thousand years had I seen this coming—my current situation. I had no clue God would work as swiftly as He did. I prayed, and He answered my prayers. It was also interesting to work in a setting where there were fewer than five African American children in a classroom. Now, that was challenging but fascinating. Each child had a unique personality and energy that was heartfelt. I found it amazing and embraced every opportunity with them; I did my best and developed a comfortable, caring, and supportive atmosphere, treating every student as if they were my own. They all had my undivided attention—with love, care, and compassion. I thanked God for this opportunity because it allowed me to step outside my comfort zone and make a difference in lives that needed love, support, and motivation.

However, in October, I experienced a discrepancy with a colleague while teaching in her homeroom class. I felt overlooked and unsupported by others. In the end, after I communicated this with the principals, nothing was done. I was down and hurt by the lack of communication and support from my colleagues. Soon after, I grew tired, felt overworked, underappreciated, and unhappy, and had a lack of interest due to this incident. I also became frustrated with not having a stable classroom in which to teach music and band; at the beginning of the school year, I was given a medium-sized, black, four-wheeler cart on which to place my supplies, instruments, and books, which was also used in the lunchroom. I picked it up each morning and went to about seven different classes a day, in the sun, and on the elevator in between classes. Once a week, I taught the younger students at their young division campus, which was five minutes from the school.

So, once a week, I loaded books and other music supplies in my car, drove it over to the other campus, parked near the street, unloaded these items myself, and walked to the different classrooms, which, thankfully, were on the first floor. The physical demands of my position began to cause me stress and dissatisfaction, which elevated my blood pressure. After I received the bad news that I would not get a stable room in which to teach music, I became frustrated and lost. I knew having a stable and secure room would improve my health, give me a break from walking around the school all day, and allow me to function. I felt I was treated unfairly and discussed this with Anthony.

Weeks passed and I continued to feel a heavy load on my shoulders. At this point in the year, I was exhausted mentally and physically. I was also coping with another legal matter—this time with a local restaurant. This caused more stress and affected my personal life. However, I stayed strong and prayerful.

Days later, I was still down and confused about my recent experiences at the school. I became ill. My blood pressure was out of control, so I visited my doctor. Indeed, it was elevated. I discussed this with my husband, and we prayed. However, the following day, I was ill, so I stayed home and reached out to human resources by email. I discussed my recent visit to my cardiologist, and she advised me as to my options. After we spoke, I was sent my contract and options for leave, but unfortunately, a miscommunication caused other issues. After a week, my immediate supervisor, the principal, reached out to me by email and asked about my absence from work. I explained my situation and asked for reasonable accommodation. She said, "Unfortunately, no." I was shocked, hurt, and upset because she had no compassion and had not reached out to me since my last day at the school—around a week ago. I informed her about my absence and medical situation, and she suggested I reach back out to human resources. I did, but it seemed no one cared about my urgent situation and need for accommodation. So, I spoke with Anthony and prayed. I still was not feeling well, so I stayed home; I didn't return to work. After a few weeks, I received another email from the principal, informing me that it was important that I report to work on the following Monday, but I didn't. My health was weak, and no one at my job cared about my mental and physical health.

Several days passed and I still had not heard from my supervisors, neither the head principal nor the assistant principal. However, the human resources department reached out to me by email and informed me that my leave of absence was denied; I did not meet the qualifications for my request based on my contract and length of employment. I was shocked and disagreed with their response.

The following day, I dropped off Kamaria at daycare and drove to a nearby shopping center to get food from a grocery store. I saw a Publix, so I parked up front and walked into the store. The moment I walked out of the store on an ordinary, sunny day and sat in the driver's seat of my car, I turned on the air-conditioning and checked my inbox. My jaw dropped. I looked down at my phone and saw an email that read, "Unfortunately, your teaching position has been terminated."

I was speechless, but then I said, "Say what? Really? No, Lord. This can't be happening… I'm lost and confused… Please don't let this be a reality. I feel like I'm sitting at the table with some president or CEO, hearing, 'You're fired.'" I looked again in disbelief, and I freaked out. It was a tough message to swallow; it was real, and I had witnessed it—words that left me down and teary. Reading the words in the email was an uncomfortable experience, like a pinch on my side but a thorn in my heart. I was hurt, but I was also thankful to God that I wasn't wounded. I was in pain and didn't believe it, like an unforeseen moment, an uncomfortable inhalation and exhalation that I had never experienced in my life. It was unbelievable news that was very difficult to accept and digest without answers. I never thought it could be "me," but I was the victim. Music was my everything, my all, and a gift so dear to my heart. It was all I knew. I was lost for words and wasn't myself until I closed the email message on my phone and called Anthony. He was also shocked and disagreed with their unbelievable actions. He said, "They didn't have to do that. They were out of place and could have handled the matter professionally, but they didn't." Seconds later, I was teary; I hadn't cried in so long—it was unexpected. Anthony encouraged me with

Scriptures in the Bible, prayed with me, and let me know everything would be okay. He also told me he loved me. I said, "I love you too, dear." He responded, "Don't worry, God got us," and I felt better. Then, I put my phone down near my purse, buckled my seatbelt, and drove out of the McDonald's parking lot to head for home.

When I arrived home, I opened the laptop and read over the email message again. I didn't know what to do, so I relaxed and continued to pray. I laid down in the bed to take a nap, but I was restless. I exercised and listened to music to stay calm and clear my head.

It was now time to pick up Kamaria, so I walked out to my car and drove on the Palmetto Expressway. I was so upset and hurt that I sped on the highway, but finally, I slowed down and continued to pray. They were in the wrong, so I contacted a few attorneys and consulted with them about the situation. I couldn't talk for long because I was on the highway. When I exited, I stopped at the gas station near Kamaria's daycare and spoke with another law firm about the matter. Minutes later, I was informed they were unable to take my case. I reached out to Anthony and informed him that I'd continue to reach out to attorneys for assistance. It was urgent and important. He agreed and supported me a hundred percent.

When I picked up Kamaria, I looked into her eyes, hugged her, and kissed her. I told her, "Daddy and Mommy love you, baby." I had on my shades so she wouldn't see my teary eyes. Besides, she would not have understood what had happened. But I was certain, one day, she would.

I felt empty and crushed, like ice, and a thousand things ran through my head—day one when I learned how to play my first instrument until the afternoon I walked out of the assistant principal's office. I saw chairs shaped like an arc and an instrument storage area that looked like a jail facility—each musical instrument was caged in a locker with a lock. I heard the sounds of this little eleven-year-old attempting to make music from what was in front of her—the clarinet. Then, my brain shifted to high school when I first played in the marching band and concert band. I also remembered making the All-County band and receiving numerous awards and certificates that my parents posted on the wall. Those were my musical days—some of them. I was lost for words, speechless, but I understood life had to continue. I had to take it one step at a time and move forward. It wasn't easy; I struggled to digest everything I'd stood against. I was shocked and all over the place because I never imagined this day in a thousand years. However, even during this battle, I knew God was in the picture; He was a part of my story, so I was comforted along the way. His grace calmed my aching heart and soul. His words soothed my mind and encouraged me along the way. I was ignited like never before. Life had struck me; it had stopped my plans. I was no longer myself; I was becoming the human being God had planned for me to be before the world started. God was preparing my deliverance, but I didn't know what it was. I had no clue what He was doing in my life, but I had confidence that He was doing something amazing and powerful. It was as if He was preparing me to encounter a new thing, a new chapter through the experience of my rejection.

I was uplifted and encouraged to push through by far the most difficult battles ever. However, as I reflect on it today, I realized this experience was out of my hands; it was the Lord at work to help save my life so that I can help you appreciate yours. I was convinced it was spiritually related beyond just a circumstance that I "had to" experience because my relationship with Christ was not healthy. My walk in Christ was weak; I was spiritually blinded like two blind men leading each other without the Helper, the Life-Giver, Jesus Christ, our Lord and Savior. I was lost, but I was motivated and I desired to be found, for God to deliver me from spiritual darkness.

I craved change and to be the change with a veil over my eyes. I didn't praise God as much as I do today, but, deep within, I knew it was temporary. I was convinced there was something bigger in my storm that God was working out. I had faith that one day the missing puzzle pieces would fall into place, connect, and fill the empty gap of confusion, allowing me to obtain a better understanding of my life. However, as I took baby steps, I knew that my faith and trust in the Lord had to be tested—which it was, and I thank God for blessing me with the strength and power to persevere and hang in there when I wanted to quit and give up. I didn't want to live; I didn't feel a need to go on, but I thank God for blessing me with a husband who supported me through it all, as I was on the edge and experiencing rock bottom. My circumstances were tougher than meat and unbearable beyond labor pains. I wrestled with my flesh, but all along, I thanked God and never stopped. If I had not experienced this day, I might have been sleeping in my grave, but God didn't permit it.

I believe He snatched me out of an environment that was leading me toward destruction and, eventually, death. On this day, something else happened, and it gave me a new perspective about life and the power of God's grace and mercy. This experience reminded me of Paul's experience on his way to Damascus. It was painful, yet impactful. In November 2017, I experienced a thorn, a powerful weapon that attacked my life from every possible angle. I was impacted by a thorn that seemed like God had authorized at the right appointed time, during such a season. I experienced a thorn that prevented me from becoming proud; I became humble as far as to my knees. It was only by the grace and mercy of God that I was saved, freed from my old life, and blessed to experience spiritual freedom with open eyes. I thank God for His grace and mercy, similar to what Paul received, as he said in 2 Corinthians 12, verses 7-9:

> *So, to keep me from becoming proud, I was given a thorn in my flesh, a messenger from Satan to torment me and keep me from becoming proud. Three different times I begged the Lord to take it away. Each time he said, "My grace is all you need. My power works best in weakness."*

I was weak, spiritually down, and disconnected like streetlights. I was at the edge of giving up. However, I didn't because hope and faith in my hell storm rescued me and replenished my heart with the Word. God saved my soul in a single day with the power of His life support. My hard work, thousands of dollars spent on two degrees, and the dedication I'd maintained over the years weren't in vain. I had faith that I had to experience numerous gains and a heap of loss to appreciate the precious value of God's word, my life, and my purpose.

My music teaching position was wrongfully terminated days before the 2017 Thanksgiving holiday—less than a year after I'd started. I had prayed for this opportunity, and I knew it was mine. God had blessed me with the job, with an upgrade, and I was grateful. Have you ever had enough faith to know something was yours or that God was going to bless you with a job or raise? He answered my prayers, but it seems there was a cost to being blessed as His child—and that cost was suffering. The circumstance was awkward. It was strange because I was literally this innocent Black woman with a kind and loving heart—one who loved her job and her career. It was unbelievable because I had just started my new music teaching position at the elementary school. I had just gotten my feet wet at my first full-time job in the music field. I had left another full-time position for this one…in the middle of the week. Crazy, right! It was unbelievable because I had never expected an ordinary day to turn into a chaotic storm, a day of hell.

It was deeper than that. I had never pictured departing from a passion I knew for years, like music. It was just about the only thing I had pursued and desired wholeheartedly. It was the only thing I knew. Studying, teaching, and performing was my love. Technically, I was fired, but though my music position was terminated in the blink of an eye, my gift created by God was never taken. It was a season beyond a life event I never thought I'd experience, like the car accident you never saw coming your way, the divorce you never planned, or the foreclosure you never dreamt of experiencing during a pandemic.

I was shocked and felt as if rocks had fallen on my head. I panicked. It was as if my flesh had been punctured by a sharp thorn—an experience of excruciating mental and physical pain and hurt like never before. It was like the mental trauma, the pain, and the hurt I experienced after losing my first, unborn child in 2006. The only colors I saw on my phone were black and white. I couldn't believe it; I used every excuse to replace my reality. I was speechless and stunned. Not only that, on this day, I almost felt as if I was going to lose my mind on the highway—on the Palmetto Expressway. I went nuts until I prayed and began to release the tension I felt in my heart. I felt torn, but I wasn't broken. I felt discriminated against for the same reason you thought; I felt like an outcast, like a woman whom no one at this institution listened to. I didn't feel that grace or mercy had been given to me except by our Heavenly Father, our Source. I felt as if someone had broken my heart. It was similar to the chaotic twelve-year relationship I had experienced.

I felt labor pains all over again. I experienced heartache on a single day in my life. I was empty, lost for words, and stunned with disbelief as to what was before my eyes. I had never expected it; it just hit me in the face. My teaching position had been terminated on an ordinary day—one I didn't see coming. But I was sure the Creator saw it. I was hurt, and I wasn't myself. I felt empty and depressed, and I didn't want to talk to anyone or fathom the ultimate reason for such a decision. At the end of the day, it was my career and a lifelong dream to do what I loved to do—teach others and perform. I literally felt numb to "Kala," the person I was at that moment before thousands of eyes.

I was on the edge of giving up, with hopes that it was all a dream. However, it wasn't. I still didn't believe what I had read, so I re-read the email until I finally realized it was real. It was my reality, and there was nothing I could do about it except continue to pray and leave it in God's hands. Seconds later, I cried as if I were in labor in the driver's seat of my car. I remembered standing in front of a class full of bright, beautiful, smiling faces who loved to learn. Then, in the blink of an eye, they were no longer before me. I remembered giving my all when I pushed the black cart with music supplies and my mobile phone throughout the day—back and forth on an elevator that sometimes didn't work. I also remembered the band practices and choir rehearsals I directed after school and the days I worked overtime.

I dressed professionally, arrived on time, and gave beyond a hundred percent in a role that required more than just showing up. It required blood, sweat, and tears—the result of real sacrifice, and I gave it. I remembered the loud voices, chants, screams, and shouts of children and teachers. Oh, what a joy it was to sit on the grass during monthly events. Everyone smiled, giggled, and greeted me each day. My first end-of-the-school-year teacher outing was at a local resort. In all my years of teaching, I had never experienced a celebration at a resort with a club in the basement. It was fun, unforgettable, and a blessing to participate in—a memorable experience.

Most of all, I remembered my final day as the music instructor at this educational facility, though little had I known it was my last day. Still, I believed God had destined this day, this life event, on purpose, with purpose, and for a greater purpose. So, even though God awakened me from this unbelievable, haunted dream of flashbacks, I was still shocked and sat in my car in total disbelief. I was crushed like ice, but not broken because of God's grace and mercy—He was during it all thankfully.

As the afternoon passed, I was still out of it. I didn't know if I could live again because I thought about what I had lost and would lose—I didn't know what God had in store for my future. I didn't know how the puzzle pieces of my life would come back together after being so scattered. I was lost without my career. I didn't know which way to turn, whether I'd stand in front of the classroom and teach again or whether I'd continue to pursue music. I also didn't know whether our daughter would ever understand or even ask, "Mommy, what's wrong?" However, I was certain that my life would never be the same. So, if you're in the middle of a turning point or a new chapter, don't worry; you're not alone. God is working in your favor and gracing you with what you need. He is shifting you where you need to be for His glory. If you're not yet convinced, hit rock bottom and embrace the experience—that moment, that season, that time in your life because God is doing something greater than you'd ever imagine. It's something I can't reveal to you; only our Heavenly Father can.

I was skeptical and anxious for answers because I was confused and clueless as to why this happened to me. Why was I the only woman, the only human being, the only Black woman chosen out of over a billion others to be fired from the classroom days before the

Thanksgiving holiday, before such a special day? Why was I the victim? I hadn't done anything wrong. I was innocent. I hadn't seen it coming, like most unexpected circumstances we experience in life. This one was a slap in the face without notice or a heads-up. I was crushed, but not broken. I felt the presence of the Lord with me every step of the way.

November 2017 was like an unbelievable movie—a dark, wild one. It was like a dream. The color before my eyes was black and blurry. It revealed not only the darkness in my life but also my relationship with the Lord. I couldn't see, not even if I wore every pair of reading glasses on the planet. I was unconscious of my spiritual walk. I didn't know where I was headed, so I served the world and praised God less. I was thankful, but I didn't express it as much as I should have, as much as God deserved.

Although God was in my life, He wasn't a part of it. He wasn't in the picture a hundred and fifty percent as I desired. I longed for a financial and spiritual breakthrough—to experience freedom from my burdens. It was an experience I desired but, more so, needed. My prayer was to find a higher-paying job where I'd receive health benefits, retirement, and a higher salary—like every person's dream. I had total faith it would happen. I knew it was possible through Christ, whose grace and mercy would make it happen. Little did I know there was, in fact, the perfect blessing. The right door opened around the corner. It was a blessing from God—the position beyond just the job I desired. It was one with the entire benefit package and more. Despite that, I made an unexpected but beneficial move. I was determined to reach my destination and experience it better. This is where growth continues, and your real faith is tested.

Working as a full-time music educator required much of my time, energy, and presence. It was serious business, and I was serious about my commitment to serve. I was responsible for several tasks all while being a wife and a mother. Everyday life was good, but I carried a heavy load. It wasn't easy; it was challenging and a struggle sometimes, but God continued to guide, strengthen, and bless me and my household. I didn't give up. We didn't give up. And certainly, our Heavenly Father didn't. We persevered and did our best. I knew one day, the change would come—God's next-level blessings and, eventually, my breakthrough. So, I coped with whatever life tossed at my family and me, and I embraced it all—beyond the sacrifices it required. We lost a lot but gained spiritual growth in the eyes of the storm. What a season. What a storm. What an experience along the journey. What a year, but more so a temporary season like no other. Boy oh boy, it was a difficult one–one that I never imagined in a thousand years, not even a guess. I didn't know how to handle it, but God did. Did you hear about it in the news? Did you see me screaming and shouting at the top of my lungs on the Palmetto Expressway in Miami, Florida? Did you hear my pulse? Was it irregular? It felt like I was having a panic attack. You didn't, but God witnessed the whole scene, the day, and even the year before I was born. So, here I am: bold and ready to speak up and speak out about the goodness of our Heavenly Father and His power. Have you ever experienced a year like no other? Yes, an unbelievable, shocking year like the one you're thinking about now? Think back to the year that took you on roller coasters, down in valleys, through storms and high waters, and up steep mountains. How about the year that took you to the moon and back, but then, suddenly, your life changed and you experienced rock bottom? If this is your year, hang in there, keep praying, and walk with me as I take you on a stroll down *my street*, my neighborhood, and my life during such a difficult time.

If you're clueless or if you feel that what you're experiencing is the worst thing ever, consider that it could be the best thing that ever happened in your walk if you have faith. However, without confidence in the will of God, unexpectedness will be difficult to appreciate and embrace; nothing unpleasant won't make sense. Like 20/20 vision, with spiritual vision, you see God in everything you experience. However, if you don't see your life circumstances as God would, things will be harder to cope with and accept. But it's okay. You're never alone. Gaining spiritual vision is a process and takes growth; it takes going through enough in life to realize the power of God and the importance of faith. I know this because God saved my soul in the job storm that opened my eyes like never before. Like the experience of taking anesthesia, God did something more extraordinary in the blink of an eye, and I'll never forget His rescue. If you're in some type of difficult situation or battle, know that God will do the unusual or uncomfortable and have you in a state of wonder, but somewhere in the process, He'll give you a clue. He'll confuse you as if you're trying to unscramble a word puzzle, but He will reveal His will. He'll guide and guard your heart in His arms until He carries you safely to where you need to be, which is in a position where you'll appreciate the "bigger picture."

In 2017, my relationship with the Lord was weak like the muscles in my body. My heart was desperate for rescue and some TLC—tender loving care. I was unhealthy and out of shape unconsciously; I was spiritually unfit, malnourished, and empty inside even though I rocked a beautiful appearance on the outside. Inside, I wasn't okay, but I kept my *makeup* on and kept it moving. All the while, though, I was out of it like a drunk person trying to walk straight. I was blind and temporarily confused because I was alive rather than living, breathing, and experiencing true life. I wasn't "Kala." I was an individual striving to find who God proposed for me to "be " before I could even start to realize who I was becoming. Man, that was challenging, but I knew there was hope, and my deliverance was on the way. I had a vision that I'd experience my breakthrough one day soon.

There was no spiritual growth, and I didn't realize it until after I hit rock bottom—yet another uncomfortable place in my life. I was tired of experiencing the same old cycles of setbacks, hardships, and pain. I was on the edge and could have given up on everything, but I didn't. I could have taken my life or jumped off a bridge and buried this book and all my other experiences in the grave, but I didn't. I didn't do what many do when one loses a job or something of value. I didn't curse the entire world, get revenge, or take my life; God's grace sustained me and kept me from destruction and danger. I didn't do what my enemies hoped or wished for, as the Almighty's power within me didn't allow it. Proverbs 19:21 says, *You can make many plans, but the Lord's purpose will prevail.* I *wholeheartedly* knew the Lord was on my side, in my business, and working things out for His glory, period. I felt it beyond the pain I experienced—in my bones. Therefore, I was certain that trusting in the Lord in these moments was greater than my problem and that one day I'd gain spiritual strength and remarkable courage to share my phenomenal voice, like the process of gaining muscles through a healthy diet, drinking milk, and taking vitamins.

The bright side of this season in my life is that in the middle of my turmoil, I discovered that my calling was greater than my painful thorn and traumatic experience. I chose to embrace my temporary circumstance; I persevered because I knew my husband and daughter needed me more than ever. I chose to let go of everything I desired to hold on to, including my life plans, to let the One who created me inside and out control my life, especially because I was spiritually unfit and bent out of shape. So, when you see me in action, it's the God in me who's directing my path and controlling my life, thoughts, and passion. It's my God who's conducting my every move and my choices, who continues to grace me with spiritual strength.

Today, I'm so thankful for going through such an experience that sometimes it's hard for me to realize what I faced. Writing this chapter and a few others was challenging, but God's strength blessed me to overcome the obstacle and offer hope in your job loss, layoff, or career change. I'm convinced you've also experienced a moment like this or are experiencing a similar situation in which it literally feels as if the earth has stopped spinning and gravity has overpowered your physical movement and brain. Over time, I realized God was transforming my mind, enriching my life, and drawing me closer to Him to develop a stronger relationship with Him, and that's a fact. I am mentally, physically, and spiritually stronger today than I was yesterday, and with open eyes, I can see.

> *"God blessed me to experience a dream, but months later, my reality became a nightmare. However, today, it's the best thing that could have ever happened in my life. God revealed my calling in the eye of a life storm."*
>
> *-Kala*

# Chapter 9

## *Life After Music*

*"Sometimes, life-changing experiences happen during your turning point, in the middle of your walk. Embrace yours when you discover them."*

**- Kala**

The next day, I opened my eyes and looked outside my window. Then, I prayed and rose to my feet. I could hear my heartbeat for the first time in months; I was well-rested, refreshed, and thankful that an unnecessary weight had been lifted off my shoulders. I could breathe without feeling like my heart was going to burst out of my body. I heard birds chirping outside my window, dogs barking, and Tri Rail minutes away from the apartment complex. I also heard school buses and my neighbors walking through the hallway and pressing the elevator button. It was strange because I was used to leaving the house before sunrise and navigating busy highways and streets. However, things changed, including my routine and lifestyle. Every morning, I awoke around 7 am, prayed, dressed, and fed Kamaria before daycare. The second I passed the school to take her there, I struggled to stay focused; it became emotionally difficult. I had disturbing flashbacks, so I drove another route to take her to school. I went to the gym, exercised, and read Scripture for encouragement. Then, I grabbed a bite to eat and returned home until it was time to pick up Kamaria. This was my routine for weeks.

I was jobless, so I had nowhere to report to or clock in at seven-thirty in the morning Monday through Friday. I didn't have to wake up and drive miles from home to park in a parking lot with a bunch of educators and school officials. I was no longer the school's K-5 music teacher, and that sucked. For weeks, I sat in disbelief and doubt, which was strange because I wasn't used to experiencing these feelings. I had faith. Well, at least, I thought I did. But that wasn't all. More occurred. I grew frustrated with the world, including myself, because the circumstance was out of my hands. I wanted to turn back the hands of time. I felt a hole in my heart like I did with my traumatic experience of losing my unborn child. I became depressed and walked in silence for months on Elm Street.

When you're depressed, you feel alone, isolated, and lost—distanced from everyone, including family. You feel alone because no one seems to understand your situation, and you are isolated every day of the week. So, now you're lost because this monster, depression, has you in this mental state. You also feel sad and hopeless because the bank denied your loan application for the second time, you lost your job, and you're dealing with financial hardship. Rent is due, your auto insurance payment is approaching, you need food, and you have to offer back to the Lord, all while trying to take a mini-getaway.

It's hard like the texture of a rock, and it hurts deeper than a bee sting. Others don't see it on your face or under your mask because it doesn't show on the outside, but on the inside your heart looks troubled. It's bleeding and needs help like a person who doesn't know which way to go in life or like a person who is spiritually blind. Yes, something is wrong, and I know it. You're down and don't know what the hell to do except store hurt and pain in your heart because you don't know how to release it, to let it go so that you can live and see again, not walk around in silence only for the world to think you've lost your precious mind. In this mental environment, you're not yourself because you're in a different but temporary world. You feel empty and useless. Everyday life is "whatever" because another voice is bothering you, telling you lies, and holding you back from overcoming this dark cage. You don't want to do anything because you don't see purpose in what might rescue you. Everything around you is quiet, but inside, you hear a thousand voices. Sometimes, it drives you nuts, but most times, it doesn't because you're used to hearing what others can't and won't hear. Everyone thinks you're weird or crazy because you're down— at a place where they're not. Well, at least temporarily. At the moment, the only thing that helps is silence, quiet time—you and the thousand voices that run across your brain, telling you lies, laughing, or whispering nonsense.

If you ever experience this uncomfortable state of mind, *stop what you're doing, go to a quiet space, inhale and exhale, and pray.* I truly mean it from the bottom of my heart. Yes, I know it's easier said than done. I said that a thousand times about a lot of stuff in my life until I began to exercise "action." What do I mean? Sometimes, we're our own worst enemy, distraction, or obstacle. We prevent ourselves from doing things we need to do to get better, to make progress. We downgrade the power and intelligence that God has given us to navigate life and all the things we face. For instance, if we see one person achieve a goal, we think just because they look a certain way, we'll never do the same. Or we think losing a job means it's all over; we'll never get another one or earn the income we once lost. That's a negative way of thinking. Stop criticizing yourself and start thanking God for who He created you to be.

Release the negative thoughts that drain you and shift you into a mental state of depression. Just do it. Think positive, starting now. When you take small steps to improve your mental, physical, and spiritual health or address financial hardships, you begin to overcome your situations in life. It all starts with your mindset. Positive thinking is one way to overcome depression. Surrounding yourself with positive-minded individuals will also help you overcome this issue and strengthen your mindset. However, you must first acknowledge that you are depressed and be willing to embrace the rescue and healing process. Why? When you are aware that you're "not yourself" and are willing to take the necessary steps to improve or get help, that's a plus; it's a great start to overcoming this normal battle. Yes, it's normal to experience depression, especially after you've faced trauma, loss, health issues, complicated relationships or divorce or if you feel worthless. But you are blessed, beautiful, and wonderfully made. Start claiming who you know you are: someone special and born for a greater purpose; an amazing individual with the potential to do great things; an imperfect human being created by an awesome and perfect God who knows your abilities, weaknesses, and strengths; a star set apart to glorify God.

To those who are experiencing depression or a mental fight, be encouraged to know you are not alone. You're dealing with a silent battle and desire to be free, to be rescued and find safety, and you will with faith. Depression didn't win because God blessed me to overcome this difficult circumstance. One thing that helped me was to start this writing journey. Each day, I release my thoughts, feelings, and experiences on paper. Writing this book was therapeutic.

If depression is your story, be encouraged to know you're not fighting alone. I was in a dark world of difficulty, hurt, pain, and confusion, but all the while long, I didn't give up and allow rejection to control my faith and hope in Jesus Christ. As a matter of fact, when I was down, I was also drawing closer to God, hearing His voice, and receiving His grace to restore my spirit one day at a time. I knew there was hope even in the middle of war, dealing with ungodly, unloving spirits. I rose on the battlefield—with a thorn in my heart—and walked with God on my side, as well as with my husband, our daughter, and my family, and I embraced the whole Armor of God, His word and promises. I let His grace and mighty power have their way to achieve victory. If you're in a fight for your life, don't give up. Stand up and know that, if you have faith, God will protect you and bless you with His grace, mercy, and favor. I am living proof that there is hope in the Hope giver. Believe in Him, and He'll show up and show out in front of any and every individual whom He created.

Be courageous when you experience something like a job loss or denial. God has greater and better things for you. Obey His word and embrace His will, both when life is going well and when it seems like nobody cares or you're suffering. God cares about you. He loves you and wants the best for you, your loved ones, and generations to come. You don't have to stay down. Stand up because you can. Stand up because you want to make a difference and encourage others in their distress. Stand up and release your untold stories, thoughts, and feelings on paper. Create a book for the world, to help others live life to the fullest, even on their healing journeys, and keep walking. Don't look back unless you're sharing your experiences with others to enrich their lives, so they know how to cope with life when they face troubles.

I would never know if you were depressed or down unless you talked to me, phoned me, or texted me, or unless I learned about it after you gave up on life. I know it sucks to walk in darkness, on a planet where you feel alone, isolated, lost, guilty, sad, or hopeless. When you're on social media, around loved ones, friends, and even co-workers, it's easy to hide your "real" feelings because no one knows what's going on. You don't want anybody to know how you're feeling, so you wear a mask. Plus, it's painful to go through memories of trauma. No one knows your battle night and day and when you're all alone in your bedroom, the kitchen, or the shower. Drops of water are part of your release to help you overcome this damn fight. From time to time, you try your best to cover it up on the outside, but on the inside, you're still bleeding and hurting because the struggle is real. If this is your story, hang in there and be encouraged to know you're never alone. There is help and hope wherever you are in this world.

> *I never knew what it meant to be depressed until I experienced it; it was real, and it sucked. But God delivered me safely to my destination.*

To even consider sharing this unexpected life event with you is like sharing what goes on in my bedroom when my husband and I are having sex or making love—it's deep, precious, and personal. So, thank you for your empathy, transparency, patience, and ongoing prayers on my journey of healing one day at a time. To write about the loss of an angel who lived in the flesh of my precious womb was difficult and took courage. I was hurt and in a lot of pain; I was down beyond the ground; I felt lonely and afraid to share it with anyone—even my parents. I didn't know who else to run to but God. It was hard, and no one knew except the Lord. Yet, there was hope. He comforted me, held my hand, and kept me uplifted to this day. He led me to the most amazing husband in the world, Anthony. So, you are never alone. I understand your pain but also appreciate your resilience and strength to carry on and endure life one day at a time with hope and faith.

My life wasn't on track, which was the hardest part to realize. I wasn't in sync with the Lord, and that was the truth. How could I embrace a situation such as this if my relationship with my Daddy was weak? I was spiritually blind and lived a distance from Him, so my faith was also weak. I couldn't hear His voice because my ears were closed. My relationship with the Creator suffered. I was weak and so was my spiritual walk. I experienced darkness and a heap of ongoing obstacles during this season, which kept me in a state of depression for a while.

That wasn't all. My social life was also impacted, and isolation was my favorite environment. I didn't have to worry about staying away from others. I was where I desired—at a distance. As a matter of fact, because I rarely had "friends," isolation was easy. However, it wasn't so much the fact of not having friends. It wasn't easy to open up and share my struggles and depression. It was very difficult. Honestly, I didn't know how to share my voice. I was uncomfortable and afraid of opinions, afraid to share what hurt the most. So, I preferred to be alone and kept silent. However, as I developed a closer relationship with the Lord, my hope and faith were strengthened. I showed resilience and never gave up.

*"No matter what I experienced, Anthony had my back and stood near my side, and he continues to do so. I'm not only one lucky woman, but I'm one blessed and grateful wife. I thank God for His love."*

*-Kala*

This turning point did more than I expected, and I'm thankful. Not only did it strengthen my hope and faith and bless me with a stronger heart but it also enhanced my marriage in so many amazing ways. My husband and I grew closer as a couple. We spent more quality time together and prayed more, which blessed us both to get closer to the Lord.

This season of my life was by far the most difficult one because it affected my marriage and household to the point that I was ready to give up on my marriage. But I didn't, thank God. I was not receiving the income and insurance I had once earned, which became a problem. It was more difficult than I can explain in words, and it put a toll on my husband and our marriage. We could no longer do things and spend how we used to. Our budget was smaller, so we had to live according to what we had. However, through it all, our love remained strong. We continued to pray for one another and our situation, and God blessed us every step of the way. Things changed, and it wasn't easy, but with love, we got through it one day at a time. Each day, God blessed me with more understanding and humbled my heart, which motivated me.

Despite my season, God kept the romance ignited in my marriage. Boy oh boy, at times it wasn't easy, but we didn't let anything interfere with our love life. As a matter of fact, we gave each other more affection and found ways to continue to spice up our marriage. We cuddled next to each other on a blanket gifted to us by a sister in Christ after Kamaria was born. Sometimes, my husband and I used it as a pillow when we were intimate. We prayed, looked each other in the eyes, and kissed. We embraced love. He called our love sessions "a party," which, indeed, they were! No matter the day, week, circumstance, or season, we embraced our marriage and the romance in our marriage, and we thanked God. This was the norm, and Lord knows I always looked forward to Anthony's affection, sincere love, hugs, and kisses. And he looked forward to mine.

We were two god-fearing lovebirds who had tied the knot and become one by the grace of God in October 2015. We strove to embrace life and live our best by the grace and mercy of God. At times, our journey seemed unbearable, but God's favor gave us strength through it all. We were always thankful and didn't take life for granted because we knew tomorrow wasn't promised. Life was precious, and we appreciated every moment, every breath together. Whatever we faced in life, we prayed together, encouraged each other, and supported one another with unconditional love and patience. We had each other's backs, as couples should.

We were determined to stay prayerful and make it last forever. For work, Anthony wore jeans, a T-shirt, and a black headscarf over his baby waves. He also wore an attractive black back brace that turned me on and gave me butterflies. I also got goosebumps, which made me smile from ear to ear. What a love scene like Romeo and Juliet: I pictured my tall, Black, handsome husband holding my body against his muscular body, in his arms, against the wall, with a bow tie around his neck. Ha-ha! Like, really? Well, I guess it wasn't a dream; it was my reality on several occasions, except one without Anthony wearing a bow tie around his neck. Yes! What a wild and freaky thought, but hey! This is my story, my life, an open book without curtains, without sheets or the color of tar disguising it. It's real, it's nonfiction. Seconds after walking over to me, he leaned over the bed and kissed me with his warm, round-shaped, brown lips as he smiled with the cutest dimples against my cheekbones. He gave me butterflies—many of them, as he did the first night we kissed on the beach while our feet touched the sand and the moon overshadowed our precious newlywed bodies. Ha-ha.

Then he kneeled over and kissed Kamaria, our baby girl, on the forehead. He said, "I love you both. Have a blessed day."

I looked up at him and said, "I love you too, baby."

Our marriage covenant was special and truly one that we embraced, cherished, and always thanked God for. We valued our love for the Lord and strove to love to like Him. We loved on purpose and for a greater purpose while doing everything possible by the grace and mercy of God to make sure we praised and worshiped Him despite the unexpected seasons we faced.

We knew our marriage was being hit by Satan, so we didn't let go or give up. We persevered and remained patient in prayer. We knew that prayer was powerful and one of the perfect ways to strengthen our marriage and relationship with Jesus Christ. We were certain that despite our dark days, our trials and tribulations, God heard our cry and would soon answer our prayers. We had faith that God would deliver us from our unpleasant circumstances in life, which we knew was a process. It would take time, prayer, and a patient heart. Our prayer life as a couple was weak, but individually it was consistent and became stronger. God made a way to continue to bless our marriage with His unfailing, unconditional love; He blessed us with His favor and protected us with grace and mercy. We continued to embrace the Light, Jesus Christ. We knew better days were here and better days would come.

As daybreak approached, the birds continued to chirp and fly past our window as the sun overpowered the dark, gray sky. I heard cars on the highway, horns honking, school buses, children running and walking to the elevator, doors slamming, and babies crying like the start of a movie scene—they were loud and unpredictable. They were bold and didn't stop until they got what they wanted. However, the moment Anthony walked out the door, the reality of my life hit again.

I felt lonely; a piece of my puzzle was missing, and my body knew it. Some days, I wished he would stay, but I knew he had to work to help support Kamaria and me. He also knew it. Eventually, I became frustrated and bored with my lifestyle. Something was missing, but I didn't know what. I was clueless as to what my heart was longing for. It was tough, but guess what? I kept going, I kept the hope, and I rose with a thankful heart. I prayed and praised God for yet another beautiful, blessed day. I knew, one day, my breakthrough and change would come, and it wasn't far away.

I wasn't motivated because I was completely lost for words. I was filled with mixed emotions and upset with the world. My mental state was scattered, but I had hope and faith that one day this would pass. I knew God would deliver me from this chaotic mess. My social life suffered, I didn't want to talk about what had just happened. I didn't feel like being questioned about how I felt and what my next steps would be, so I distanced myself. It took a while to adjust, but eventually, God gave me the strength to face the uncomfortableness of life like my fears—one day at a time. So, if you're in a season of depression, you're not alone. It's temporary, but until you let God transform your mindset, you'll never see a way out or hope to be rescued. Desire to overcome this "false scare" and be bold. Be courageous and never think less of yourself. You'll get through this dark season when you're ready to take God with you on this journey of healing and overcoming life one day at a time. If you're determined to help others in their struggles with depression, release your feelings or experiences on paper; write a book to inspire others. Many are walking in silence, so I'm certain they'd love to hear about your journey—it's different from your neighbor's. It might be hard at first, but when you stand up and help others, God continues to heal and help you in many ways. It's amazing and comforting.

I wished for my situation to be as if it had never happened and to receive an email that allowed me to return. However, that didn't happen. Months later, I was still one unhappy individual—another intelligent Black woman without work, living in a dark, crazy, damn world. But I wasn't alone; I knew many were also experiencing job loss, unemployment, or layoffs. So, now what? I had a choice: to give up and let Satan defeat God's plan or to push through and persevere. I no longer received direct deposits bi-weekly, so days after my dismissal, I applied for unemployment benefits and my 401(k) retirement funds. I took a leap of faith because I was determined to receive what I earned. Ultimately, though, I wanted to get back on my feet and work. I didn't know how long that would take, but I had faith that God would reveal it to me one day.

During this time, we removed Kamaria from the daycare. Because I was no longer at the school, we enrolled her in a closer daycare center, which worked out well. During her transition, I received my retirement benefits, but I struggled for over a month to obtain unemployment benefits. I experienced several denials and appeals, which frustrated me. However, I didn't give up; I endured until I won. Months later, I was finally approved for unemployment benefits, including back pay in late January 2018. This was the longest I ever had to wait for unemployment benefits, but we were thankful for

God's grace and mercy. I was nearly broke without financial stability or a new job. But it wasn't over.

After research and prayer, I obtained an attorney to take on my wrongful termination case. It was tough and became tiresome from the afternoon I reached out to the law firm to the day my life and background were impacted.

During the week, I emailed documents and additional information to the attorney, and throughout the month, I met with the attorney for litigation and other hearings. It was difficult to hear others talk negatively about you—people whom you thought cared about you. It was unbelievable. However, I stayed strong and prayed. I knew I was experiencing a hell battle and the only way I would succeed was by faith, prayer, and persistence.

After months of emails, litigation, hearings, and phone calls, I drove down to the courthouse and sat in a small room with school officials, the head principal, and my attorney. For a few hours, I was asked many questions. Then I walked from room to room while a decision was made. It was one of the hardest days of my life. I was intimidated and put down, and I became very emotional and cried. Finally, my attorney and I talked, and I asked about my case and teaching position. He didn't have all the answers because the other party was still discussing the case and settlement. I asked him if there was a chance for me to get my position back. He wasn't sure, but he informed me that most clients who experienced this type of case moved forward in a different career path. I had the choice to take the case to trial, which would be challenging and risky. At this point in my life, I was tired, both mentally and physically; I desired peace and to move forward with what God had in store for me.

Eventually, the other party joined us, and they discussed the final settlement amount. It wasn't much, but it was more than what I had in my savings and pockets. To me, it wasn't about the money; it was about receiving justice and being treated fairly, which did not happen. Based on their opinions, false information, and outlook, the school officials documented that I could no longer work at the elementary school, which would also cause other issues down the road. They also gave my attorney the final settlement amount that would be provided upon my approval and signature. After I was informed about the final amount, I reviewed the documents and signed the settlement amount letter. I was speechless and my heart sped. However, after I stood and prayed, God calmed my heart. I thanked my attorney and, as I walked out of the room, I looked around at everyone else. I took the elevator downstairs, exited the courthouse, and walked to my car. There, I prayed again and called Anthony. We spoke for several minutes. Then, I drove off and went home. What a day I had experienced—one that was totally unexpected. However, I knew deep down that this was just the beginning of new blessings and opportunities. Better days were on the way, and I expected God to reveal my purpose in life.

That night, I surrendered to God. I trusted He would guide me in the right direction. I knew He would take care of me and guide me safely to my destination. I had faith He would do the impossible and blow my mind, so I let Him have complete control over my life, my thoughts, and my actions from that day forward.

In February 2018, God opened my eyes like never before. I tossed and turned at night, unable to sleep due to my recent job experience. However, God's greater purpose for my life overpowered that moment. I removed the covers and picked up my mobile phone. Then, I clicked on the notes sections on my phone and started releasing my feelings and recent job experience. Hours later, I'd written over five pages of words I longed to share with others. It wasn't easy, but it was fulfilling. I was free, and I finally had faith after years of walking in darkness. The veil was removed. At that moment, when my husband and daughter were sound asleep, God blessed me with spiritual vision. I wasn't the same person; God had renewed my mindset and blessed me with a new way of thinking. My identity was different—I was no longer conducting my path. Instead, God was directing my walk.

As with any difficult, unexpected life event, the aftermath can be tough, like meat. Eating a piece of steak can be challenging, but accepting an unimaginable event can be worse and more difficult to digest; it can leave an impact beyond just a "shock" effect. It leaves a scar that, unlike a pinch on your finger, takes a lifetime to heal. Life events aggravate that puncture, and, in most cases, they leave something behind like a reminder. These reminders bring on flashbacks like the "perfect" storm or earthquake I experienced that did the unbelievable in my life. My life wasn't the same. It changed physically, mentally, spiritually, financially, and socially, and I didn't see it coming.

When I unexpectedly lost my job, I also lost my salary, which was one of the most difficult, painful experiences ever. Within a few years, my salary went from $6.50 an hour to $12,000, $17,000, and $43,000-plus a year, and then to zero. Yes, zero bi-weekly direct deposits except for the leftovers from retirement. I was shocked, hurt, and speechless, and I said aloud, *"All these years of schooling, education, and work experience, and now this. Wow. Now I gotta start from the bottom."* I never expected to lose what had seemed like the "perfect" salary, the perfect job. It was a dream job, and God had blessed me to experience this reality. Then, when this happened, I was lost for words. However, it didn't make me second-guess the thought that I had been graced with the job. I had prayed for the teaching position, and God had answered my prayers and blessed me with my wants.

As with any painful experience, hardship, or sudden loss, I was torn but not broken and destroyed. However, it felt as if someone had stuck a knife in my heart, pinched my soul, and tossed me out a window.

Losing my salary impacted not only my finances but also the income of my household. It also affected my personal life and marriage. My husband and I started to lose valuables and had to quickly adjust to a strict budget and less spending. Also, Anthony had to pay a greater portion of the rent. There was only one income, and I was determined to help support my family as best I could, so I pawned my precious clarinets to pay bills and buy food. This hurt. I had never imagined having to pawn my musical instruments, each of which cost me $2,500. That was more than what I was given in the store, which was around $450 to 600 each with interest. However, I had seen an opportunity to get funds to help with important bills in my household, so I rose and did what I could to assist.

The money wasn't enough, though. Every time we turned around, there was something due, including life and auto insurance. We also had a small co-pay for our medications. Every dollar counted, and we had to make sure it was spent wisely.

Weeks later, I pawned my clarinets again, but after several months, and with incoming bills and the interest, it was hard to get them back. The last time I pawned one of the clarinets and missed a day to pay for pick-up, the store manager had no compassion and sold it. So, the morning I drove to the pawn shop to retrieve it, an assistant manager told me that the instrument had been sold the day before. I was shocked and hurt. I walked out, informed Anthony about what had happened, and contacted the company's district office, but they weren't helpful. I prayed, and when Anthony arrived home, we prayed together. I cried and was down for several days. However, God began to comfort my heart. He whispered, "Everything is going to be okay. Both of your clarinets are in the hands of others in need." After the Spirit confirmed this, I was strengthened. One day at a time, I healed from this loss, though the process was in no way easy; the sacrifice was one of the most embarrassing and painful experiences ever. I gave myself grace and room to be human. After all, I realized, no one has a perfect, storm-less, or struggle-free life, even with a load of money in the bank, the biggest homes, stocks and CDs, and no debt. Everyone struggles with life and experiences tough choices, but the individual who acts bougie and is prideful or who walks without humility will never be appreciative and thankful for the grace of God.

This season of my life was also difficult because we had to pay for daycare if Kamaria was enrolled in the school. We prayed about it and eventually removed her from the daycare. I decided to oversee Kamaria for a few weeks to a month until our finances improved and we found an affordable and nearby daycare center. It was hard, but we had to make a wise decision for our household. We didn't give up. Our communication and romance suffered, but it didn't fail. As a matter of fact, we drew closer to God and each other, and our love life grew stronger than ever. We stayed prayerful and continued to trust in the Lord for guidance, strength, and His provisions, and we embraced every unforeseen circumstance.

The struggle was real for my family and me. However, we fought the good fight and prayed hard without giving up. Because of our faith, our eyes stayed on the Lord, on His word. Not only that, but God always made a way out of no way and continues to do so. He has kept us covered by the power of His grace, mercy, and love since day one. To this day, we've gained more wisdom and grown stronger in love and in the Lord—and it's not over. He's still working in and through us—our lives.

> *"I was a walking bomb, a human being clogged with so much stuff in my life that I was near a breakdown, an uncomfortable explosion. Well, it happened, and God blessed me to overcome it, to get through such a difficult climax in my walk."*
>
> *-Kala*

My personal life with Christ stank; it was weak, dry, and ineffective, which affected my life. I'm sure it wasn't pleasing to God, either. My spiritual walk was not in harmony or balance with the Lord; my mind wanted one thing, but my heart desired another. I can certainly testify that I wasn't concerned about spiritual discipline, obedience, saving, financial growth, becoming debt-free, and strengthening my marriage. I was spiritually and physically weak. My priority was work, money, and my family. I went through the motions; at my workplace, I arrived early and typically stayed late for other activities until, one day, my body became weary and nearly shut down. There were days when I was tired, lacked physical energy, and experienced elevated blood pressure. After I experienced back issues, a lack of rest, and high blood pressure, that was it.

One morning, I stepped out of bed and couldn't move for several seconds. It took me more time to walk to the living room area than it ever had in my life. I was frightened, but that didn't stop me from persevering and giving up until my body nearly shut down. I couldn't continue working in these conditions. So, I visited my physician and, before I left the office, was prescribed medications to help control my blood pressure. I was stressed, and I wasn't at my best—I was physically weak. When I asked for reasonable accommodation, I was told, "Unfortunately, no." I was shocked to my knees, speechless and hurt. I was disturbed by the responses and the overall situation. I continued to receive unbelievable emails that didn't sit well or make any sense. I was spiritually weak; up to that day, my eyes had been closed, covered by a veil. So, that day changed my life. It was the turning point. A burden lifted not only off my shoulders but off my life. I could breathe like releasing after an orgasm—an amazing feeling of the most pleasurable sigh. God also opened my eyes. I once was blind, but now I could see!

My spiritual vision was clear despite my circumstances. I was confident there was no turning back. Besides, I had been spiritually blind because I wasn't conscious of myself as a woman, wife, and mother; I hadn't understood my purpose here on earth nor had I executed my life calling. I know this because I wasn't content, and I didn't feel fulfilled. I didn't let God work through me to get the glory.

I didn't praise Him as much as I do now. I didn't tremble in awe of God at any point during the process because I didn't have a healthy relationship with the Lord and with His will for my life. I never understood this Scripture until I walked in Paul's shoes (except a size smaller). I would never have imagined in a thousand years that I'd face something that made me reflect on Paul's experience more than what I experienced in 2017 leading into 2018. I couldn't fathom the goodness of God or His blessing during this chaotic event. I walked each day for over a decade until this day when God did the unbelievable, yet the imaginable—He opened my eyes. God blessed me with a greater understanding of my situation like the burst of a beautiful, blossoming flower during the perfect season. God allowed me to recognize and discover the true jewel that He had placed inside me before I knew my name—one that revealed my identity.

Have you ever walked in my alley or on my street? How was it? Where did you go? Whom did you run to or call? Did you endure or give up? If you're in a fight, you must struggle until you overcome life. Face your obstacles until you win, and be thankful in the game.

Well, one could argue all day that struggling from one end of a pool to the other is hard because they "heard" about it or saw it on TV: It's a piece of cake. However, to experience the reality of what it really takes to swim from one side of a pool to the other requires experience; no one knows the strength and obstacles it takes to breathe, kick, paddle, and repeat with such skills in the deep waters of life without walking in your footsteps. I experienced the other side of the fence because I was supposed to. It was "my turn" to be the victim—an experience I never imagined that I'd face in a thousand years. However, God's favor overruled the experience. Life was challenging as I continued to adjust to "the norm" or this "new way" of living. It was difficult, without a doubt. I didn't know about tomorrow; today was enough to cope with. Each day became just another blessed day.

Still, the struggle was real! I was no longer in the classroom, which was difficult, so I had to constantly motivate myself. Otherwise, I would have given up. I was now back in a state of depression; this was the lowest I'd been, and it wasn't easy, but God guided me closer to Him and blessed me with His grace. Writing was my blessing in disguise. It was the only gift I could connect to and embrace. I didn't know about the future, but I knew who held the future.

After I experienced an unimaginable day before the holidays, not only did my journey change but I could see—spiritually. The next morning, my eyes were open, and I felt free. It was as if a load had been lifted off my shoulders. I no longer felt imprisoned like a caged bird, which I had experienced in my twelve-year relationship battle. I could breathe despite the messy, yet much-needed shift in my walk. The unnecessary weight of life was released when "I" was released—when I let go of myself and the desires of this world and let God control my steps, my walk, and my mindset. He renewed it. This created room for God's grace and mercy to overpower my old ways, my old life, and my carnal mindset. Different areas of my life began to change, like my health. I started losing weight. After I dropped off my daughter at daycare, I exercised for thirty to forty minutes because I was compelled to improve my overall health.

If I improved my diet, my blood pressure would improve as well, though this didn't happen overnight. I was determined to be productive and make use of this time to improve my health and lifestyle. So, I journaled, applied for jobs, read Bible study plans, and spent more time with my family. Each day was consistent unless I ran errands for our household, had a job interview, or went out with my husband and daughter.

I was a different person because God did the extraordinary: Renewing my mindset as I tossed and turned that night, in the middle of change. The blessing was that God kept me uplifted and calm; I was down but not low enough to that point that I forgot about the goodness of God—His unfailing love, grace, and mercy. He rescued me from an unhealthy pit of darkness and destruction. He encouraged me with His remarkable and trustworthy Word. He opened my eyes and comforted my mind, body, and soul through His almighty power. He blessed me with His favor.

God humbled my heart and blessed me with spiritual understanding. As a result, I slowed down. I was no longer the woman who sped 100 miles per hour in Miami and around Florida. I was more cautious about my surroundings and embraced the small things of life. I no longer chased the things I had desired before my life changed. I needed money, but putting in long work hours instead of spending time with my family and God was no longer interesting to me. I cherished the value of God and my family and no longer wanted to work a job or career that prevented me from building a stronger relationship with the Lord and my family.

When my attitude and heart changed, God continued to bless me. In mid-2018, I applied for a full-time position at United Way of Broward County and received an amazing position working as a campaign associate, which I loved, including my colleagues. They were friendly and supportive since day one. However, it was a temporary contract. I had the opportunity to speak to small and big businesses and companies and develop my public speaking and customer service skills. I was honored and blessed to have worked with such a remarkable organization. In December 2018, my contract ended, and I continued to write and self-publish books.

In 2019, I applied for an academic advisor position at Miami Dade College Wolfson Campus and received the great news that the department was interested in scheduling an interview. Days later, I attended the interview and met great and good-hearted individuals. It was now several years since I had worked at the Kendall Campus, so my return in this season of my life was on time. They discussed the position title, role, requirements, pay, and potential start date. I also had the chance to see my potential office. It was spacious and clean, and it included a computer, filing cabinets, an office phone, and a comfortable chair. It seemed like the perfect role, and the pay was more than what I was earning as a self-published author.

After a month, I started my new role as a part-time academic advisor at MDC Wolfson Campus, and I loved it. Anthony worked early mornings and got off work at 4:30, and Kamaria was in daycare, which she attended near the house. The schedule was perfect, but the drive wasn't the best. I had to leave extra early to bypass most of downtown Miami's traffic. However, it worked out and things went well.

As an academic advisor, I assisted students with creating a course schedule, IEPs, graduation applications, adding/dropping courses, and course overrides. I also participated in on-campus department events and early registration and assisted dual enrollment students. I had a big role with little pay, but after I spoke with my supervisor about my background, experience, and degrees, I received a pay raise. It was a blessing, and I was grateful.

I loved my position and inspired every student I met. Everyone had different backgrounds but entered my door for the same reasons: to strive, thrive, and succeed. I did more than my job requirements; I made a difference, encouraged my students with hope, and motivated them to have faith and never give up. As a result, my schedule was booked with students—young, old, and fresh out of high school. They left with confidence and enthusiasm to further their education. A few were homeless, but they were determined to make it, to overcome their difficult obstacles and lifestyles to win and assist others in their families and communities. Every day, I was prepared to impact lives and bless others with the power and wisdom that God blessed me to possess. If a student needed assistance beyond my responsibilities, they received it and were satisfied.

I knew my storm was temporary and God was doing something bigger and better in my life, so I made the best of each day. I let go and let God have His way, as I was tired of handling life my way. I saw this as an opportunity to let God do something remarkable in my life. I had faith that His call on my life would be greater than I ever imagined. I was lost and frustrated and wanted peace. I wasn't myself, and I knew it; I was out of it and nothing could have cheered me up except maybe getting my job back. But honestly, I don't think I'd be as happy, grateful, and fulfilled as I am now if I had stayed in such a toxic workplace and environment. I wouldn't be the same person, and my lifestyle would have been imbalanced. I struggled with anxiety, fear, doubt, and low confidence, and it wasn't fun.

I did whatever it took to help put food on my family's table. I was dedicated and worked hard for my earnings and other blessings; I did it all with hopes of getting to where I desired to be in life, for the better of my family and myself. If there was an opportunity for overtime, I took advantage of it. If there was an opportunity to earn extra money or a stipend that year, I went for it and committed myself a hundred and fifty percent. If I had to sweat, I endured it because I knew that was what it took to reap blessings. I had faith that I was getting somewhere. However, I wasn't concerned with the essentials of life. My mental, physical, spiritual, and marriage lives were being impacted and taken for granted. If I had known about the path I was headed toward, I would have prayed on purpose, with purpose, and for a greater purpose. I would have embraced my husband and our beautiful daughter more. I would have put my family over a job, over my career. I would have embraced my marriage more. I would have planned more time with my family. I would have saved more money and spent less. Most importantly, I would have sought Jesus Christ and desired to develop a closer relationship with the Lord by submitting my life, ways, and wants to Him. And I would have walked with more humility.

This job took over my life. If I was working and grinding, I was okay; bringing home a "sweet" salary and living out loud was fine and acceptable despite the issues it caused in my spiritual growth, finances, and marriage, but I thank God it all happened. Now I have a better understanding, and God did more than I could have asked for—He blessed me through my unexpected life event. He did the extraordinary because He's that kind of God—the Almighty, powerful One who knew the power of a thorn attacking my life. I have faith that He knew it had to happen. He knew I needed to feel every pain from the thorn. He knew this would be the perfect storm. He knew without this storm, I probably would have given up my life. He knew I could have lost my life. He knew I could have dug a deeper hole in my destruction. He knew I would lose my mind and then some. He knew I would continue to walk in spiritual darkness without eyes to see and a heart to turn over my life to Him.

In 2019, I self-published my first book, *Run Your Business in Ten Essentials for 365 Days and Beyond*, with no self-publishing experience. I was excited about finding ways to share my story and business tips and to glorify God, so I didn't waste time releasing this book. It was my first book but not my last one. I reached out to a publishing specialist, and they assisted me in self-publishing this book. It wasn't as successful as I thought it would be, but I was okay. I was thankful I had the courage to do what many feared because of doubt. I sold books but not a million copies. Still, I had faith and hope that, one day, God would let it happen.

I worked during the day, wrote content on my breaks or any time I was free, and continued in the evening. I was determined to grow my brand and book business while writing full-time, so I continued to work at the college until God saw fit to carry me in a different direction. However, I didn't plan to resign from my day job. I let God guide my steps and continue to reveal my purpose.

In August 2021, I found a remote literary agent position at a publishing house in Atlanta, Georgia. The benefits were great, though the pay was only by commission. I seemed to be a great match, so I applied for the position and received a response within days. The notification I received on Indeed from the publishing house invited me to participate in a remote Zoom interview with other candidates for the position. Days after I received the initial welcoming email, the Zoom interview happened on August 10. The following morning, I received an email congratulating me on being selected as one of the literary agents for the publishing house. I was excited and thanked God for this amazing and unexpected blessing. Also, I informed Anthony about the great news. The email informed me that the publishing house's director would reach out to me to arrange a virtual new hire orientation. The next day, I received an offer letter. I signed it and returned it to the company. After the orientation, which lasted about three hours on a Saturday morning, I began my new role as a literary agent. Not only did I feel valued, but it was an incredible accomplishment. I thanked God for His grace, mercy, and favor and for answering my prayers.

Days later, Anthony and I celebrated by going out to dinner. We talked about the position and looked forward to my new role. I updated my work status on my social media pages and attracted many potential clients. However, I didn't earn an income unless a new client or author signed a contract. This was the challenging part, but by the grace of God, I obtained one client and assisted another author with completing her publishing process, which allowed me to earn something as a start. After a month in my new role, I reached out to the directors of the company with an interest in an hourly salary. They informed me there was an administrative position open, and they provided me with the requirements, hours, and pay, which worked with my schedule. However, after days in this position, I didn't receive pay. So, I reached out to the employer and informed them I was no longer interested in this additional role if I was not paid on time and fairly.

They understood and provided me with a list of potential clients to contact, and I did, but many weren't interested or were not ready to publish their books. However, I did speak with one client who was interested in our ghostwriting services the following year. Every week, I followed up with potential clients, but still, no one was interested in signing except for one amazing individual and author who committed at the time. However, the function of the company began to seem strange. I wasn't paid on time and didn't receive a bonus gift card I had earned for reaching out to potential clients. That wasn't all. In the middle of coping with an auto accident, I met a potential client who seemed to have the desire to sign with the company but didn't for several reasons. As a result, I started to question the company's professionalism and organization. Things weren't working out. They were dishonest and lacked concern for taking responsibility for the functioning of the publishing house and providing me with my earnings. Finally, I emailed the company my resignation letter and moved forward with confidence in my quest for God's will in my new chapter.

Despite another unexpected circumstance, I stood strong and continued to push forward with focus. I didn't give up or reconsider working with the employer, especially after what I'd experienced. I deserved better and knew my value, so I knew without a doubt God would do a new thing, open a better door, and continue growing my book business. I didn't complain. I was relieved and thanked God for rescuing me from another unhealthy workplace— somewhere I didn't belong. I was okay. I knew where I was headed, so I persevered and continued to climb Jacob's ladder as God saw fit. God ultimately destined to have me shine and glorify His name.

If you can relate or are in a similar situation, you must know your worth, your incredible value, and your purpose on earth. God has better for you and will continue to allow you to experience unexpected situations that draw you closer to Him and shift you into an environment to shine and glorify Him. If you are employed and unhappy, this might be a sign that you are not operating in your calling, walking in your purpose for God's glory.

However, if you are jobless but seeking work, a career, or for God to reveal your calling, there is hope. Never give up! Start with faith and self-evaluation. Ask yourself: What can God do to help me improve my financial health or situation? What can He bless me with if I put forth just a little more effort and motivation? What can I do to thrive in the middle of my unexpected circumstances? For example, brainstorm your gifts and talents. Then, ask yourself: What am I great at? What do I enjoy doing? What is my passion? What makes me happy and satisfies my heart? What can I do with my voice or hands that I enjoy and will potentially make an impact?

Next, while you are praying and actively seeking employment, *get to work* with everything before your eyes—in proximity to you and your environment. You never know what you will discover or see that will motivate you in a powerful way if you let go and just do it. However, you must put forth effort and find the courage to do so. If you find that reading books aloud is interesting, work on it daily, then brainstorm ways to begin a service for this interest. Or if you discover that you enjoy cooking healthy meals, exercising, painting, or writing stories, make use of your time, energy, and effort, and embrace these hidden gifts. Don't continue to hide them. Make them known to others by starting a business! Proactive and positive thinking will change your life. Your gifts and talents will open amazing doors and opportunities for you if you believe more than you think. Remove negativity, doubt, and fear from your circle and atmosphere. Set your mind on positive outcomes and helpful results, and keep at it; be consistent with your efforts and energy to make something of yourself rather than waste your precious soul by sitting on the couch or giving up. Remember, your income was cut, you lost a job, or you got laid off. This isn't the grand finale; it's a great beginning for you to get yourself together—to actively get back on track without excuses releasing from your heart. God will help you, but you must be willing to help yourself. God will elevate you in due time.

After I searched for work and prayed, I received another job opportunity—one of the best days of my life. I tutored children in my area for months until I realized I was serious about writing more books and building my book business. I was working only three to five hours a week and earning fifteen dollars an hour. I put in my two weeks, stopped working with the tutoring company, and continued to focus on growing my book business.

It's never easy to accept God's decision. You must choose to accept His will. There's always a slight hesitation before we're able to say yes or no. My flesh was hesitant about letting go, but the Lord knew my spirit was craving to release "myself" so that I could experience freedom. Indeed, I needed rest, to let go and let God take over the wheels of my heart and my life, to direct my path. My heart needed to breathe, and this was the perfect opportunity. It was by far one of the hardest decisions I had to make, but it was also one of the greatest things that could have happened in my life for the glory of God.

I think one reason why letting go of something of value is so hard is because of the closeness, the time, energy, and hard work it took to begin at square one. Losing someone or something is often difficult, especially, if it's a loved one or something of great value. It hurts. It's traumatizing, and sometimes, it doesn't make sense; one plus one doesn't equal two as it should because you're in complete shock. Every day, someone loses a loved one, a car, a job, a relationship, a home, money, their health, their mind, and even small possessions like car keys. It's certainly not easy "losing" or having something or someone taken away from you. However, in some cases, losing is okay and does the mind, body, and soul good. For instance, losing a home that was worth more than one's salary or losing a car to repossession can be a blessing. It can be the blessing you need to experience freedom or a burden lifted from your life. It can be the blessing you need to relieve stress. It could be the blessing you need to bless you where you are today.

There was more to the picture than experiencing such a life event; the moment was bigger than I'd ever imagined. There was something more to just losing a job, and it was so great that I didn't "see" it in the moment. However, as I look back, I realize it was for a greater reason—to do the unbelievable, the unthinkable. Studying music hadn't been a dream of mine until years after I began studying in junior high. Then, it became a goal to further my career. I obtained both my bachelor's and master's degrees, which was not easy. I spent a fortune on both degrees and worked hard in the music education field. I was dedicated and passionate about performing and teaching, and I never let anything stop me from succeeding and furthering my education and network. However, things changed once I arrived at an unexpected halt in my life. Letting go of my career, the job I desired to pursue, was by far one of the most difficult things that ever happened; it was an involuntary, unexpected release. However, it was a blessing that not only was destined to happen but that needed to happen for God to reveal my life calling, my assignment here on earth. Otherwise, I would have still been just living rather than being alive on purpose in my calling today. There are blessings when you let go and let God conduct your life—mentally, physically, spiritually, and financially. From the moment I released my mind, heart, and soul to the Lord, I felt a significant difference in my spirit, and an uncomfortable burden lifted off my shoulders. My life wasn't the same.

God did the unexpected yet unimaginable when I placed my trust in His arms. Not only that, I had faith that God would come through. I knew He hadn't forgotten about me in my weakness, low days, and moments of frustration. I remained patient in prayer and exercised my faith and gifts. I strove during months when I was without work, especially in the summer—for years. It was a difficult and ongoing scare that I faced with hope, faith, and determination. My goal was not to live on the government and purchase food with food stamps each month. I desired better for myself and my family, so God turned my pain into my purpose. I've been writing books ever since, but it wasn't a skip and a hop, a microwave scene.

I experienced a lot of trials and tribulations, faith tests, and mental hurdles, on my journey, but every time I prayed and turned to the Word for my rescue, He turned my situation into a positive outcome. When I grabbed my Bible and turned to a Scripture for encouragement, it brightened my day and made me stronger. I strove to apply His word in my life, and He renewed my strength and fueled me with hope and faith to calm my anxious heart on difficult days. My Heavenly Father sat me down and gave me enough strength to pray and allow Him to comfort my hurts and pains. His powerful words kept my focus on His promises, His will, way, and word. They kept me on fire to experience the power of His word and to want a closer relationship with Him no matter what. I turned to the Word when I wanted to stop and do what would not have pleased Him, and I felt better afterward.

During this turning point in my life, He gave me a reason to not look back, to look forward and trust in His sovereign power to guide me where He had planned before I was born. He opened my eyes and revealed my purpose, my greatest calling, and made my heart smile. I knew then, after I experienced this extraordinary event, it was time for me to put the rest of my life in God's hands.

# Chapter 10

## COVID-19

*"In May 2022, my family and I experienced COVID-19—an unexpected storm we never imagined since the beginning of the pandemic in 2019. It was a tough battle, but God's grace and mercy carried us through. He delivered us from this monster, from what could have destroyed us. He turned it around for us, for His glory. We're forever thankful for His unconditional love."*

*-Kala*

It was the 2020 new year, and everything seemed to be going okay, including my job at the college, until suddenly, out of nowhere, I received multiple text messages on my phone about a global pandemic: COVID-19. I was shocked and saw information about the pandemic on my computer screen. Then, my supervisor sent out emails to staff about the unexpected situation. Everyone was surprised at what was going on. I immediately prayed and texted my husband, who was also at work. He didn't know much about what was happening except the fact that whatever it was, God had us and would protect us from any hurt, harm, or danger.

The following message was from the college president. It contained important procedures and information about the school's next steps to ensure all students and staff were safe. We were informed to clock out at a specific time and monitor our phones and emails for updates and reporting details.

After I clocked out of work, I left the college campus and picked up Kamaria from her daycare, which provided me with further information about the temporary closing of the school. I was shocked but not worried. I knew everything would be alright. Hours later, I received text messages and emails that the college would be closing indefinitely for most faculty and staff. I received a separate email with information about who was to report to the college the following day. I was not included. Also, Kamaria's daycare was closed until further notice. Later that week, I received an email from my supervisor, stating that staff would be assisting students with registration and answering questions remotely until further notice. Immediately, I panicked because I didn't know how I'd be able to work, answer phone calls, participate in meetings, assist students, and oversee Kamaria. I reached out and obtained clarification about my duties, which wasn't so bad but required me to remain on standby.

For months, I assisted students remotely, cared for Kamaria, and carried out my other responsibilities as a wife. We also reached out to our family to make sure everyone was okay. However, in May, I received disturbing news that my sister, Allison, had experienced ongoing heart attacks and been rushed to the hospital. Anthony, Kamaria, and I rode the train up to meet my mom at the hospital. I panicked and prayed when I heard it was true. Days before her tragedy, we had spoken, smiled, and laughed at each other. I was down but hopeful about God strengthening and healing her.

To show love and support, we traveled up to Palm Beach County almost every weekend for months. It was difficult mentally and physically, so we started visiting Allison and our family several times throughout the month. We knew Allison needed all the support possible, including my parents, niece, and nephew (Allison's children).

During this unbelievable season, many became ill, lost their jobs and businesses, or had to make significant decisions like I did. The education system experienced drastic change, which affected children and families like ours. I was blessed to have the opportunity to work from home, but this was also one of the most difficult and stressful times of my life. Still, I embraced it and started writing content for my next book. I knew the world's aches and pains were temporary and that God was doing amazing things in my life to glorify Him.

As with every storm I'd experienced, I learned to cope with and embrace unforeseen situations like the pandemic, especially those out of my control. I did exactly that while overseeing Kamaria. When her daycare closed, I had to make unexpected adjustments, mentally and physically. I had to persevere and endure. I also had to adjust my exercise routine and writing schedule to assist our daughter while at home. It was challenging, but we prayed, and I did my best and pushed through it—months of chaotic *change*.

Months later, I became overwhelmed by work and everything else that I was coping with. After careful consideration, prayer, and a discussion with my spouse, I decided to resign from my work position. It was by far one of the most difficult decisions I had to make, as most of my income came from this workplace. However, I chose to do it because I was stressed and became unhappy with the workload, physical demands, and challenges. After attending several meetings, I found that more was added to my plate than expected. Working past my normal hours became an issue and began to interfere with my personal life. My load was heavy, and I felt it. I wanted peace and to be free like a prisoner or caged bird.

After I received my 401(k) and last check from the employer, I felt that a load of responsibility had been lifted from my life. I was the happiest woman on earth again, on my street, and in our apartment. I was free to focus on my book business, and I did. In 2021, after I was denied my first traditionally published contract, I was inspired to self-publish my first poetry, prose, and inspirational quotes book, *Words from the Heart*. It became a success and has earned me great reviews and compliments to this day, to God be the glory. However, it wasn't enough for me to retire. I had hopes of writing full-time if I could save up enough money to assist with my book business, so I did my best and strove, every day, without giving up. At times, it was challenging but not impossible. I kept my faith and leaned on the Lord for His guidance and grace.

I continued to write and was inspired to pen a book about my experiences during the pandemic, under the title *When You Rise*. In March 2022, I self-published the second edition of *When You Rise,* which was also a success. Many were touched by the poem and could relate to my thoughts and experiences. I didn't need approval to do something positive with my unknown stories. I had confidence in my ability to overcome fear and challenging hurdles. I found ways to swim through deep waters and turned my successes and failures into inspirational and motivational books. During this season, I experienced adversity and a loss in income, but I was relentless. I refused to give up because I was born an overcomer. I wouldn't stop living unless it was my time. I was determined to rise and continue making the best of each day, to embrace God's will, way, and Word through it all. This gave me hope and fuel to stand up and be resilient.

In May 2022, my family and I faced another unexpected life storm: We became ill with COVID-19. Moments after I opened my eyes, I saw Anthony walk into the bedroom. He jumped into bed and smiled at me. He kissed me with his warm lips and said, "Happy Mother's Day!"

I smiled and said, "Thank you, handsome."

Soon after, our princess awakened. Kamaria looked over and said the same thing with the most beautiful smile ever! It was a beautiful moment, one we'll never forget. She said, "Mommy, it's a beautiful, blessed day," and I said, "Yes, it is, baby!"

It was almost time for Children's Church (Sunday School class for children of the Hope Church of Christ) at our place of worship, on Zoom, so we helped her get dressed and prepared her breakfast. Her class was awesome, and she enjoyed it. This was among the best forty five minutes of her lifetime as she learned about God and had fellowship with her brothers and sisters in Christ. After Children's Church, we headed to the worship service nearby. We arrived safely and sat down, but Anthony looked tired; he held his head down and stayed quiet—not that he was a talker during service. I asked how he was feeling, and he said, "Not so well." So, after worship service, we left and drove down to my mother's house to meet up for lunch. We arrived safely, but Anthony didn't wanted to rest and didn't have an appetite. He ate soup and rested at my mom's place while we enjoyed Mother's Day lunch at Golden Corral. It was delicious and we laughed and shared some memories. Days later, Anthony complained, yet again, about a severe headache, so we didn't waste time; we jumped in the car and drove to the nearest hospital, which was minutes from our home. It was the same hospital where Kamaria was born, which was a blessing and benefit; we'd stayed in the same apartment complex for eight years. The hospital was within walking distance, and we could literally see the facility from our windows. When Anthony walked out, he said that, yes, he'd caught COVID-19. Where and from whom, he didn't know. It was impossible to track who had given him this nasty virus.

Throughout the night, I noticed Kamaria's elevated temperature—she was beyond warm. It was unusual as I felt her warm body rest on mine. The next morning, I awoke and felt nauseous. I wasn't myself and knew something was wrong. My head was also hurting, and I felt weak, so I drove back to the hospital and had the doctors check Kamaria. She was, indeed, sick with COVID-19 as well. I never got checked, but I was informed that because my daughter and husband were sick with the virus, I was more than likely also sick with COVID-19. So, we prayed and quarantined. After two weeks, my husband re-tested at a local COVID-19 testing site. His results were negative, to God be the glory. However, my results and Kamaria's were still positive; we were both still ill. About five days later, we re-tested and were finally negative, glory to God. Wow. Wow. Wow. What an experience. But God turned it around for His glory! We were so thankful and jumped with joy. We did continue to experience minor after-effects—coughing and brain fog, but we improved and were fully restored. God blessed us and kept us safe, sound, and in good health until we were fully delivered.

Is this your story? Did you also overcome COVID-19? If so, praise God for His grace and mercy, for His deliverance, unfailing love, and compassion. He saved you. But for God, it could have been you in your grave. But for God, it could have been you in the hospital on a ventilator. All kinds of stuff could have happened, but it didn't. God saved you and gave you another chance, not by chance or luck but by His grace and mercy. You are blessed and favored. It wasn't your time, and that's worth glorifying our Heavenly Father.

Because you overcame this virus, you must encourage someone else who is coping with this serious monster. Someone is open to hearing your story. They're down and need practical advice, encouragement, or wisdom. Share words of comfort to help soothe their mind or uplift their spirit. Many have become depressed and on the edge of giving up; many have suffered and lost their minds, but you haven't. You're sane and physically sound because God is awesome like that. And you didn't lose your job or have to apply for unemployment. You're earning a living, and your business hasn't shut down; your money-maker is still running. There is no "Now Closed" sign on your business door. You're not lucky; you are blessed. Each day, God continues to give you the strength to inhale and exhale without fainting, sweating, vomiting, coughing, or losing your taste. Your immune system is stronger than ever, and your blood pressure is regulated. You don't need ventilation because His life support is sustaining you. God's grace is continually prevailing over your unexpected circumstances in life, so why not give Him praise, glory, and honor? He's worthy of praise! Yes, be thankful in the name of Jesus. He is awesome. There's nobody like the Lord; can't nobody do you like Jesus and can't nobody cover you like the Lord.

# Chapter 11

## *Prayer*

*"I prayed, but it wasn't intentional and effective,
and I'm certain. But God's grace made a way out of
no way every time I faced a struggle."*

*-Kala*

When I was a child, we moved to our second residence in Delray
Beach, Florida on 14th Street, in front of a Church of Christ. I
remember sitting in the church service around a bunch of men,
women, and children. Everyone's eyes were on one man who stood
behind a podium and spoke loudly. At five years old, I didn't know
what he was saying. Later, I learned he was a pastor who preached
about the Gospel. He read Bible Scriptures and sang, and five men
stood in front of his podium with baskets. They walked around, and
I saw many people put money and coins inside these brown baskets.
It was strange but interesting. My sisters and I smiled and talked
during church service, amazed at how everyone wore fancy dresses,
hats, and shoes. One Easter Sunday, I wore a pink dress with white

shoes and walked around saying "cheese" to everyone. I loved to smile with my long, black, Indian hair.

I also saw men and women with their heads bowed and their hands together. Some closed their eyes and kept their heads lifted, and some closed their eyes and held their hands toward the sky. I always wondered why they did this more than whom they were doing this to or for. It happened every Sunday—in children's church class and just before church service was over. However, I'm certain my parents prayed. I just don't remember until we started going to another church location, 15th Street Church of Christ in Delray Beach, Florida. Not only did the pastor say that prayer was important, but my mother also encouraged my sisters and me to do the same. So, we bowed our heads, closed our eyes, and waited until the paster said "Amen" to open them. In the time between when we closed our eyes and opened them, the pastor thanked God and prayed for the sick and shut-ins, members of the congregation, and the world. He also prayed before communion and collection.

From that point on, my outlook on prayer was a way to express to God my gratitude; I didn't think much of it because I didn't understand the importance of praying. When I was an adolescent, I'd watch my mom pray before we ate breakfast, lunch, and dinner, but that was about all.

I didn't begin to understand prayer until we moved and began attending church service at Lake Ida Church of Christ, also in Delray Beach Florida and years later, Hope Church of Christ. I'd just started high school. We attended as a family—my mother, sisters, and niece. I began to have a clear understanding not only of prayer but also of God and His Word. In addition, we learned about prayer during young adult class, at lectureships, and during Wednesday night Bible Study class. I loved learning about God and how life began—the creation of the world. Sometimes, before class was over, I was asked to pray. I was shy but overcame this fear and started to become comfortable with prayer. After I was baptized in 2004, my prayer life strengthened, but it still wasn't effective. This was because I continued to walk in darkness. I was a Christian who still wore a veil; I continued to sin and unconsciously live carelessly. Also, my prayer routine was expressed to God without purpose. However, I didn't give up. I had hopes that God would not only hear my prayers but also answer them.

During my college years, I prayed, but it wasn't intentional. I prayed for a better relationship, but I continued to satisfy my flesh and have premarital sex. Living how I desired was more pleasing to my body; it felt better to serve my temple than to worship God and live a wholesome, Christian life. That was challenging, but I stayed hopeful and never stopped praying. I also prayed for God to improve my finances, but I continued to take out student loans and spend without having a budget. I prayed for a financial increase, but I had no discipline. Most importantly, my heart longed to be delivered from sin, so I expressed my desires to the Lord through prayer.

Years later, my prayer life continued to suck; it was still weak, like my heart, and ineffective. I did not take prayer seriously, so I suffered the consequences. I prayed when it was convenient; it wasn't as strong as it is today. But that's not all. My relationship with the Lord wasn't strong before I was dismissed from elementary school. Therefore, my life wasn't in sync with Christ. I was separated from the Lord like a married couple or a mother and daughter. My faith was also weak. I believed what everyone else said, but I didn't have faith in my Heavenly Father and His power. My belief didn't align with my life because it wasn't active.

I wasn't connected with the Word, and because my prayer life was weak, my day was odd, like the experience of watching *Odd Squad*. My mornings were a challenge. However, Grace prevented my mind, body, and soul from losing it. He made a powerful way; God's favor kept me strong.

Seconds after my usual talk with Jesus, Kamaria awakened. I kissed her and told her how much Anthony and I loved her, but also how much more God loved her. She smiled. I put her clothes on, prepared her snacks and bottles, and fed her oatmeal, which she loved. I also ate a bowl of homemade oatmeal covered with Greek yogurt and fruits. Then I prepared myself for yet another complicated and busy day at work, which sometimes I looked forward to and some days I didn't. Facing this reality became more and more of a struggle. It seemed as if I were walking in a circle. I didn't question God; I continued to walk with the hope that one day, things would get better—this burden would rise off my shoulders, and I would experience freedom. Anthony and I continued to pray, and I encouraged myself. I was motivated and determined to rise, to stand strong, and to trust in the Lord's will. Other than the loss of zeal I began to experience in my position, I continued to have a busy and sometimes hectic life. The conditions in Miami did not help. Miami's highways were unpredictable; they weren't my best friend in the mornings or the evenings, but I learned to cope. God blessed me to make it to my destination safe and sound, scratch-free and alive.

I was beyond thankful despite my outside environment, situations, and circumstances. Through my experience, I've learned the more we appreciate the uncomfortableness of life, the more we learn to embrace each moment God gives us, so I complained less and praised Him more. I thanked God in silence through my perseverance and endurance on the journey. Life was strange but amazing once I gained a greater appreciation of Christ, so hang tight to the Lord when the journey gets bumpy, overwhelming, and stressful. God gotcha. Don't worry.

Pray through your unexpectedness of life and never give up. Prayer and faith were my weapons. We weren't created to live perfect, stress-free lives. We will struggle and experience things we don't like, for a greater reason. Perhaps it's to teach us to have more patience or to learn to be more thankful; to bring us closer to the Lord; to get us back on track; to prevent destruction; or to help save a life. Or maybe the situation is designed to help encourage others or the lost and blind.

We all have dreams and aspirations to hone something or a business, to become doctors and lawyers, hair stylists, brokers, authors, musicians, athletes, etc. Everything we expect to happen might not happen or go as planned, but if you learn to accept God's will on your journey to your destination, you'll experience fulfillment. Your heart will have peace no matter what blows your way or attacks your spirit. You'll grow to appreciate and embrace whatever blows your way with contentment. So, that was my typical day, morning, and week. Little did I know that the next moment, the next day of my life, would be an unexpected, unbelievable one. Lord knows I may have been better prepared—physically, mentally, spiritually, and financially—but that wasn't the case.

If it wasn't for the favor, grace, mercy, and love of my Heavenly Father, I wouldn't have made it this far. I would not have had the strength and guts, the confidence to even begin to unite my fingers together like "criss-cross applesauce," like two joining to become one, to share my journey, including things you never knew about me. Most of all, I would not have been able to free my heart to help yours; to offer you hope and comfort in your storms or trials and tribulations; to empower you to overcome fear by having faith and getting to know the person in the mirror.

Writing this chapter and memoir took more than I'd ever imagined. There were times when I felt like procrastinating another day, month, or year, but my drive to get it out of my soul—my story—motivated me to get it done.

To have the finances to self-publish this book was also a blessing, but it wasn't a piece of cake. I had to continue to write books, self-publish, sell, market, promote, organize book signings, and search for opportunities that would open doors for me to gain and grow. I couldn't imagine keeping every word stored in my heart only to have it buried in the grave so that others could write my story. I chose to be selfless, to think about you and generations to come. I knew God's grace would make it happen and make an impact greater than staying on mute.

When we experience life events or unexpectedness, we hesitate to be thankful for our circumstances. Often, the power of grace is overlooked or disregarded unless we "see" it. However, through experiences, expecting grace is a great sign of faith. By being grateful in the storms, chaos, battles, and hardships of life, we learn to appreciate life more than ever. When God blessed me with work or opportunities to earn income, not only did that motivate me, but I was super thankful.

My faith grew and I cherished every moment, every opportunity God blessed me with. Most of all, grace blessed me in ways that surprised yet touched me. I didn't expect it, but I knew God would come through and make a way out of no way. I knew He would bless me when I least expected it. So, if you're in a difficult situation and worried about hope, have faith because God will show up. You're not alone. I know this because, at times, I thought I was, but I wasn't. The closer I grew to the Lord, the stronger my faith became and the more He revealed my purpose in life.

# Chapter 12

# Neck and Back Surgery

*"The moment I stepped into the outpatient surgery facility, I panicked. Minutes before the procedure began, my heart rate sped as if I were in a race. But there was nothing I could do at that point. My life was in God's hands. The car accident I experienced was unimaginable, one heck of a day and season, and honestly, difficult—the entire process. But God blessed me every step of the way."*

*-Kala*

In the blink of an eye, an ordinary day turned into an unexpected one. I felt my entire body go forward in the parking lot of a local coffee shop due to the actions of a careless driver in July 2021. This young man hit me with his company's vehicle, causing my entire body to be pushed into the steering wheel with a heavy impact. I was shocked and upset because I had been hit by a man who had jumped in his truck while talking on his phone without leaving the parking lot. Slowly, I lifted my head from the steering wheel and stepped outside my car. Then, I called 911. I hesitated to do this for several reasons: I was nervous about calling the paramedics because I always had a fear of them checking my vitals and transporting me to the hospital. So, I did not request first responders to transport me to the nearest hospital; I bypassed seeing their faces that morning. But it wasn't over. I had plans to seek medical attention afterward.

The young man walked over to me as if he didn't know what had happened, and he apologized. Right after, my blood pressure became elevated as I stood against my car in the hot sun, sweating with an anxious heart about what lay ahead. My mind was all over the place. I thought about the ambulance, doctor visits, rental cars, and explaining this accident to my husband, who was at work at the time. I had just dropped off Kamaria at daycare, which was a few minutes away from the accident scene. I became dehydrated and frustrated at such a preventable scene. The driver's senseless act was unbelievable but also believable because I had experienced another unexpected accident.

When the police arrived, I was asked the usual questions. I explained, in one breath, what had happened. I was nowhere near at fault—the driver took full responsibility for his actions, which was great to know. It was such a hectic morning that caused me to stress out and experience anxiety. Because I refused to be transported in an ambulance, I drove myself to a chiropractic office. The long, extended journey began. It was tiresome and time-consuming, but I had to attend; I needed the therapy. Then, weeks later, not only was my back aching, but my right leg had weakened to the point that, some days, I struggled to walk without having to rest beforehand. I struggled with my right arm and hands as well to the point that it affected my strength to write, so I wrote less.

My lifestyle changed, and there was nothing I could do about it. I had been involved in an unexpected car accident, which was now the issue on my shoulders. My schedule was disturbed, but I was determined to get through this challenging phase in my life. After I dropped my daughter off at daycare, I drove to my chiropractor's office and received therapy. For weeks, I was stressed; my blood pressure was elevated, and my heart rate was over a hundred beats per minute. I was advised by the office's medical doctor that I could not be seen until I had scheduled a visit with my cardiologist, which I did on the same day. I phoned the office and explained the reason for an urgent visit. They approved my visit without hesitation.

When I arrived at my cardiologist's office, I walked upstairs and walked in. They requested a co-pay with my insurance, which I didn't expect but still provided. My health was more important, so I did not complain. The medical assistant called me to the back room, where they weighed me and asked for the reason for my visit. The assistant took my vitals, which weren't good. My blood pressure was elevated but not as high as it had been at the chiropractor's office. However, my heart rate was elevated. Minutes later, the cardiologist examined me and suggested I continue taking my high blood pressure medicine and arrange an appointment for a stress test. Before I left the office, I scheduled the stress test, and they ordered blood work. My cardiologist also advised me to rest, exercise, and maintain a healthy diet. I did my best, and my heart rate improved. However, my blood pressure was still elevated. I took a week off from therapy to work on my blood pressure, which improved by the grace and mercy of God. I was now able to start therapy and treatment for my injuries.

After my therapy sessions, I went home, cooked lunch, and worked on books. Then, I rested, prepared dinner, and, sometimes, picked up Kamaria from school. Anthony was a big help during this season of my life. He ran errands, washed clothes, picked up Kamaria at daycare, and drove us to worship service. On his days off, he dropped off Kamaria at school. I was determined not to let this unexpected season disrupt my life, including my book business and family. My back and neck injuries did not improve, nor did my right leg. Due to the accident, I had trouble sitting for long periods, which caused pain in my neck. Then, weeks later, my right leg became weak. Some days, I struggled to walk. Finally, I reached out to my attorney, and I was advised to consult with my chiropractor. After weeks of therapy, I was referred to an orthopedic surgeon, who examined my spine and right leg. Then, I was sent out for X-rays.

Days later, I followed up with the specialist and was informed that I could continue to see a chiropractor, or a C4-5 and right L5-S1 microdiscectomy with laminotomy would remedy my issues. I was frightened but glad to know there was a solution. However, it would require outpatient surgery, which I had not experienced since my C-section in 2016. My thoughts were all over the place, so I discussed it with my attorney and husband that afternoon. I had never been a fan of anesthesia or surgeries ever since my first surgeries as an adolescent—I had my tonsils and adenoids removed and underwent eye surgery.

After weeks of praying and discussing the advantages and disadvantages of this procedure with my husband, I found that the Spirit led me to move forward with the surgery. Monday morning, I met with my attorney and the staff at the surgeon's office and notified them of my decision. The surgeon, his assistant, and the staff consulted with me and provided details about the procedures, including the date and time of the surgery and postoperative details. I was also asked medical questions and signed an agreement to have the surgery.

On October 15, 2021, an Uber driver picked up me, Anthony, and Kamaria and drove us to an outpatient center in Broward County. I was nervous, but Anthony encouraged me with Scriptures, and we prayed. When we arrived, my mom was there. She sat in the waiting room with Anthony to oversee Kamaria. That morning, I also took a COVID-19 test before the procedure. Just before the nurses escorted me to the back room, Anthony prayed. I hugged my mom, kissed Kamaria and Anthony, and told everyone I loved them. I was not to drink, take any medications, or eat anything past midnight. As they prepared me for surgery, my heartbeat sped, and my blood pressure rose. I was informed to undress and place a gown on. Afterward, I lay in a designated bed until the nurses moved me. Then, I prayed again. God calmed my anxious heart and comforted my soul. Minutes later, they moved me to the operating room and began providing me with anesthesia. I panicked again and my heartbeat raced. I overheard one of the doctors say, "Why is her heart beating fast?" At that point, I remember closing my eyes and then awakening in a recovery room. It seemed like everything had happened so fast, but it hadn't. Thirty minutes to an hour later, I was placed in a wheelchair and headed home. I wore neck and back braces and expected a follow-up with the surgeon in a few weeks. During this time, Anthony and my mother supported me, as did neighbors, who helped drive Kamaria to school. I was ordered not to operate a vehicle for at least a few weeks. That sucked, but I followed orders for successful healing.

Anthony assisted me with walking, showering, putting my clothes on, cooking dinner, grocery shopping, and caring for Kamaria, and he did a great job. I had no issues except for pain the first few days. This eventually stopped. I had never liked medication, so I did not take pain medicine; I endured the temporary pain with faith. I knew each day I would feel better and experience less pain. As time passed, I began doing things on my own, like cooking, showering, and walking, which was a blessing. I walked every day for at least thirty minutes, read Bible plans, wrote, and praised God for His grace and mercy. I knew God would heal my body and restore my health one day at a time.

Since then, I have been better than on day one. However, I am not a hundred percent; I still experience challenging days of pain, but I've learned to endure it all with the hope that one day I'll fully recover. I expect my deliverance because I know God is more than able and has the power to do anything and everything man cannot—the extraordinary, and I'm forever grateful.

I am certain many of you have experienced a difficult auto accident or traumatic life event that has left you in pain or distress. If so, hang in there. Healing is a lifetime journey for many, so give yourself grace and take life one day at a time. It's comforting to know I am not alone on my healing journey. With faith, God will get us there, closer to overcoming an illness, health issue, depression, poverty, low self-esteem, or any life storm. He'll bless you to experience His grace and mercy. Your breakthrough is on the way. I believe it, but do you? You must believe before it happens; see your breakthrough before you experience it. It'll motivate you every time. Wherever you are on your journey, keep trusting in the Lord and have gorilla faith. God is doing something greater and beyond your understanding even during the odd, unexpected things in life.

I knew there was a greater reason for this event, so I never questioned God. I thanked Him for the message in the storm and the blessings He had in store for me to share with you.

# Chapter 13

# My Calling

*"Living is boring if you don't discover one of the greatest and most satisfying experiences ever."*

**-Kala**

I never imagined God would bless me to discover my calling, but it happened, and it changed my life. My passion to write books and inspire others along the way is unexpectedly fulfilling and worth pursuing. I say this because not everyone witnesses the power of God's favor in the middle of a storm, fight, or unpleasant circumstance. So, I give all praise, glory, and honor to God for choosing me, for blessing me with opened eyes to realize He did a mighty thing in my life. Everyone is in sync with the Almighty and has that close relationship to testify about the goodness of God. However, that doesn't mean you'll never experience the other side of what you're coping with today. I didn't magically get here or roll an eight-ball to write this book. Someone, not anyone, more powerful than my entire body, imagination, and the world—God—did the extraordinary without the power of man. At times, it feels unbelievable, like beyond a dream come true. This experience, and more so, new lifestyle tastes better than ice cream, and I'm forever grateful He used me to share His mighty grace and power—on purpose. He chose me to be the victim and blessed me at the same time, which is an experience worth having.

Honestly, I am humbled and at peace to have finally arrived at this page—a journey more than a move that took a lot of prayers and perseverance unlike anything I ever executed in my life. And it wasn't a dream or wish. God blessed me and chose me for a greater purpose, and I want you to be encouraged to know He's also working for you and on your journey. Believe in doubt and your abilities. Work smart with patience, not hard with bitterness in your heart. Rise with appreciation and enthusiasm to achieve your goals—yes, the one or two God is bringing you through. And walk anyway, no matter what they say. I had a vision, and I was determined to experience the reality of what I hoped for, and this is it—God made it happen in due time. He blessed me with a new thing: the power to courageously operate in my calling as a passionate young woman and entrepreneur who runs a book business, KJL.

With zero employees, except for family assistance, I earn less than Facebook's annual revenue, temporarily, and I don't get paid every Friday like I did when I worked part-time or full-time jobs. I usually receive a monthly or, sometimes, bi-monthly check from KDP based on my book sales. So, if I sell a few books, I receive a percentage of the sales in my bank account. If not, I don't receive anything. However, if I sell books in person, at a book signing, or at a local event, I receive direct pay, which varies depending on the event, the audience size, and the cost of each book.

With my first book, *Run Your Business in Ten Essentials for 365 Days and Beyond*, I sold very few copies, but I didn't give up. I sought ways to improve my writing skills, book presentation, book titles, and overall book business with faith, determination, and resilience. When I lost, I bounced up and tried again—with greater purpose and gratitude for opportunities to reach my goals, sell more books, and produce more powerful book titles.

I didn't give up like many do when they don't sell as many books as they desire, gain a million followers and readers, or self-publish the book of their dreams. I accepted my call to write books for a living with a commitment to God that there was no giving up or turning back on a path that wasn't in His will for my life. I pushed through every unexpected obstacle you could think of as an inexperienced author and business owner. I knew that, over time, God would continue to open doors and grow my passion and desire not only to inspire others but also to glorify His name.

Since then, I've grown to embrace God's blessings and will for every situation in my life—not overnight but one day at a time. I used to clock in on computers and registers that recorded every second of my life, including lunch breaks when I worked in corporate, at fast food restaurants, and in the educational system. Not anymore, at least for the time being, unless God sees fit. Lord knows I got tired of that routine, with hopes of shifting away from being monitored for eight hours or, sometimes, less. I say this with humility and confidence, unapologetically, because it's the raw truth. Being ten minutes late had an impact on my check, as did clocking in late from lunch. I became unhappy and unsatisfied and knew God was working in my favor to get me to a place of satisfaction sooner or later.

For those wondering about my new journey, I don't only somewhat like my career or kind of like what I'm doing in my new chapter. I'm in love with where God shifted me and everything that comes with being a Black and sassy creative woman who loves to write about her experiences and topics that interest the world while helping others have the courage to share theirs; to write stories and self-publish because it does the body beyond good. It has a significant impact on the human body and, of course, it's promising, unlike traditionally publishing a book. I had a choice to overlook being fired or to offer hope to those who'd just lost their jobs and needed encouragement on their journey of this painful experience. So, I did; I have faith I made one of the wisest decisions in my life. Not only am I proud of myself, but I'm more grateful to God for His grace, will, and guidance.

What's funny is that one of the hardest things I struggled with when I started my business was speaking out about *behind-the-scenes*—the story, the day my job was taken unexpectedly. Who goes around telling the whole damn world they just lost their job and now what? Well, many do—for whatever reasons. I don't know why it happens, but it was hard for me. So, writing captured my heart; it gave me the greatest opportunity to share so much on paper that I never imagined until it happened. I went for it with courage like a *badass* woman. I wasn't so concerned about having a business as much as I desired to share my thoughts and feelings on paper with strangers, family, friends, and those in need. Every time I faced obstacles, I reminded myself about *who* rescued me from an unhealthy lifestyle that could have taken my life and *why* I am so passionate about writing stories and sharing them with the world.

Knowing my *who* and *why* motivates me and keeps me spiritually focused. Here's a secret: I love my purpose and calling more than I ever imagined. I am not a millionaire, a woman with a perfect lifestyle and credit score; a business owner with her bills all paid up and zero debt; an entrepreneur who has it all together and knows every single solution on the planet. Nope! As a matter of fact, it's deeper than that. I never dreamt of having the perfect life in which I didn't have to work to earn a living, strive to succeed, and grow. I knew success required effort, determination, and a commitment to never give up. I never prayed to God to "have it all together" because I knew it wasn't a desire. I was certain it would be stressful trying to fake it until I looked like someone who appeared to have the perfect life. However, if it was God's will for me to earn as much as I had ever made or prayed for, then I'd gladly and humbly accept His will. Other than that, I knew my worth and the value I was blessed to have and deliver to others. I wasn't just anyone; I was somebody special, wonderfully and fearfully made, and highly favored. No one could change my mind except God, who transformed my walk and restored my spirit.

Writing books and helping others sharpen their writing skills to craft together and deliver something interesting about their lives felt good to me from day one. Since that morning, God has woken me out of unconsciousness, from being asleep to an unimaginable place deeper than my wildest dreams. It was all fulfilling, and that was the truth. I needed to get myself together because I was broken, not torn. I was fixable, and I had faith. I was motivated and encouraged to glorify God and experience satisfaction in His will. I was no longer alive or sucking up air because I had to. I was now living on purpose and for a greater reason, consciously, and I was grateful for such an experience.

In my shoes, it's nowhere easy. As a matter of fact, it's more challenging than having a team of a hundred employees. I've been running my business since the morning God revealed my calling, and I've been "open" ever since. In April 2018, I started my book business as Visible Voice Oh Yes LLC but later, I removed the LLC for personal reasons. Years later, I changed my business to my full name: Kala Jordan-Lindsey. I performed my first poetry and prose read that month in front of a small audience because I had the desire to share my story about the life event I experienced and to encourage others that they weren't alone. It was amazing! Sometimes, I look back on that very first engagement that God blessed on my heart to put together and thank Him. I was determined to speak out and share my story to help others who also experienced a difficult job loss, failure, storm, or unexpected life event. I knew it would make an impact from that day on, no matter how many showed up. I started and didn't give up.

I was motivated to move forward despite what I recently faced and the investment I had to put into this journey. That afternoon, I touched lives, encouraged many, and, most importantly, glorified God. Discouragement, frustration, and hurt could have stopped me from standing up from rock bottom, but it didn't. I chose to move forward with my life in pain, disappointment, and change. It was one of the best decisions I made, and I'm proud of myself for being brave; for being courageous; for being strong; for being resilient. No matter what you face in life, know that you have the power and strength to rise and overcome your obstacles with effort and faith. It's a mindset I've learned to embrace the more I struggle and face unexpected storms. It's key to find ways to think positively and push through some of the most difficult things in life. Stay focused, as otherwise, the distractions of the world and what others are doing will discourage you. Find peace, joy, and fulfillment in your calling, in your purpose and assignment here on earth, and nurture it with gratitude and appreciation. If you abandon it, you'll become depressed, frustrated, angry, or lost because now you're no longer executing your passion. You must embrace your precious calling that God blessed only you to pursue and share with the world. Otherwise, your voice will remain on mute. No one will hear you, recognize you, and value what you have to offer. You can do it. Motivate yourself. Celebrate your accomplishments. Be courageous. Don't be afraid to live on purpose and pour out all you were built to do—unapologetically.

I've been writing, self-publishing, organizing book signings, participating in conferences and other events, assisting others with their book-writing journey, and building my business brand one day at a time, and it has been a blessing. However, as with any major shift or change in life, my new direction hasn't been easy or a piece of cake that melts in your mouth. I no longer earn a paycheck; instead, I earn most of my living through every product or book I write and self-publish, which isn't as easy as it sounds. My books and services are my earnings, so I'm constantly brainstorming new book titles and writing books to grow my business and increase my earnings. During the week, I work on multiple books and prepare future titles so that I can grow my library, which I enjoy and embrace. Every moment I get to write a book, jot down notes, or complete a manuscript is satisfying and motivates me to keep going for a greater purpose.

I had to change my lifestyle and shift my mindset, to change gears. If I want to continue earning a living and making money, I must constantly produce books, find book clients for consultations, participate in vendor opportunities, provide an editing service, etc.

I am the product, so unless I create books and provide services, I earn zero, which I experience some months. Every month or two, I receive a royalty check.

Over time, my frame of mind changed from a *corporate way of thinking* to an *independent, creative's way of thinking*; the "clock-in at 9, fifteen- to thirty-minute lunch break, and clock-out at 5" routine, plus overtime, shifted to a *constant producing mode to earn a living and survive*. Everything I do, from the time God blesses me with another chance to live and pursue my purpose from the time I fall asleep, consists of producing, writing books, brainstorming my next works, watching videos of encouragement on YouTube, revising manuscripts, editing, helping clients share their stories, posting encouraging messages on social media, and doing anything related to executing my calling. It isn't easy; it's a daily process that requires prayer, strength, resilience, determination, passion, motivation, and focus to achieve my goals—to climb higher than I did yesterday and fulfill my assignment on earth.

I've also realized my outlook on life and social circle has changed and continues to do so the closer I get to Christ and develop as an individual, woman, wife, mother, and author. Often, I find myself switching gears to concentrate if I'm distracted or when I experience unexpectedness. At the same time, I am growing with more love and appreciation for my reality—a hundred percent more than yesterday. Every day isn't promised, each moment passes by like the wind, and time never stops. So, every chance I have above ground as I operate in my purpose, I'm thankful. I cherish every experience, moment, and memory like a valuable keepsake and my loved ones.

Earning a living in my shoes has been a challenge, especially with little exposure as a Black indie author, but it's not impossible for those who have a God-given calling to write books, own a publishing business, or create valuable content for an audience. I encourage you to go for it and let negativity from others motivate you to stand firm and accomplish your goals. It's possible. With confidence, pursue your purpose and the calling God reveals to you. Commit to executing your passion for His glory, and never give up. In your tough seasons and days of confusion, God will grace you to gain stamina, resilience, and power to help you rise and get through adversity and mental war when doubt or fear attacks your heart. Transitioning from a lifestyle in which I received bi-weekly, weekly, or even monthly income to earning as I self-publish books or create products and assist aspiring writers has been a journey—a mental and physical adjustment. I am constantly striving to find ways to generate recurring streams of income. Before my turning point, I didn't have to work as hard as I do now to earn a paycheck. I earned a stable income, and sometimes a bonus check and salary increase, if I performed my duties and worked my hours. I didn't have to write books to earn a living because I worked for others. I gladly accepted my earnings and looked forward to receiving them again— the same amount or more, not less.

Today, I'm a full-time author, but my earnings aren't a typical full-time, forty hours of set pay. This means how I earn my income is quite different from how someone who works at a grocery store or teaches full-time at a university earns an income. Writing books full-time as a dedicated entrepreneur demands more time, energy, strength, and commitment to consistency. It requires a *selfless and unique mindset* to accomplish goals and daily tasks and persevere when there is a loss or no sales, clients, or traffic.

Writing books, self-publishing, and booking clients for a consultation or editing service is my happy space and contributes to my weekly or monthly earnings when it's successful—done the right way. It also touches lives. I don't receive income unless a product or products are sold, so I am constantly repeating the *KJL earnings formula* and a *unique strategy* for earning royalties from book sales for a lifetime. It starts with faith, nothing less, or else you'll bury your experiences and wealth in the ground.

Writing books and self-publishing is satisfying and worth every moment of my life, but it requires a different *mindset discipline* to succeed, focus, gain, and grow. It allows me to be creative, produce the most interesting and inspirational books, and build a legacy.

My journey has been a roller coaster but amazing with the help and strength of God. It has been one with blessings and benefits, with more ups than downs; one with unexpected grace from my Heavenly Father. From day one, I taught myself how to do a lot of unusual and uncomfortable tasks while exercising my innate skills and knowledge. Every challenge has been rewarding and fulfilling. I spend my time, days, energy, and earnings wisely and enjoy every part of my business, especially writing, which is more precious than gold or anything that isn't in God's plans for my life.

However, troubleshooting through life isn't always easy. Sometimes, it can be a headache, like the week I didn't have a Wi-Fi connection. I fought to fix technical issues days before a book event in May 2023. It took more than I imagined and encouragement from my husband to push through and do the best I could to solve the matter, which I did by the grace of God. I was on the edge of buying a new cellular phone because my memory storage was maxed out and there was nothing else I could think of to troubleshoot my way to getting what I needed. Thankfully, my husband offered a great suggestion, and it worked. Hours after so much confusion and frustration, God's grace blessed me with everything I needed to have a successful event the next day.

Troubleshooting can be a challenge if you're clueless about what to do or how to handle unexpected situations. If the issue looks impossible, you freak out and feel lost and confused. But listen to me: There is hope even in the middle of chaos and struggles. Never doubt. Have faith no matter what.

In some cases, you might feel discouraged or even hopeless, especially after you've tried multiple times to overcome a problem. What I've learned through experience or trial and error is that if I am struggling to overcome a task or job, I must not focus on the problem and never give up. I must embrace the challenge, gain, grow, and learn. If it takes you a week or longer to figure out an issue, push through it but not alone. Pray and ask God for strength, patience, and direction, and explore all you can while you fight your way to success. Remember: You didn't get this far to fail. You're doing great, so keep it up and keep striving for excellence.

From day one in starting my book business, I have continued to learn and apply the knowledge and skills I obtain and have primarily for the glory of God; to offer wisdom to others along the way while building my legacy and book business for generations to come. I'm certain my writings will inspire others and make an impact for as long as the earth rotates, the sun rises, the birds chirp, and the sun sets.

I develop titles and content for my books based on thoughts, experiences, current events, issues, different environments, storms, and everyday circumstances. I'm observant, so my brain is constantly brainstorming ideas for books to write, including content, to share with you to enrich your life and help you embrace yours ten times more.

Months after I started writing in 2018, I wanted to create a website to help market and share my story, but money was an issue; we didn't have the funds to hire someone to create a website. So, my spouse and I prayed about it, and I decided to teach myself how to design and build a website. During the week, I browsed other authors' websites to get a general idea of what to include, watched YouTube videos, and Googled information on how to create a website, and it helped; my efforts and determination to create something valuable for others and help spread the word about my story and grow my book business were inspired by the discovery of my calling, and I thank God I didn't give up. I was humbled by the website I created—a blessing that was original, creative, and engaging.

After sleepless nights, long nights and mornings, and perseverance, I saw the glory of God and the progress of my website, and I smiled. I was thrilled and motivated to do more with my God-given skills, talents, and abilities, and I had faith God would continue to make a way out of no way for me to succeed.

I received positive feedback from my husband, family, friends, and readers on how creative and professional the website looked. That made my day! Days later, I shared my new website link on my social media pages and with family and friends, and I noticed traffic.

I was thankful because God had blessed me to do something that many fear and doubt due to a lack of faith. He empowered me with the courage to create something powerful that would help others while glorifying His name. God's grace, mercy, and favor worked through my situation, which could have turned into a stumbling block but didn't. Instead, it motivated me to trust in the Lord with all my heart. My God blessed me and satisfied my heart's desires.

Each day, I worked on different sections of my website and added general segments to make it as professional as possible. And I performed this task with no experience and background in website design.

As an entrepreneur, I prepare monthly newsletters, social media write-ups, assist clients on their book-writing journey, prepare other marketing materials and videos, and offer a seasonal developmental editing service. My duties are time-consuming, and it requires patience, focus, rest, energy, and flexibility. Most important is faith. *Your business is bound to function as you treat your mind, heart, and soul—it has the potential to become malnourished, stand without purpose, and be weak. You might become discouraged, or give up. But no matter what, be resilient and keep the faith. Keep going. You will succeed.*

When I started my book business, I began from scratch. I had nothing to begin the journey. The only thing I could do was activate and execute what God had built in my heart to release through the tips of my fingers. This took a different level of faith and focus, which wasn't a piece of cake. However, to share the "good news" about my calling, I was moved to take a risk, invest, and dedicate my time. I did this by the grace and mercy of God, especially during my first trial of creating a website. I had no website experience, so I Googled "how to create an author website" and, as I mentioned, browsed the sites of a handful of other professional authors, and it helped! However, I desired to be authentic and create one from nothing. I wanted something unique and engaging.

My desire to write, self-publish, and share my stories motivated my spirit and was greater than my inability to create something perfect. My obstacles fueled my heart to persevere, and I did so from the day I picked up my phone and started writing.

Some of the challenges I experience and strive to overcome as a self-published author are getting exposure, new clients, and opportunities to share my books and services with a wider audience. I've noticed that the rich and famous or those with significant views and subscribers receive the spotlight or exposure over others. That's a fact. However, this reality hasn't affected my love and passion for consistently writing and doing the best I can do with the grace, mercy, and strength God gives me daily. Because I'm an indie author, most of the work involved in getting my books in front of an audience falls on me. I am constantly updating information and troubleshooting tasks during the week. The most fun and satisfying thing about this process has been taking on the challenge and being determined to improve my writing skills, grow my clientele, and build my library. However, at times, I wanted to give up because it seemed like so much work. When I decided to self-publish, I didn't realize the investment needed to start and run the business. I saw only the product or book, not the journey it took for the author to publish the book. Yet, grace made it happen. I'm a living testimony to the fact that, no matter what, "I can do everything through Christ, who gives me strength" (Philippians 4:13).

So, what's next? For years, I worked many 9-5 jobs. And no, not what you're thinking, ha-ha! I worked "real" jobs, a lot of them, in the corporate world, food industry, and education field. A handful of my work experiences were part-time and seasonal, or on-call. However, a few were full-time, in public, private, and institutional workplaces where I got my feet wet and settled, but not for long, unfortunately.

I constantly searched for steady, reliable work like a man who searches for life. Some jobs were okay and some I just wasn't interested in. However, as I reflect, I'm sure God had greater reasons; I'm convinced the calls I didn't receive weren't God's will and that the emails replying, *Unfortunately, we've decided to move to the next candidate*, were triggers to greater blessings and new beginnings to come. I started to realize this as I received more of them. As a matter of fact, I stopped applying because I had faith that God was trying to tell me to stop worrying about a job and start focusing on what He had already created for me to pursue and execute: my calling.

Since then, God has continued to provide and make a way for my family and me to survive. We're not millionaires yet, but that's no worry. We're trusting in God to continue to bless us with an increase in all areas of our lives, and we believe it will continue to happen.

If you are job hunting, don't worry about rejection or all the phone calls and emails you don't receive. Celebrate and keep it moving! Stay positive. If you have faith, you'll understand that God is working in your life and through your circumstances to prepare you for His best yes; His best deliverance for you for His glory and your benefit. What you don't have might be what you didn't need in the first place—whether it's a relationship, job, career, or pay raise. God knows best. He knows what He's doing and where He's shifting you because He created your life, story, and destination. Trust in His will, and everything will be alright one day at a time. You'll receive what's for you no matter how long or wherever you are on earth. God is sovereign and mighty and has all the power in His hands to do the unimaginable, to turn your darkness into a path of light.

I've experienced being out of work for nearly a year and sometimes longer. However, not only did these stumbling blocks not halt my efforts to push forward and be resilient, but God gave me confirmation in the middle of many situations or times when I was without work; He said, "Everything will be okay."

I've been in situations in which I was desperate for work and thought about settling for anything just for the pay. However, I knew I wouldn't be happy; it would be temporary satisfaction. I experienced it every time I deviated from my calling. I received the same old response. Either I didn't meet the qualifications or the job description seemed too demanding, so I didn't move forward, or the employer moved forward with the next candidate. I wasn't comfortable or happy. I continued to let God's will control my steps. What's so amazing yet eye-opening is that each time I thanked Him for my calling and focused on my true passion, I felt His confirmation; I felt a whisper over my life from my God—one that always guided me in the right direction.

On the other hand, I'm beyond excited and grateful to have landed on this page at a time in my life when it took more than I'd ever imagined to make it here, to arrive at such a stop, in a new chapter of my life. I never dreamt of sitting at my desk for hours writing and building a book business, building a website from scratch, and assisting others along the way. Nowhere on my desk, in my journals, or on my phone will you find this dream. But I think the power of God is amazing and too great to understand. Where I am now changed my mind and life. It's an experience I hope and pray you witness as well.

I am convinced God knows I'm just as excited as you are about sharing many more years of my unexpected journey and experiences, book-related stuff, and book releases. Thank you for letting me be genuine. I think one of the hardest things about writing a nonfiction book is releasing the truth; sharing with courage over doubt; encouraging others in your own pain, hurt, or storms; and motivating others with hope where you are. I certainly look forward to settling here for a while until retirement, ha-ha! I pray that you gain, grow, and give to others during this journey with me. We're all works in progress and need encouragement every breath we take. He carried me on the other side, and I'm forever grateful. I can exhale. I'm free. Yes! To God be the glory.

# Chapter 14

# My New Chapter

*"No one lands anywhere by mistake; I don't believe your experiences happen without reason, except for a greater purpose."*

**-Kala**

I'm here now after walking for years in the same chapter, the same circle of life, to God be the glory. He finally blessed me to experience a thorn that opened my eyes and graced me to enter a new stage of my journey, a different direction than where I was headed. I've entered a new beginning that feels good and nothing less, a new position with a different mindset, appreciation, and a clearer perspective on life. I am overjoyed and grateful because I made it to my long-awaited destination—not just anywhere on purpose, not to the end of my journey, but to a new chapter of my life. It's a place I'm experiencing only by the grace and mercy of God—the power of pursuing my calling.

So, when you see me around town at your local library, on social media, sharing some encouragement on YouTube, writing at my desk, at a conference with my favorite pen, signing books, giving a book talk, or doing anything book-related, know it's not happening by luck or chance but by the grace and will of God. Not only am I grateful, but I also have joy in my heart because I'm still here and still standing.

My walk is living proof that God made no mistake in my turning point. I realized God was stirring up something bigger and greater than my imagination to get me here, at this phase of my life. The next time you encounter unexpectedness or a difficult situation, be encouraged to know God is preparing to bless you with a "wow" experience. He's permitting something beyond your understanding. He's blessing you to experience a "new thing." He's doing something amazing in your life, something you might not understand until after He gets you to where you need to be. That's so true. So, if you're not there, it's okay. You'll get there one day, Lord willing. We're all striving to get somewhere in life, at a place of peace. Stay hopeful and never give up on the desire to experience this "wow." When things seem dark, seek the Light, prayer, and God's word. He'll help you and guide you in your new chapter. He'll comfort you and lift you when you're down. He'll strengthen you when you're too weak to say or do anything.

I chose to trust His will over my situation and new "change" despite the obstacles I faced along the way. So can you if you want to enjoy all the benefits of experiencing true love, joy, peace, and happiness; if you want to experience fulfillment like never before; if you want to gain the courage to make an impact in the lives of others.

On that note, I am humbled to say I am finally enjoying my life like never before after years of desiring to be free like a caged bird. However, I am still a work in progress; I am climbing Jacob's ladder daily, and it's satisfying for many reasons: 1) I get to enjoy the process. 2) I get to take on unforeseen challenges along the way. 3) I'm learning and gaining in the process. 4) I get to experience God's grace. 5) I get to testify and share the goodness of God. It's an experience worth having.

I have freedom, and you can experience the same. I can breathe and have a burden lifted off my shoulders and removed from my life, and you can taste the same. I don't have all the answers, nor do I have it all together, and nor am I perfect. However, I am better, stronger, and wiser than I was yesterday, years ago, glory to God! I once was lost, but now I'm found. I once was blind, but by the grace of God, I can finally see. And I'm certain it's not a fluke; I didn't make it here by mistake or by rolling an eight-ball. God's plan overpowered mine, and that's a fact. So, what am I saying? I strongly believe God allows us to "go through," "cope with," "struggle with," and "experience" unexpected storms in life not only to shift us to where we need to be but also to bring us closer to Him and closer to our destination; to glorify Him; to open our eyes to the power of His sovereignty, grace, and mercy; to carry us exactly where we need to be without destroying us; and to elevate us when we're at our lowest. So, this is a new chapter not only in *The Turning Point* but also in my life. I'm humbled and overjoyed that I arrived safely, especially because it could have turned out otherwise. It could have been, should have been, or would have been a total wreck, but grace rescued me at the right time.

Can you think about a recent life storm you faced? If so, how did you handle it? Even better, have you ever realized the best part about experiencing this major life event is the blessings in the middle of the storm? Did you consider this could have been the best thing to have happened, that if you hadn't lost your home, you would not have had the chance to meet your spouse and pay off debt?

I am certain God knew my journey before I was delivered from my mother's womb. In fact, He created the pages of my life before my life was written. How awesome! Often, when we face obstacles in life, we're shocked; when life happens, we never expect the unexpected because we assume it doesn't fit us or "this isn't me." But ladies and gentlemen, storms were designed for a greater reason beyond human understanding. Our unexpectedness is created so perfectly that God is never amazed at anything. We remain clueless as to why an event happened or why things are falling apart.

Life happens for us to give God the praise, glory, and honor for His grace and mercy and His unfailing love. God knew in advance that I'd arrive at this "new chapter" in my life. He knew I needed this new chapter before the turning point in my life. He knew my pain would bring Him glory. He knew my depression would bring Him honor and praise through my deliverance. My Heavenly Father knew I'd submit to my calling not just for my pleasure and joy but also to help others; to offer hope and encouragement to those who are weak and tired of being tired; to be the vessel that testifies to the goodness and grace of God after hell storms or even success; to inspire many with a reason to keep going and embrace their imperfect journeys. He knew I'd impact and touch lives. He knew I'd encourage millions around the world by sharing an unbelievable and unimaginable story. Memoirs offer a different perspective on life. My Father knew what I needed to heal my mind, body, and soul.

Often, we miss the "bigger picture" in our life storms because we're so focused on the problem. The drama and mess attract our hearts more than our Heavenly Father, who's our Rescue. We assume our circumstances will get better if we keep our attention on the issue rather than pray and trust in the Lord for deliverance. I encourage you to focus on Jesus in the storms of your life. They're created to test your faith but also to strengthen your faith. Rejoice with confidence and have faith that our Lord is taking you higher. He's carrying you to a new chapter in your life. Embrace every moment—the good and bad, the happy and sad, and the difficult ones.

You must cope with each page of your life with hope and sound faith in the Lord—and never waver. Trust in the process and never give up. And give God all the praise and glory for your story—the one He created before your eyes opened.

I never thought I'd experience something like this. It's hard to believe, but it's the truth; it's my reality and I'm finally okay with it. I'm inspired by my own story. Be encouraged to know: "But those who trust in the Lord will find new strength. They will soar high on wings like eagles. They will run and not grow weary. They will walk and not faint" (Isaiah 40:31). Keep the faith when the Lord says, "For I am about to do something new. See, I have already begun! Do you not see it? I will make a pathway through the wilderness. I will create rivers in the dry wasteland" (Isaiah 43:19). I believe in His word and embrace it all on my journey. To grow, you must start doing the same no matter how challenging it might be. Submission to Christ is vital, or you'll stop growing like a flower without sunlight and water. I experienced life, but I was determined to continue to grow in my pain no matter what happened.

Are you equipped with the Armor of God and determined to grow in your hardships, storms, or unexpectedness? Without it, expect to struggle in a way that might lead to disappointment. With the Armor of God, my life hasn't been anywhere close to perfect, but my journey has been a blessing. Pursuing anything in life requires faith.

When God does it, He does it big, on purpose, and with purpose. If you're experiencing a life event, have faith; be convinced that God is preparing you to do great things, a "new thing" in your life—a blessing that will glorify Him and help others along the way. When this happens, God will continue to enhance your life; He'll fill your life with blessings on top of blessings. You're bound to make an impact and help open human eyes. Believe it and expect God's best along the way, even during your storms. I never expected to face a turning point, but I did, and it was one of the greatest things that could have happened in my life.

It's funny how God works in mysterious ways. Ever since I was a child, I have loved to write. Reading wasn't my strongest point; I struggled with this thing called reading comprehension. We fought like two boxers in the ring, and it took me a while to improve and win. Learning to read was challenging, like riding the tricycle in kindergarten. It was hard, but I persevered. I embraced this hindrance. I was determined and took every opportunity as a blessing to improve my reading and writing skills. I tried, and that's what matters. I loved to write, which allowed me to express my thoughts and feelings without using my voice. This continued for years. Later, I continued to have a passion for writing. One of my dreams was to build a music school, so I wrote a business plan, which was fun! Then, I journaled for some time and started writing regularly in high school, through college, and afterward, especially when I began to struggle with life and face unexpected hardships.

I released my feelings on the page, which felt good. It was fulfilling. It gave me comfort and relief. When I was a professor, I organized and authored a 300-page PowerPoint and provided original, supplemental material to my students; it worked and made a great impact. I fell in love with it, but after I became pregnant, I resigned and stopped writing regularly. That wasn't the end, though; after I experienced an unexpected storm, when my teaching position was wrongfully terminated, my life changed. Months later, I picked up my phone and began to write. I haven't stopped, and I never will until God says, "Well done." Now, this new chapter in my life hasn't always been easy; I struggled along the way, but I continued to release my gift and passion on paper. I continued to write and self-publish my life experiences. I say this because I believe God has a way of stirring up a new thing in your life on purpose so He can put fire in you to help open eyes and touch lives; so you can carry out His will such that others may praise, glorify, and honor Him as well.

# Chapter 15

# *When Things Happen*

*"My life experiences—the good and the uncomfortable accounts of my journey—inspired me to turn my memoirs of encouragement to help and heal your heart and offer hope to you on your amazing yet unpredictable walk. Be inspired because you were born to fail and overcome life on purpose; to be human and face what God has planned for you to get you where you need to be. So, give yourself grace and celebrate anyway."*

*-Kala*

As I reflect on my personal and professional experiences over the past decade, I am convinced there were no mistakes on my journey, not one, not even if I changed my mind minutes before things popped off in my life. Now that I'm older, my outlook on life is not the same as it once was. My viewpoint on life circumstances is different now because I have experience and a deeper, more intimate relationship with the Lord than I ever had.

No one knows what their life would be like if they were to go back in time and erase everything bad, uncomfortable, or unpleasant about their journey to make it perfect. It's impossible to relive what you've experienced unless you're writing a book, sharing your story, or acting in a movie. No human being on earth has the power to relive yesterday in order to correct the mistake they made and thereby white out what has already happened. If we had this power, I think many would do things differently. However, I wouldn't, as I believe unexpectedness, unforeseen life events, or life storms are created for that individual and for greater reasons, which sometimes takes years to even partially understand.

I thank God for my uncomfortable and satisfying experiences in life because things could have been worse; a lot of other things could have happened, but God saw fit for them not to. He graced me with enough strength to hold on, endure, and embrace my imperfect journey unapologetically and with gratitude for the opportunities to encourage you to never think less about your crazy, unbelievable, difficult life. You must see the bigger picture in everything you experience. Each day is a blessing.

The loss of a job dear to my heart in 2017 hit differently. It touched my life in a way unlike any other difficult experience. It made me think twice about getting my life together and developing a closer relationship not only with the Lord but also with my husband, daughter, and family. I desired to improve my mental, physical, and spiritual health, so I made a commitment to the Lord that I would do better with His help and strength.

I remember sitting in a room with school officials, strangers, and familiar faces, trying to decide: Should I fight and go through more hell, backlash, and stress than I was already experiencing, or should I let go and let God direct my next steps, my path? This was by far one of the most difficult decisions ever and one that I knew would impact my life. So, that morning, I prayed silently and informed my attorney I did not want to take this case to trial without providing him with all the details. My decision to do this was between me and the Lord, my God. Afterward, I felt a sense of relief, and a weight lifted off my shoulders. I looked at my attorney and took a deep breath. **The experience was like God whispered to me, "Let it go. Everything will be okay. I will handle your enemies and bless you with peace beyond their imagination. I got you, so don't worry. You have won the fight. Move on."** When this happened, God comforted my spirit, calmed my soul, and gave me more than a hundred reasons to trust in His will for my life and embrace where He was carrying me. I left not getting what I wanted, but I walked away and gained more than the disturbance—losing a job in a career field I'd studied for over fifteen years. I had a new spirit, mindset, and desire to worship Christ more than ever.

Before my struggles and unexpected life events destroyed me, God intervened. He stopped me in the middle of my plans, tore me into pieces, and allowed what I thought were the worst situations ever to open my eyes. After I discovered my calling, He slowly put me back together, renewed my mind, and restored my stubborn, imperfect heart. It was like watching a surgeon close an incision after open heart surgery, and it gave me a reason to follow Him, not my flesh; to have faith; to glorify Him; to praise and worship His holy name. Choosing to let God take the wheel of my life and direct my path was an experience like no other. It changed my life. He removed the veil from my life and gave me a reason to activate my faith—not in myself but in Him.

When things happen, like uncomfortable experiences in life, or when something unexpected occurs, it's normal to freak out or become shocked. Many people become emotional—upset, sad, or angry. That's life. Everyone experiences this at some point on their journey. However, often, those who think carnally, without thinking about God, who has the power to turn their unbelievable situations around, give up or lose their minds.

I've realized that, when uncomfortable things happen in life, the "thorn or pain" impacts the mind and sometimes leaves one feeling hopeless, like it's all over. It might seem impossible to stand up and persevere, or overcome life. The heart becomes weak, and the individual lacks the motivation and energy to do anything and move forward. Like a pinch, the heart is attacked and feels like a weight is overpowering victory. This leaves faith as the last resort, and better days impossible to envision—in the moment.

If you experience this, beware. It's a FALSE MENTAL TRIGGER—one that attacks every human being and overpowers one's thoughts and actions unless you use your weapon: faith. When this happens, think about the goodness of God; think spiritually. Read a Scripture, go to a quiet place and pray, and activate your faith, not fear. With a firm foundation in the Lord, God will bless you with peace even in the middle of a life storm. He will let His word sustain your mind, heart, and soul. You will be okay.

If you can relate, you are never alone. I experienced this for years until I realized I was unconsciously walking in darkness; I was spiritually blind and did everything without the guidance of the Holy Spirit. Like a drunkard, I wasn't living the life of the person whom God built me to be. I was all over the place; I didn't walk in sync with my Heavenly Father because I wore a veil for years, which caused me to suffer and struggle within. Some years, I felt like I was the only person in the ring fighting to live and survive. I bumped my head more than fifty times and put myself in a lot of preventable situations. However, I strongly believe I had to experience pain for the power and grace of God to rescue me, to put me on a healthier path.

When things happened, I did more than freak out. I panicked and experienced anxiety because I didn't have a strong relationship with God and wasn't seeking His obedience to get back on track. I got baptized and became a Christian, but my actions didn't prove my faith. I was an individual who desired a breakthrough, a change that would bless my walk and improve my lifestyle. However, I didn't know what to do, so I continued to struggle without God. Yeah, I prayed, but it wasn't authentic and specific because I didn't know how to pray and communicate with God.

I went to church, but my worship with God was weaker than the muscles in my body and my health. I thought church was simply going to a building, putting money in a brown basket, singing, hearing the Word, and repeating the same thing each Sunday. I didn't understand communion, offering back to God, fellowshipping and developing healthy relationships with others, and serving God. However, when I hit the ground again and faced another storm, I craved a closer relationship with God. I wanted to know Him and what I needed to do to improve my life.

Do you worry about a thousand things, like what's next and how you're going to survive or make it through difficult health or illness? Do you stress about bills and earning enough to take care of your family and retire? When you lost your job, did you lose your mind, attempt suicide, or run to your friends? When I faced this difficult time in my life, I chose to not run to everyone in my circle, outside of it, in my family, or even my husband. I knew it was time for me to surrender my life to the Lord, so I ran to Him. I knew He already knew what had happened, why it had happened, and how He would deliver me from this scary, dark tunnel. I trusted Him with all my mind, heart, and soul.

Are you one of the handful of people who also hesitate to move forward with their lives, who experience fear or even doubt God's sovereign power, His remarkable hands? If you can relate, don't feel embarrassed or ashamed. Also, there's no need to point fingers, as we all experience seasons of discomfort and difficulty. Relax and don't lose your mind; you need it like the air we breathe. I almost lost mine, but the grace of God held me, comforted me, and strengthened my heart and mind before I lost control.

When unusual things happen, stay calm and pray. See the good and blessings in your mess, the chaos, and the situations out of your hands. Get in Christ and never abandon your relationship with Him. There's always a better way to cope with or handle uneasy situations in life. There are also lessons to be learned, wisdom to gain, and life nuggets to appreciate when you face terrible times like the season you're in now. Think positive and use unexpectedness as a blessing to grow and gain in the middle of your afflictions.

When you experience rejection like a credit card denial, job loss, or relationship refusal, see the bigger picture. Look beyond what's in front of you and what you are going through. It wasn't easy for me, but through prayer and letting God have His way in my loss, I began to think spiritually and see the overall image of the problem. So, from here on out, look at whatever is bothering you, terrifying you, or getting the best of you as a blessing and grace from God.

My denial from my teaching position and a second chance to teach at this educational institution prepared me for God's best for my life and destination.

The next time you receive a *no*, be happy and grateful. Not only is this circumstance getting you ready for a redirection closer to where God sees fit, but something amazing will happen in your life, and your story will encourage and inspire many. Yes! The experience that you thought was horrible will be the one that touches lives and does the remarkable, even for your enemies. I'm living proof, a survivor of the goodness and grace of God in what should have been but didn't happen to destroy my soul. Instead, this unbelievable event turned my life around and blessed me ten times more than I had ever imagined, to God be the glory.

So, when you get to your lowest, know that your neighbor and I have been there and experienced most of the effects of loss, hardship, struggle, or chaos that you're facing. Have faith without wavering or being concerned about whether things will work out according to your plans. When you make a U-turn in the middle of a storm, have faith that God is guiding you in a better direction.

Trust in God's plans, and you'll experience more joy, peace, and happiness on your journey in life, even when things don't go your way. Trust His word more than your intuition. God knows best and never makes mistakes. If your employer lets you go or fires you unexpectedly, it will hurt and cause you pain *if you understand*, but don't be discouraged. God's will is greater and more powerful than you think. Don't panic.

If you're a person who worries, then reflect on all the many ways you're blessed and a survivor. Ask yourself, "Why do I worry?" and find ways to improve your mental health or position yourself in a healthier state of mind. Otherwise, you'll drain your overall well-being—seriously. So, be encouraged and smile. Don't let the bad stuff or struggles of life get you down. Rise. Pray. Have faith and trust in the guidance of the Creator. When things happen, don't complain. Embrace your imperfections, and God will continue to bless you with His wisdom to carry you through the storm(s). God will turn your denial into one of your greatest yeses. Yes! You'll experience peace like never before and a happy heart, as I did!

He has the power to turn chaos and a disaster into a story that changes lives and offers hope to those who feel like giving up; to those who want to quit; or to those who feel worthless and useless. When I first experienced my job loss, I had no idea what God was doing nor where I was headed—until I began writing this book and previously published books. The more I expressed myself and self-published, the more I felt a desire in my soul to spread the good news and light about the Light of the world. I started writing down my thoughts, the experience of receiving an uncomfortable email from a principal, and the mental headaches that went along with this unforgettable experience.

The word "no" is always hard to digest. It's like a slap in the face or a door slammed before your eyes. When denial rests in your ears, it's like a thorn in your flesh; it attacks your heart, and it never feels good. It's painful. However, through experience, it becomes powerful. There is always a purpose in rejection.

Things happen, and that's the truth. I've learned more than I ever imagined. It took me a while to realize that, but I thank God for bringing clarity to my life and allowing me to appreciate His will. However, to be realistic, the truth of the matter is that, for human beings, life isn't easy when we face something we never experienced. It's tough to digest. When things happen, we experience the unexpected, not expecting x, y, or x to occur. What do you do in circumstances like this? What have you done or how are you handling unforeseen things in life? Do you get upset or angry? Do you pray? Do you phone up a friend and complain and boo-hoo? Or do you do what many fear, look over, or desire not to do? I know it's not an easy answer because it wasn't for me at first.

I didn't know what the hell to do because I was so accustomed to experiencing the same old things that I naturally persevered. I was so used to struggling with life and going through difficulties that when things happened, it was not a huge shocker. I continued to embrace my mess and move on until I realized everything I was going through was for the glory of God, to help others, and for my good.

Once you reach a point in your life where you accept God's will and embrace situations when they happen, you'll start to see the good in all things and appreciate where you are; you'll start to have a better understanding of the storms you experience and a positive attitude toward the situation. I know it's easier said than done. So, over time, I've learned to accept and embrace my uncomfortableness twice as much as if I hadn't experienced something because I know it's powerful. I know who's really in control and has the power to fix my issues. I know there's only so much I can do by making wise choices. It's a battle I've chosen to leave in God's hands, like the life event I experienced in my last season.

At thirty-seven years old, I am no longer the person I was since birth. I am mentally, physically, and spiritually stronger and healthier than I was yesterday. However, I am not perfect. I am a work in progress and beyond grateful because God rescued me and saved me from near-death experiences.

When you experience pain, take a deep breath and let it propel you to enable the grace of God to work in and through your situation. Don't be afraid to discover His word, your passion, or ways to improve your life one day at a time. He can deliver you from any unhealthy situation or envirement and restore your life, health, strength, and spiritual vision. Have faith, and let your painful experiences carry you into a territory of more love, peace, joy, and happiness. God will turn your life around and open doors you never thought would open. With faith, God has the power to get you back on your feet and direct your path—from your thoughts to actions. He'll turn your stubborn ways into words of hope and encouragement to help and inspire others to turn their lives over to Him.

Today, I have a clearer perspective on life and am thankful for the greater purpose of the storm. I am one day better than the morning I faced change and experienced pain out of this world, mentally, physically, and emotionally.

This life event blessed me with more gain than loss, more strength than hurt, and more gratitude than expectation. Along the way, I've realized that God makes no errors in the things we face. He gives you power in your weakness for His glory. Our Creator knows our destination, and you should never feel ashamed or embarrassed about the difficult things you experience. When things happen, be encouraged to know you're never alone, but also realize things will happen when you least expect them to. I didn't expect to lose a job, but as I look back, I realize this experience was bound to happen. No matter the month, day, or year, this was going to happen. I would lose what I cherished the most, and there was nothing I could have done in the power of God's plans.

I believe when we experience unexpected life events, struggles, or pain, they're destined to happen no matter what we do, what we eat, or how many times we relocate to a new residence. Whatever you faced yesterday was planned to happen, and whatever you experience years from now was bound to happen. The amazing thing about it is that no one knows except God Himself, the Creator, who created every human being on the planet. When things happen that shock or frighten your spirit, you must relax, pray, stay calm, and know God is in control and will bless you to overcome your situations in His will with grace and mercy. If we knew what was headed our way, it wouldn't have the same impact as it does when we experience unexpected circumstances. When things happen, like an unforeseen life storm, it's never easy to digest, especially in the beginning. It's a process that takes time or even a lifetime for many. When you discover God's purpose for your life, be grateful and glorify Him; give it your all, commit to what God has called you to pursue and execute, and appreciate the powerful things God will have you do to inspire the world.

As I continue to strive and thrive in an imperfect world filled with possibilities, unexpectedness, and change, I've learned a lot of lessons through my complicated and fascinating life experiences. No matter what you experience—good or bad, pleasant or unpleasant—every experience is intended for your good because you are loved and created to live a happy, healthy, and spiritually rich life. The goal is not to hurt or harm you but to position you in a healthier, more satisfying place in life; to change your carnal thoughts into actions that produce obedience, right living, and a desire to follow Christ in the eyes of God; to equip and nourish your mind with God's wisdom for everyday life, obstacles, and painful experiences; to inspire you to discipline your mind in a way that pleases the Lord; to demolish your life and build one that reflects and models Christ; and to empower you to impact and touch the lives of others in a way that glorifies God.

# Author's Note

Thank you so much for reading my personal and inspirational memories, *The Turning Point: Memoirs of Determination, Hope, Faith, Loss, Love, and Resilience.* I hope your spirit is renewed, refreshed, and replenished with words of hope and encouragement to help you embrace God's will and grace on your unpredictable journey. Also, I hope He opens your eyes with a new perspective on uncomfortable situations you might experience. I pray that you embrace the transparency of my story and let your situations inspire you to unapologetically celebrate your turning point, calling, and success.

My life experiences ignited my heart with more gratitude and love than ever and led God to open my eyes in order to reveal my passion. In my pain, I discovered my greatest calling, and so can you. I'm a survivor and blessed to be a recipient of the goodness and greatness of God's grace, mercy, love, and favor.

Thank you so much for purchasing this book and for walking with me and gaining a greater appreciation for what God is doing and will do in your life on your phenomenal journey. If this book has touched your life, please consider leaving a review on Amazon, or recommending it to a friend, loved one, colleague, organization, church congregation, or educational institution.

Cheers to you for a happy, healthy, peaceful, satisfying, and prosperous journey in the Lord.

Love & Blessings,

**Kala Jordan-Lindsey**

# Acknowledgments

Writing the personal memoirs of my life took more courage and strength than I imagined. The process was challenging but fulfilling and more rewarding than the day I held my first book in my hands. None of this would have been possible without God, my Heavenly Father. I am thankful for the grace, mercy, and favor He blessed me with to release another part of my heart and for the opportunity to share my unsung stories with you, loved ones and strangers.

I am beyond grateful for the love of my life, my husband, Anthony Lindsey, who motivated me to go for it and complete this book. He cheered me on when he looked over my shoulders and congratulated me during every milestone of the process. He prayed for me and blessed my heart with God's word. He also supported me during the editing phase and assisted me with marketing tasks, including our beautiful daughter, Kamaria Lindsey. I am grateful for them both, for their contagious and creative spirits that motivated me to never give up on achieving my book publishing goals.

I am sincerely thankful for my close friend and sister in Christ, Dr. Belinda A. Dalton, who touched my life in unimaginable ways and inspired me on my journey to write one of the most inspirational and life-changing books of all time. She motivated me to take my writing to the next level and encouraged me with wisdom and great feedback. Since the afternoon we connected on LinkedIn, she became one of my first readers. Belinda is an ongoing loyal supporter, inspiration, and motivation in my life.

I am also genuinely grateful for my close friend and sister in Christ, Veidra Johnson, who inspired me in many ways to keep going and never give up despite my unexpected life event. She cheered me on, prayed for me, and continues to be a great example of a real friend and good-hearted sister in the Lord.

Writing a book about your life is a remarkable process and one of the most outstanding achievements ever. I'm forever thankful to my publishing team, including my phenomenal copyeditor, and developmental editor, Cassandra Vann, for their editorial assistance, honest feedback, and outstanding support in bringing my memories to life. They helped me from start to finish and blessed my life.

To my lovely parents, Jefferson and Evetta Grisby Jordan, who have been two of my biggest fans since day one. They have blessed me and been a part of my life journey since birth, and I'm forever grateful. They supported me during my music career and now in the new chapter of my writing journey.

And to my amazing and loyal readers. Thank you beyond a hundred percent for your support and special connections. Each one of you continues to make me smile and laugh, encourage me, and bless my life and new journey. Cheers to you and everyone above. God bless.

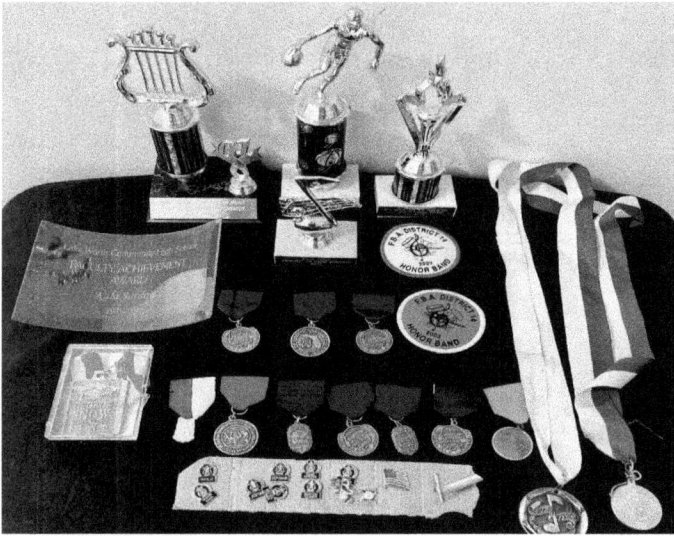

I received many academic and band awards, plaques, medals, and pins in middle and high school, including a trophy for participation in the Lake Worth High School 2002 Summer Basketball Camp.

I also received many academic and band certificates in middle and high school, including a spotlight in the Palm Beach Post and a certificate of participation in the Candlelight Processions and Massed Choir Program, in 2002.

My mother joined me each semester at my high school's academic breakfast. When she arrived, my face lit up, and I thanked her for her support.

I was awarded these plaques at the Annual Lake Worth High School Trojan Sound Band and Color Guard Banquet.

I participated in the Mic Speaks' Women in Business & Power event at Expansive Biscayne.

I received my Bachelor of Music degree on this day. It was one of the best days of my life.

Hubby and I are at our church's holiday event. I was also pregnant with Kamaria.

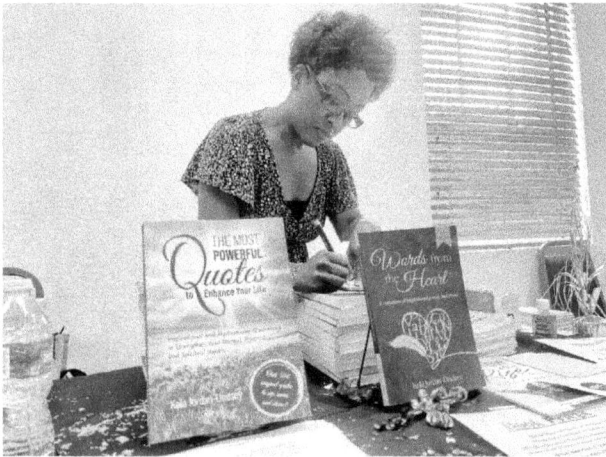

I participated in the 9 to Thrive Women's Business Conference in Miami Lakes, Florida, in 2023. I enjoyed speaking, selling inspirational content, and signing books.

Dad and I with my precious and beautiful bundle of joy, Kamaria.
This picture was taken after worship service, one afternoon.

One of the most memorable and special days of my life, my
wedding day.

We rode on the Jungle Queen Riverboat in Fort Lauderdale, Florida, months after we met. We loved it and walked away with unforgettable memories.

We enjoyed an evening of fun, food, smiles, and good convo at my sister's place.

It was intermission, so I decided to have someone take a picture of me in the pit orchestra. I don't remember which orchestra this was, but it was a local pit orchestra in Miami.

I performed with the Miami Wind Symphony somewhere in South Miami.

This picture of Allison (left), Heather (center), and myself (right) was taken around Easter at a Sears in Florida. This photo was one of our first holiday memories together.

I took these pictures of myself holding Kamaria at a shopping center in Hialeah. I adored having my little princess in my arms. Kamaria always smiled.

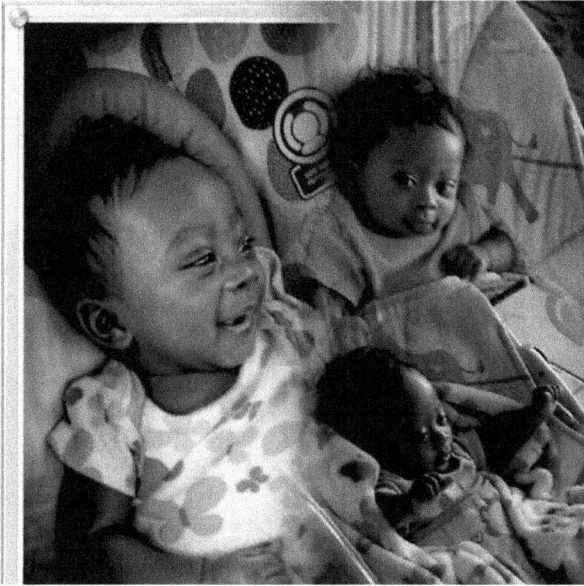

Kamaria was a happy baby and loved to smile, play, and watch cartoons. She also enjoyed watching me play the clarinet.

I took this picture in my mid-20s during my undergraduate years.

My mother took this picture one sunny Easter Sunday after church service.

My parents took this photo after my graduate clarinet recital at Florida International University Modesto Campus. It was a long but enjoyable performance.

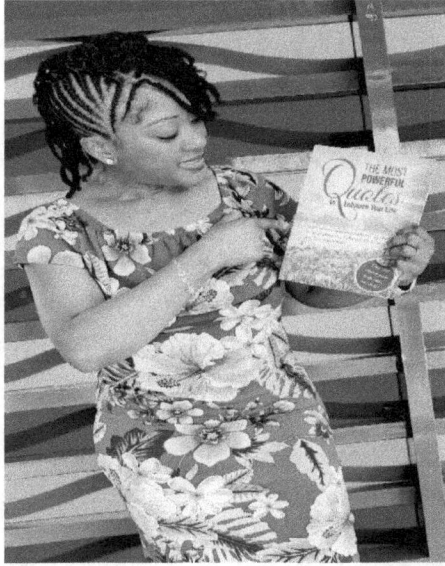

Anthony took this beautiful photo one afternoon near a local Chipotle, in 2023.

I am posing with my clarinet and a beautiful red rose.

I am posing with my clarinet and rocking black leather boots.

I included this photo in my graduate clarinet recital program.

Dad and I had a great time with Kamaria at a local park in Miami.

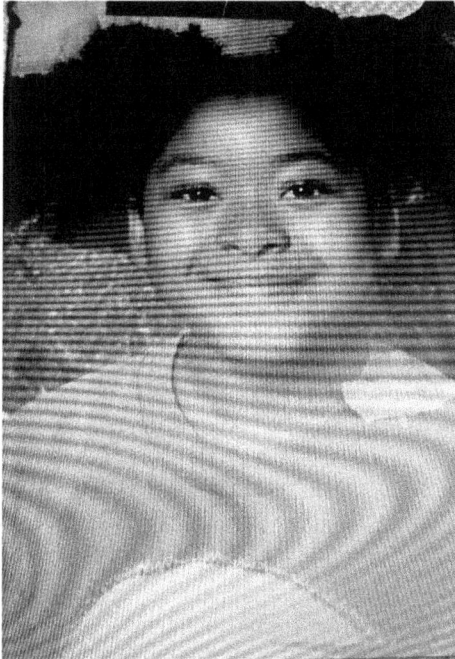

I proudly wore my seal shirt and rocked my afros for Picture Day
at my elementary school.

I loved taking photos with my clarinet.

I bought this purple dress at one of my favorite clothing stores at a local mall.

I am in a practice room preparing for my graduate clarinet recital.

I had the privilege and blessing to travel to Pittsburgh, Pennsylvania, and audition in a local orchestra. The Theater Square was one of the sites I visited during the day.

I was excited about taking this picture in my polka dot dress.

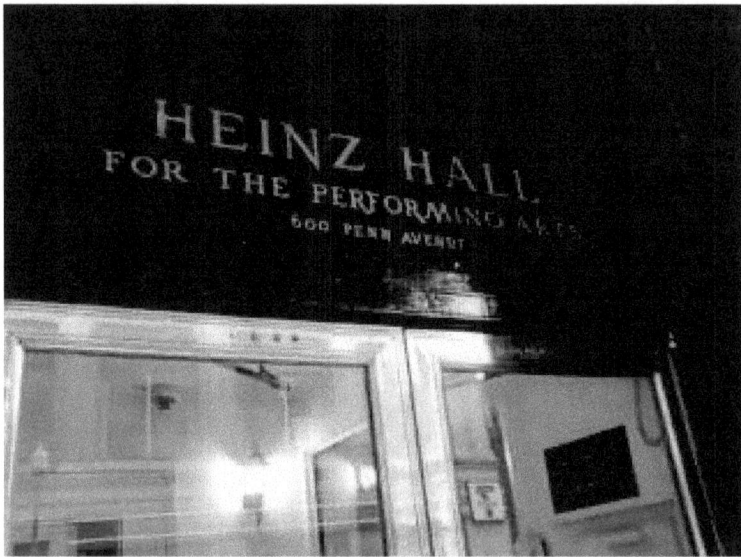

I had the privilege and blessing to travel to Pittsburgh, Pennsylvania, and audition in a local orchestra. I auditioned on the clarinet in the Heinz Hall.

I was a high schooler.

I adored my clarinet.

This evening, I performed in the New York Summer Music Festival's wind ensemble in Oneonta, New York. It was a fun concert.

I performed clarinet with the Miami Wind Symphony.

No matter what I experienced in life, I always smiled.

It was a beautiful day at the beach.

I loved the sand at the beach.

My beautiful daughter, Kamaria, is holding my book of
inspirational quotes.

My beautiful mother.

I enjoyed the phenomenal hospitality at Westin Pittsburgh.

During a teacher's retreat, I took this selfie in my lovely resort room.

Allison and I loved to wear fans. I took this in middle school.

My beautiful mother at the park.

A selfie just before work during my teaching years.

Hubby and I after lunch one Saturday.

I took this after I arrived home from a lady's day event in 2023.

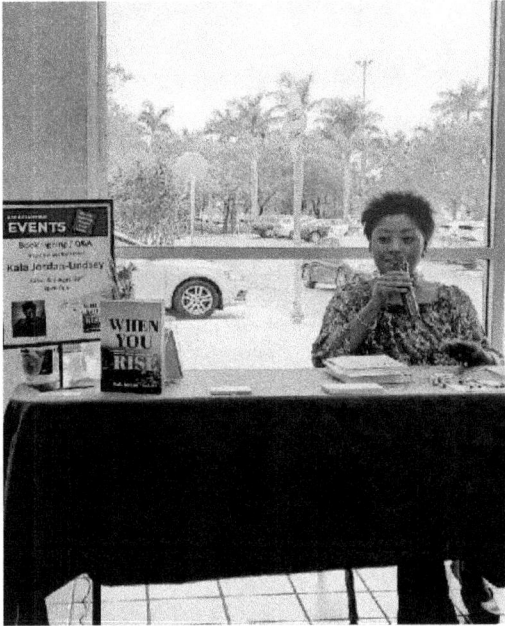

My first book signing at Barnes & Noble was memorable.

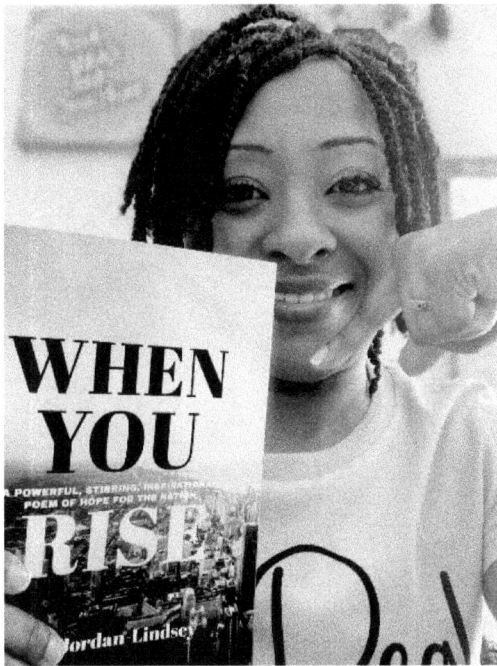

I was in the mood this morning to take another selfie.

My hubby and our beautiful princess, Kamaria, celebrated his 45th birthday at Golden Corral.

Kamaria loved to touch the tone holes and keys on my clarinet.

My beautiful mother on my wedding day in 2016.

My beautiful mother.

Hubby and I were in the dining room area of my mom's house.

Anthony and I attended our minister's appreciation celebration in Delray Beach, Florida.

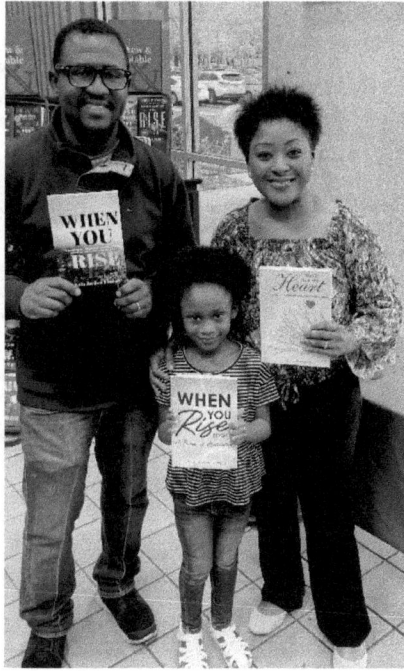

My first book signing at Barnes & Noble with hubby and our beautiful daughter was successful. To God be the glory.

My beautiful mom and I on Christmas in 2022.

My beautiful parents are on their honeymoon.

I had just got my hair washed and styled by a gifted hair stylist in
Delray Beach, Florida.

My baby sister, Aimee, took this in 2020.

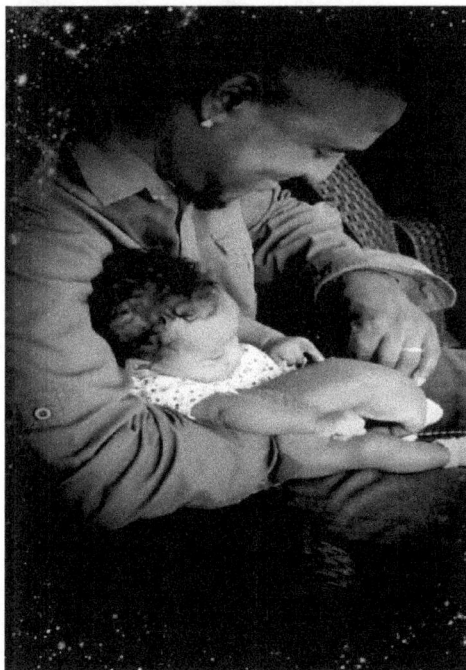

This is Anthony and our beautiful daughter, Kamaria. I took this
photo weeks after she was born.

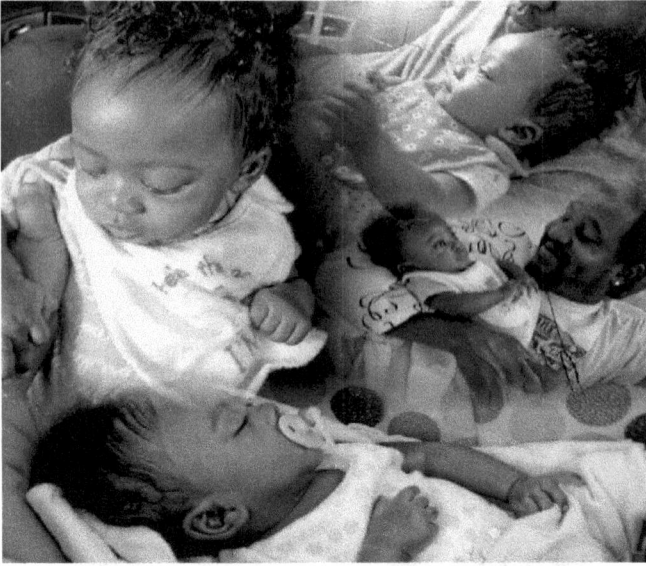

My special blessings, Anthony and Kamaria.

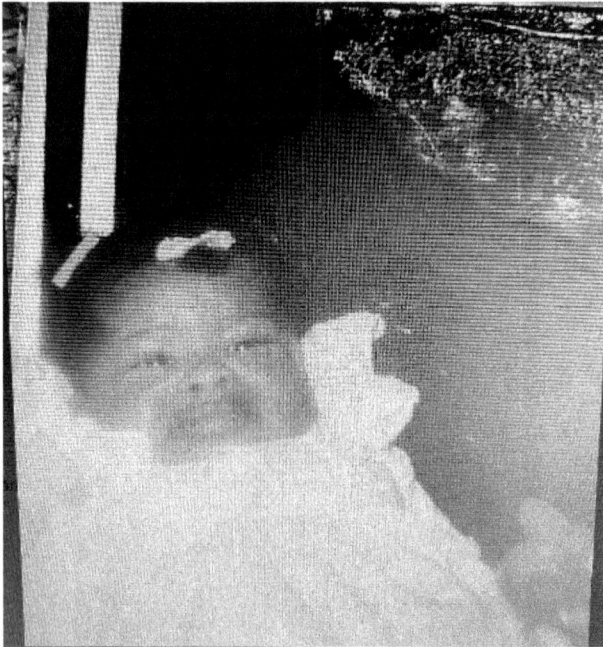

This photo is of me as a baby.

Mom and I on a beautiful sunny day.

My beautiful mother wore her favorite color shirt.

My beautiful mother and I were at my first book signing at Barnes & Noble.

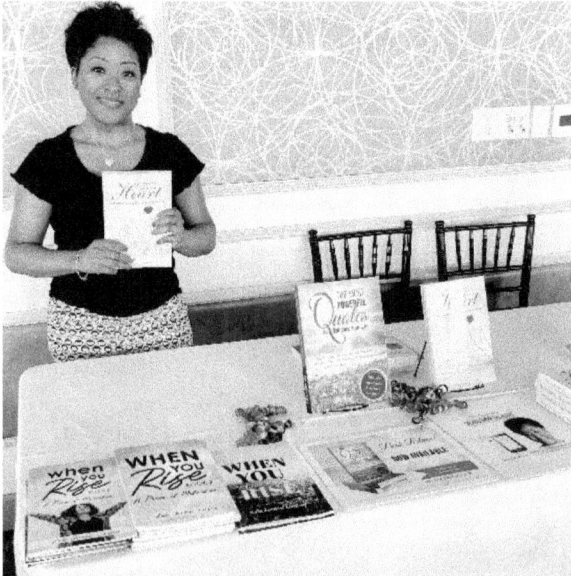

I participated in the Stand with Black Women event in Miami, Florida and had a great time. I listened to great speakers and signed books.

I participated in the Mic Speaks' Women in Business & Power event at Expansive Biscayne. I also shared some words of encouragement this evening.

Me, myself, and I.

I created this inspirational shirt and wanted to display it to the world.

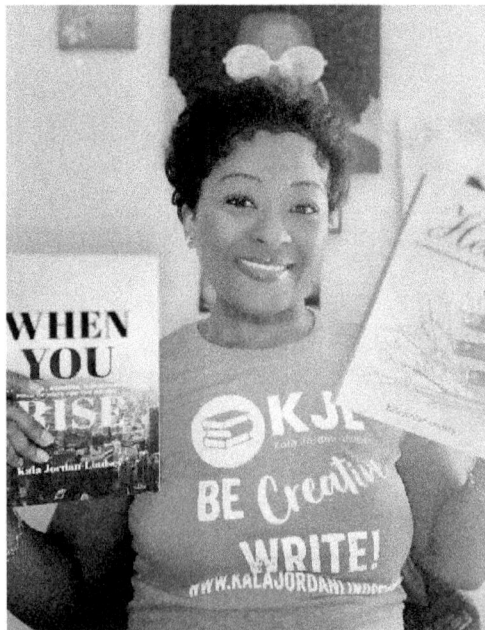

It was another blessed day.

My handsome partner and spouse, Anthony. Our big wedding day.

Our beautiful wedding day at Lake Ida Church of Christ.

The man of my dreams, my handsome husband, Anthony.

Our special wedding day.

My mother, Evetta, and beautiful sisters. Mom (center), Jennifer (top left), Allison (top center), myself (top right), Heather (right center), Aimee (lower right).

A selfie after work at Miami Dade College.

I was a mama's girl.

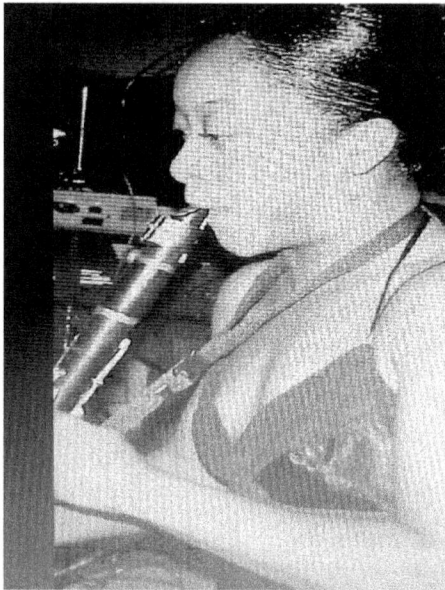

I performed clarinet at my church's holiday banquet at the Marriot
in Boca Raton, Florida.

Today was his 45<sup>th</sup> birthday.

It was Valentine's Day weekend, and my amazing husband,
Anthony, stood behind the camera.

www.ingramcontent.com/pod-product-compliance
Lightning Source LLC
Chambersburg PA
CBHW071856090426
42811CB00004B/624